HOW TO
TRAIN
AND
DEVELOP
SUPERVISORS

HOW TO TRAIN AND DEVELOP SUPERVISORS

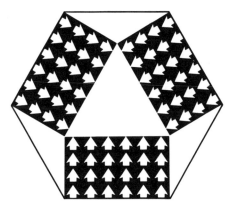

DONALD L. KIRKPATRICK

amacom
American Management Association
New York • Atlanta • Boston • Chicago • Kansas City • San Francisco • Washington, D. C.
Brussels • Toronto • Mexico City

This book is available at a special
discount when ordered in bulk quantities.
For information, contact Special Sales Department,
AMACOM, a division of American Management Association,
135 West 50th Street, New York, NY 10020.

This publication is designed to provide accurate and authoritative information in regard to the subject matter covered. It is sold with the
understanding that the publisher is not engaged in rendering legal,
accounting, or other professional service. If legal advice or other expert
assistance is required, the services of a competent professional person
should be sought.

Library of Congress Cataloging-in-Publication Data

Kirkpatrick, Donald L.
    How to train and develop supervisors / Donald L. Kirkpatrick.
       p. cm.
    Includes bibliographical references and index.
    ISBN 0-8144-5148-9
    1. Supervisors—Training of. I. Title.
HF5549.12.K57 1993
658.4'07124—dc20   93-9249
                                        CIP

Portions of this book appeared previously in A Practical Guide for Supervisory Training and
Development, published by Addison-Wesley, and How to Improve Performance Through
Appraisal and Coaching, published by AMACOM, a division of the American Management
Association.

Printing number

10 9 8 7 6 5 4 3

Contents

Preface

Supervisory training and development continues to be a critical issue for managers in all types and sizes of organizations. Training and human resources professionals consider this to be one of their top priorities. Changes of all kinds necessitate continuous updating of knowledge and skills as well as changes in attitudes. The situation is common, not only to industry but also to government, hospitals, and retail organizations. The question is "how to do it effectively" and not "whether it should be done."

The term *supervisor* has been used throughout this book to describe the first level of management, whether in an office or factory. In some organizations, it will be synonymous with the term *foreman*. Emphasis has been placed on "how to do it" by describing practical principles, techniques, and examples. In the last section of the book, eleven case studies describe what a variety of organizations are doing to train and develop their supervisors.

The terms *training* and *development* are usually used together. I have not tried to distinguish between the two. In general, the term *training* refers to the teaching of specific knowledge and skills required on the supervisor's present job. The term *development* is broader and contributes to the growth of the individual and preparation for higher-level jobs.

The principles and techniques described in this book are designed to meet the challenges that face supervisors in the 1990s. Three of the most common ones are: diversity in the workforce; the need for quality improvement; and employee empowerment, with emphasis on self-directed work teams.

All organizations have had and always will have diversity in the work force. Not only are there differences in race and gender, but also in attitudes, education, emotional stability, skills, and many more physical and personality traits. I have been conducting training classes since 1949, and I have always emphasized the need to understand employees and respect their differences. The same need exists today and will exist in the future. The current emphasis reflects the increasing percentage of the work force made up of women, minorities, immigrants, and the disabled—which makes training in this area particularly important.

But the principles of training remain the same. The whole concept of "determining needs" is based on the challenge to help supervisors be more effective by giving them the knowledge and skills they need. This certainly includes the importance of understanding their employees. Programs on such issues as human relations and leadership are designed to change attitudes as well as teach important knowledge and skills.

There is also nothing new about the need for quality improvement. Organizations have always had an objective of producing products that meet the quality standards their customers require. They have had to balance quality with quantity, cost, and meeting the schedule requirements of their customers. With increased competition from Japan and other nations, they have had to upgrade their quality standards or else go out of business. One of the first concerted efforts was to adopt the "Quality Circle" concept, which has been so successful in Japan. Getting employees to participate in improving quality (as well as reducing cost, improving productivity, and making other improvements) was the basic approach. Many organizations then realized that more needed to be done, so they implemented "statistical process control" as recommended by W. Edwards Deming. Currently, "total quality improvement" and "Total Quality Management" have been widely accepted as a philosophy and have been implemented in many organizations. Because of these changes, "quality" has received a high priority in determining the training needs of supervisors.

The terms *leadership, empowerment,* and *self-directed work teams* have become buzzwords in books, articles, and the language of business and industry. Warren G. Bennis has expounded the philosophy that *manager* and *leader* are separate and distinct terms. In doing so, he has obviously used the term *manager* to describe a certain type of manager who is not a leader. This simply emphasizes what we training professionals have always tried to do: Develop/ improve leadership qualities in supervisors and higher-level managers. As for the term *empowerment,* this has simply added another dimension to the ideas of "participation" and "involvement," which have been emphasized for many years.

There are four basic approaches for a supervisor to use in making decisions. All four should consider the quality of the decision as well as the acceptance by those who will implement it. The four approaches are:

1. Decide without getting any input from subordinates.
2. Ask subordinates for input, consider it, and then decide.
3. Conduct a problem-solving meeting with subordinates and lead them in reaching a consensus.
4. Give subordinates the power/authority to make decisions without the leadership/influence of the supervisor.

The last of these is "empowerment" with the formation of "self-directed work teams." In his 1981 book *The Change Resistors*, George S. Odiorne stated: "The best option for change is one created by the people who must implement it, or one for which the implementers can claim ownership." In 1963, Norman R. F. Maier emphasized the need for involvement. He stated that the greater the need for acceptance on the part of those implementing a decision, the more the need for participation. "Quality Circles" is built on involvement. The only thing new about empowerment is the degree to which employees participate. Some organizations have found involvement to be very effective in terms of improving quality, increasing productivity, reducing costs, and otherwise benefitting the organization. They have also found that it has improved morale and the quality of work life. Other organizations have found that using empowerment has *not* been successful. I think that Tom Peters and others have gone overboard in dramatically describing empowerment as the answer to all productivity and morale problems or at least recommending it without reservations. In some cases, a stated objective is to eliminate a level of management.

I strongly urge top management to be very cautious in implementing a "self-directed work team" approach. They should consider the following factors in deciding how much of the "empowerment" approach to adopt and force on their supervisors:

- The culture of the organization
- The urgency of the decision
- The scope of the decision
- The need for acceptance by those who will implement the decision
- The attitudes of the employees toward the idea of helping the organization
- The qualifications of the subordinates in terms of knowledge and experience
- The desire of the employees to participate

I like the words used in a policy statement by Honeywell, which encourages supervisors/managers to delegate decision making to the lowest *appropriate* level. This encourages involvement and possibly empowerment, but still gives supervisors/managers the authority to decide what is appropriate.

In addition to diversity in the work force, total quality improvement, and empowerment, much emphasis is being placed on the need for teamwork. This requires special attention, especially by top management. Supervisors are under pressure to build teamwork among their employees, while top management frequently does not practice it. The following example illustrates the point. In my "Management Inventory on Managing Change," I include the following item to be answered "agree" or "disagree" by supervisors:

Most managers in my organization would welcome ideas and suggestions from people in other departments.

I have been surprised and disappointed to find that 89 percent of the supervisors who answer this question mark "disagree." And these supervisors are from organizations that send supervisors to management training programs. It is a terrible indictment of top management that most of them won't even listen to ideas and suggestions from others. The discussion of the item reveals that most managers have put up a barrier with such attitudes as: "If I want your advice, I'll ask for it," or "Don't tell me how to run my department," or "What makes you think you are qualified to offer me advice on how to run my department?" And these same managers are telling their supervisors to build teamwork! The attitude of supervisors usually exemplifies the famous saying by Ralph Waldo Emerson (paraphrased here): "What you do thunders so loudly I can't hear what you say."

It is also interesting that 100 percent of the supervisors who complete the "Management Inventory on Managing Change" test answer "agree" to the following item:

Managers should welcome ideas and suggestions from all sources.

The difference between this item and the previous one is the substitution of the word *should* (theoretical) for *would* (actual).

Upper-level managers must exemplify teamwork if they expect their supervisors to build it in their departments. Training managers must impress this on their upper-level managers in addition to training supervisors in principles and techniques for building teamwork.

This book was written especially for human resources and training professionals. It describes classroom programs as well as on-the-job approaches including "Performance Appraisal" and "Coaching." Many references have been included. Of special interest will be the description of eleven of the most comprehensive books listed in the Bibliography.

Executives and middle-level managers will find the following chapters of special interest and application:

Chapter 2. Responsibility and Authority for Supervisory Training
Chapter 9. Getting Maximum Benefits From Outside Supervisory Development Programs
Chapter 10. On-the-Job Performance Appraisal
Chapter 11. Coaching for Improved Performance
Chapter 12. Selecting and Training New Supervisors
Chapter 15. A Twelve-Day Certificate Program for Supervisors

Acknowledgments

I am grateful to the late Dr. Russell Moberly, who hired me right out of college to teach supervisory training courses at the Management Institute, University of Wisconsin in Madison. I am also indebted to Brad Boyd, Earl Wyman, Ron Bula, and the late Norm Allhiser with whom I worked at the Management Institute, both in Madison and Milwaukee. In addition, I'd like to thank my many friends and colleagues associated with the American Society for Training and Development who have contributed to my knowledge and growth.

PART I

Planning, Implementation, and Evaluation

1

Why Supervisory Training and Development?

Very few organizations are satisfied with the performance of their first-level supervisors and foremen. Research conducted at the University of Wisconsin's Management Institute indicates that supervisors are from 50 to 65 percent effective—as evaluated by mid- and top-level managers. The main reasons cited for such limited effectiveness are that they lack:

- A clear understanding of what is expected of them
- The proper attitude and motivation to do their best
- The knowledge and skills that are necessary to do the job

Which of these causes for inadequate performance can be corrected by effective training and development?

The first one—not understanding what is expected—is a communication, not a training, problem. It can be corrected by clear and complete communication between supervisor and boss. The second condition—poor attitude or lack of motivation—can be improved through training and development. And the third—lack of knowledge and skills—clearly can be corrected by effective training.

Improving Performance on Current Job— As It Now Exists

Training and development can be important in improving the performance of supervisors in their jobs as they now exist. Attitudes, knowledge, and skills can all be improved. Such improvement can change the job behavior of supervisors, thus producing better performance and results.

Recently, I conducted a short training course for supervisors at a small Wisconsin shoe manufacturer. The objective of the program was to reduce turnover, and the main focus was on effective induction and train-

3

ing of new employees. At the end of the program, we evaluated it by asking the participants for their reactions. They were less than enthusiastic. Typical comments indicated that "the ideas that Kirkpatrick expressed were good, but they don't agree with the way things are done here."

These reactions prompted a research study in which I was asked to interview supervisors to determine their attitudes toward the company as well as extract their recommendations. In the personal interviews I asked four questions:

1. How do you feel about your job?
2. How do you feel about the company?
3. What are your main problems in doing your job?
4. What suggestions do you have for improvement in the company?

The earful of complaints I received about many aspects of the company reflected a general feeling of frustration and low morale on the part of the supervisors—negative attitudes that were probably reflected in the attitudes and performance of their subordinates. Clearly, the attitudes of these supervisors, as well as their knowledge and skills, had to be improved if the morale and productivity of the workers were to be improved.

After I completed the interviews, I gave the company executives a report. They began to take steps to correct the policies, procedures, and practices that were causing poor supervisory attitudes.

This example illustrates three points about supervisory training and development:

1. The attitudes of supervisors can have a significant impact on the effectiveness of the program. I'm sure that my ideas and recommendations were not accepted by the supervisors of the shoe manufacturing company because of existing management policies and practices that had created low morale.
2. Negative attitudes of supervisors must be changed if the workers are expected to improve performance and increase productivity.
3. Negative supervisory attitudes can't be corrected in the classroom if they reflect unsatisfactory job conditions such as low pay, an inadequate work force, poor management policies, delays in getting raw materials, and excessive pressures for production.

The main thrust of supervisory training and development should be to improve the performance of a supervisor on the current job. Attitudes, knowledge, and skills can be improved and immediate payoff can be obtained in improved performance and productivity of the workers they supervise.

Improving Performance on Current Job— As It Will Exist

A second need for training and development exists if the job of the supervisor is changing with changes in the organization. The content of this training should include both the technical and managerial aspects of the supervisor's job. In the technical area, a supervisor may need to learn more about computers, automatic equipment, quality control, the labor agreement, raw materials, manufacturing processes, and other technical subjects related to the job and the department. The managerial aspects may focus on the latest and best approaches in such areas as leadership, motivation, decision making, performance appraisal, quality improvement, teamwork, and employee involvement and empowerment.

Preparing for Advancement

If the current supervisor is being considered for a higher-level position, new training needs emerge. These, of course, are related to the job of middle management instead of first-level management. The technical needs may include increased understanding of computers, automation, Statistical Process Control (SPC), and Just-in-Time (JIT). The managerial needs might include organization development, personnel planning, delegation, styles of leadership, decision making, and strategic planning. These are in addition to better understanding of motivation, communication, the development of subordinates, and Quality of Work Life (QWL). The higher the level of the manager, the more emphasis should be placed on managerial skills as opposed to technical knowledge.

Summary

There are three main reasons why supervisory training and development are needed. First, training can improve attitudes, knowledge, and skills and increase personal effectiveness and that of the department.

Second, the jobs of most supervisors will be different in the future. Therefore, new knowledge—technical and managerial—must be acquired in order to perform effectively the first-level management job as it will be.

Finally, some supervisors will be promoted to middle-management jobs in the near future. Training and development can prepare them for effective performance on the new job when the promotion occurs.

Time and money spent on supervisory training and development are not an expense. They are an investment in the future of the organization in the recognition that people are an organization's most important asset. Benefits should be viewed as a return on the investment. The extent of the benefits will depend on many of the factors that are covered in this book.

Benefits to the supervisor can include improved attitudes, knowledge, skill, performance, and rewards. Benefits to the organization can include increased productivity, improved quality, reduced costs, improved morale, and greater profitability.

It must be mentioned that training may not be the answer to improving supervisory performance. The well-known Peter Principle[1] (every employee tends to rise to his or her level of incompetence) must be considered. The term *incompetent* implies that no amount of training or coaching will help. In these cases, the supervisor must be removed from the job or the job modified to fit the supervisor. Peter Drucker suggests that you remove them from the job, but treat them right. Easy to say, but sometimes difficult to do.

---

1. Laurence Peter and Raymond Hull, *The Peter Principle* (New York: Morrow Publishing Co., 1969).

2
Responsibility and Authority for Supervisory Training

Four different people in an organization can be held responsible for the training and development of a supervisor: the supervisor, his boss, top management, and the training professional.

1. *The supervisor.* It is generally agreed that each supervisor is responsible for his own development. Some supervisors accept the entire responsibility and lay out their own program for self-development; the majority do not. Therefore, it is not advisable for organizations to adopt the philosophy that development is the sole responsibility of the supervisor.

2. *The boss.* It is a well-accepted principle that every boss is responsible for the development of subordinates. This seems logical because the boss is responsible for the performance of subordinates, and that performance depends largely on their training and development. Most job descriptions for a department head, superintendent, or other middle-management job spell out the responsibility for training and developing subordinates, with particular emphasis on improving performance on the current job.

3. *Top management.* Policymaking executives in an organization have a special responsibility for the training and development of first-line supervisors: They must provide the proper climate for growth and development and also provide time and money. If the organization is large enough, professional staff should be added to the payroll to plan and implement effective training programs. Professional staff may be full-time training and development specialists. In smaller organizations, the personnel or human resources manager may be assigned this responsibility along with employment, salary administration, and other duties.

4, *The training professionals.* Training professionals are paid to see that effective training is carried out. They, too, are responsible for seeing that supervisors are properly trained to do their jobs. As "experts," they should understand how supervisors learn and the type of training that will help them reach their maximum potential. Their success depends on their ability to work effectively with managers without the power to force their ideas and programs on line management. Influence, not power, is their key to success.

If supervisors, bosses, and policymaking executives all carry out their responsibilities, chances are great that supervisors will be effectively trained and developed. In accomplishing these results, it is important to recognize the amount of authority that accompanies the responsibilities.

The Supervisor

The fact that a supervisor has much of the responsibility for her own personal development does not necessarily mean that she also has the authority for it. On personal time, of course, she can attend a seminar, read a book, or take a correspondence course. However, she probably would not have the authority to spend the company's money or take off a workday to attend a seminar.

The Boss

The boss, on the other hand, usually has much authority. He can send the supervisor away for a day or a week to attend a seminar on company time. He can assign the supervisor a book to read and give special job assignments in order to improve knowledge and skills. In other words, the boss has the authority to tell the subordinate what to do and when to do it, and he can usually commit company money and time.

Top Management

Top executives also have authority, especially to establish policy and approve budgets. They must make it clear that they support supervisory training and development. They should establish a written policy that explains their philosophy. Budgets for training and development should reflect their support, and these budgets should not be trimmed indiscriminately when business becomes slow. Some organizations clearly demonstrate their lack of commitment to training and development when training professionals are the first to be terminated when profits are reduced or budgets are cut. Top executives must recognize and support the idea that training is an investment, not an expense.

In addition to a written policy and adequate budgets, top executives must provide company time for supervisors to attend training classes. This shows that supervisory training will benefit the organization, as well as the supervisor who receives it. Such a commitment to training creates positive attitudes on the part of supervisors. These positive attitudes are necessary if maximum benefit is going to be realized from the time and money spent.

Tuition refund plans should be established to pay all or nearly all of the expenses for training courses that supervisors complete on their own time. Three possible approaches are:

1. The organization pays all fees if the course is completed with a passing grade. The supervisor pays for and keeps all books that are required.
2. The organization reimburses tuition costs as follows:
   If the supervisor gets an A: 100%
   If the supervisor gets a B: 90%
   If the supervisor gets a C: 80%
   If the supervisor gets a D or F: 0%
   The supervisor pays for and keeps books that are required.
3. The organization reimburses 75 percent of the tuition cost if the supervisor passes the course. The supervisor pays for and keeps books that are required.

Many modifications of these approaches are used by various organizations. Examples are described in Chapter 6 under "Educational Assistance Programs."

In all of these approaches, the organization pays most of the costs, while the supervisor spends some of his own money as well as time. The organization strongly supports training and development but expects the supervisor to contribute something because both parties benefit from the training.

Training Professionals

Training professionals have no authority over the training and development of supervisors. They must sell ideas to the boss as well as to the supervisors themselves. Influence must substitute for authority. There are four possible approaches that training professionals can use: (1) provide whatever help the line manager requests; (2) help the line manager determine the training needs of the department and help develop a program to meet these needs; (3) develop an effective training program and sell it so that the line manager will want it; and (4) develop an effective training program and sell it to top management so line management will not dare disapprove. Let's look at these four possibilities, one at a time.

1. *Provide help as requested.* This is a desirable approach, especially if line managers are oriented to training. If enough line managers are desirous of help, the staff professional does not need to do any selling; he will be kept busy providing training help as requested. The professional must be sure that the training is effective. When other line managers learn about the effective program, they will also request training help. At some point, the training department may be expanded to meet the needs. Line managers who are being served will be most supportive of such staff additions. This is an in-house consulting approach.

2. *Assist in determining and meeting needs.* This approach, part selling and part providing help as asked, can be very successful. The professional should stimulate the line manager to think about problems and help determine which problems can be solved, in whole or in part, by training activities. The professional is helping the line manager solve problems. In so doing, he must communicate and sell training know-how and capabilities to the line manager. The line manager will use training professionals if it will help meet objectives without costing too much time or money.

Three strong qualities are needed to implement this approach, as follows:

a. A thorough knowledge of training principles, approaches, and available resources
b. Skill in selling ideas
c. The ability to deliver a quality program

A professional with these qualifications can be very successful. Line managers are usually willing to give this kind of a staff person a try. If the results are good, they will probably ask more supervisors to go through the program. And one line manager will tell another that it is a good training program. As long as line managers are convinced that the professional is providing a service that is worth the time and money, they will continue to ask for help. This is also a consulting approach.

3. *Develop a training program and sell it.* The success of this approach depends on the training professional's ability to develop or purchase a training program and to sell it to line management. The staff person

should be sure that the program meets the needs of the supervisor. One of the best ways is to involve line managers (and perhaps the supervisors themselves) in the decisions related to the program. For example, several alternative proposals can be made to line managers, and the final decision can be left to them. Or the professional can recommend and sell a specific program that she is confident will meet the needs. Obviously, a history of successful programs will make it much easier to sell programs to line supervisors. Therefore, the professional should do a thorough job in planning programs that will be effective.

4. *Develop a training program and force acceptance.* Some professionals are able to carry out their training responsibility by enjoying the status and power that make line managers reluctant to refuse help. Under this approach, the training professional develops a program, sells it to the top executive, and then puts it into operation. Line managers will participate whether they think it's effective or not.

The initial program may get started because line managers don't dare refuse to participate. If it is successful, the situation can change into one of the three that have been described. Power and status may become irrelevant, and the professional will be effective because of the acceptance and enthusiasm of line management. But if the initial program is ineffective, the status and power of the professional will disappear, and one of the other approaches must be used.

Summary

The responsibility for the training and development of first-line supervisors should be shared among the supervisor, the boss, top management, and training professionals. The supervisor should be responsible for wanting to improve and for requesting assistance. He should also be willing to contribute some time and money for personal growth. The boss has the responsibility and the authority to stimulate, encourage, assist, and follow up to see that proper training is given. The boss should be held accountable for the on-the-job development of subordinates. Top management must provide the climate, philosophy, policies, time, and money for supervisory training and development. If the organization is large enough, professionals should be hired to plan and implement effective training programs. And the training professionals have the responsibility (usually without authority) to see that effective training is accomplished.

3

Philosophy, Strategy, and Guiding Principles

To be effective in training and developing supervisors, it is important to have and communicate philosophy, strategy, and policies related to the development of employees. Following are examples from six well-known and respected organizations.

DANA CORPORATION, TOLEDO, OHIO
LARRY LOTTIER, DEAN, BUSINESS SCHOOL, DANA UNIVERSITY

Following are some of the policies of the Dana Corporation that relate to the selection and training of supervisors.

People

We are dedicated to the belief that our people are our most important asset. Wherever possible, we encourage all Dana people within the entire world organization to become shareholders or, by some other means, own a part of their company.

We believe people respond to recognition, freedom to participate, and the opportunity to develop.

We believe that people should be involved in setting their own goals and judging their own performance. The people who know best how the job should be done are the ones doing it.

We believe Dana people should accept only total quality in all tasks they perform.

We endorse productivity plans that allow people to share in the rewards of productivity gains.

We believe that all Dana people should identify with the company. This identity should carry on after they have left active employment.

We believe facilities with people who have demonstrated a commitment to Dana will be competitive and thus warrant our support.

We believe that wages and benefits are the concern and responsibility of managers. The Management Resource Program is a worldwide matter—it is a tool that should be used in the development of qualified Dana people. We encourage income protection, health programs, and education.

We believe that on-the-job training is an effective method of learning. A Dana manager must prove proficiency in at least one line of our company's work—marketing, engineering, manufacturing, financial services, etc. Additionally, these people must prove their ability as supervisors and be able to get work done through other people. We recognize the importance of gaining experience both internationally and domestically.

We believe our people should move across product, discipline, and organizational lines. These moves should not conflict with operating efficiency.

We believe in promoting from within. Dana people interested in other positions are encouraged to discuss job opportunities with their supervisor.

Managers are responsible for the selection, education, and training of all people.

All Dana people should have their job performance reviewed at least once a year by their supervisors.

We believe in providing programs to support the Dana Style. We encourage professional and personal development of all Dana people.

Organization

We discourage conformity, uniformity, and centralization.

We believe in a minimum number of management levels. Responsibility should be pushed as far into the organization as possible.

Organizational structure must not conflict with doing what is best for all of Dana.

We believe in an organizational structure that allows the individual maximum freedom to perform and participate. This will stimulate initiative, innovation, and the entrepreneurial spirit that is the cornerstone of our success.

We believe in small, highly effective, support groups to service specialized needs of the Policy Committee and the world organization at large as requested. We believe in task forces rather than permanent staff functions.

We do not believe in company-wide procedures. If an organization requires procedures, it is the responsibility of the manager to create them.

Communication

We will communicate regularly with shareholders, customers, Dana people, the general public, and financial communities.

It is the job of all managers to keep Dana people informed. Each manager must decide on the best method of communication. We believe direct communication with all of our people eliminates the need for a third-party involvement. All managers shall periodically inform their people about the performance and plans of their operation.

FLORIDA POWER CORPORATION, ST. PETERSBURG, FLORIDA
V. W. THURN, MANAGER OF EMPLOYEE DEVELOPMENT

The training philosophy of the corporation includes the following:

Effective training could be defined as a process which enables persons to do something which they could not do before they were subjected to that process.

Properly designed training is job-related and changes on-the-job behavior if the immediate supervisor stimulates the employee's interest and the training must be reinforced by line management.

The modern concept of training is therefore seen to be performance-oriented and is based on sound principles of learning and aimed at achieving behavioral change in order to meet clearly defined organizational job needs.

Performance Orientation

To be effective, training must have supervisory involvement in order to improve job performance. It is essential when preparing any training program that the job be analyzed carefully. This analysis will determine what the learners must do and what they need to know to be able to perform effectively.

Principles of Learning

Educational and industrial psychologists have, as a result of their extensive research, been able to establish that learning depends mainly upon three factors: the learner, the learning resources, and the learning technique.[1]

1. *The learner.* The learner decides if she will learn. It is therefore essential to provide a learning situation that motivates the learner. This is best achieved by satisfying the learner's needs for accomplishment, responsibility, and recognition during the learning process.

2. *The learning material/resources.* To ensure that learning is effective, the learning material/resources must be meaningful, presented in logical sequence, and in optimum-size steps (not too big or too small).

1. Carl Rogers, *Freedom to Learn: A View of What Education Might Become* (Columbus, Ohio: Charles E. Merrell, 1969).

3. *The learning technique.* The following points are important when selecting a learning technique:

- ▸ Learning is most effective when it is applied in practice. Passive learning should be avoided and active participation encouraged.
- ▸ A feedback system should be built into any program.
- ▸ Feedback must be an ongoing process and should enable learners to identify and correct their own errors.
- ▸ Learning is reinforced by practice, and controls should be reduced as performance improves.
- ▸ Those in control of the learning environment provide direction during the learning process and do not attempt to control it.
- ▸ The learner should be encouraged to practice what she has learned in as many different situations as needed.

Learning Objectives

If learning is to be effective, it is important that the learner and the trainer should know precisely what is required on the job. Clearly defined objectives stating the performance/action required, the conditions, and the required standards are essential. The Criterion-Referenced Instruction (CRI) approach developed by Mager and Pipe has been the basis of the process we used.[2]

Systematic Approach

The systematic approach is show in Figure 3-1. The terms are used as follows:

diagnosis   Essentially, an analysis of a performance problem in order to determine whether training is the most economic and effective method of improving performance.

preparation   What takes place after training has been selected as the best solution. The course developer(s) determines the objectives (using analysis data) and performance standards, measures existing skills, and selects the method of measuring when competence has been achieved by each learner.

development   Selection of the best learning materials, techniques, and strategies. The feedback system is considered during this state and is an integral part of any well-designed training program.

implementation   Testing the training program or system on members of the targeted population.

evaluation   The final step, which consists of evaluating the training so that the efficiency and effectiveness can be determined and the program improved as needed.

2. P. Pipe, *Objectives—Tool for Change* (Belmont, Calif.: Pitman Learning, 1975).

Figure 3-1. A systematic approach to training programs.

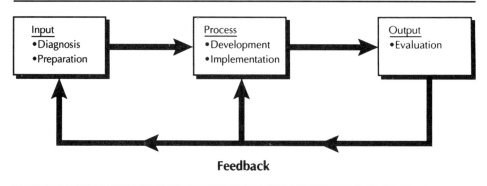

The new role of the first-line manager is described in the following excerpt from a white paper, "The Changing Role of the First-Line Manager," prepared by the

IBM, ARMONK, NEW YORK
ROBERT G. MacGREGOR, CONSULTANT-MANAGEMENT DEVELOPMENT

IBM has shifted to become a "Market-Driven Quality Company." This change has directed IBM's attention to responding to the customer's needs with total solutions. With this focus, IBM has undertaken a major restructuring of the business and has changed the role of all managers in IBM. With this change, management education focuses on four areas:

1. New emphasis has been placed on the importance of the basic beliefs and values of IBM. John Akers has been quoted a number of times that "everything about IBM can change except the basic beliefs and values."
2. IBM has increased its focus on leadership with a series of course offerings that were introduced in 1990 and will continue well into the 1990s. These offerings include "Transformational Leadership," an awareness-level course; "The Journey Continues," a skills development course; and "The Leadership Commitment," a series of offerings in the areas of empowerment, teams, risk taking, and change management.
3. The area of general business management has been given increased attention. Managers are being asked to manage their areas as if it were their own business. Courses have been developed to provide managers with the necessary skills to be general managers and entrepreneurs.
4. A continued emphasis is placed on skills in managing people. Managers in IBM are expected to continue to demonstrate the strong people management skills that have been required in the past. The focus in this area has not changed.

The new role of the first-line manager is described in the following excerpt from a white paper, "The Changing Role of the First-Line Manager," prepared by the

Corporate Management Development staff with input from IBM managers around the world:

> The first-line manager continues to be responsible for preserving and implementing our Basic Beliefs, recognizing employees' contributions, performance planning, counseling, and evaluation in our human resource programs, and day-to-day interaction with employees regarding issues, support, guidance, coaching, and nurturing. That has not changed.
>
> What has changed is the delegation of many management prerogatives to the individual closest to the customer. For that person to make good business decisions in managing customer relationships, management must share some of its responsibilities—controlling, communicating, and understanding business directions—with employees who are not managers.

Empowerment

In today's IBM, the manager should motivate and guide employees to address customer needs effectively and to ensure customer satisfaction. The customer must come first. This is nothing new. What is new, or at least different, is that the responsibility for satisfying and delighting the customer now belongs to every IBMer, regardless of position or job title.

We are moving toward this goal worldwide by removing excessive or inappropriate levels of approval and increasing delegation to the person closest to the customer. Information must be shared freely, so that individuals have the knowledge to make and implement IBM decisions, and people must be held responsible for the quality of their decisions.

In this environment, the first-line manager is more like a coach. Rather than calling all the plays, the manager must empower employees by giving them a clear understanding of their responsibility and authority and how best to respond to customer needs, both internal and external. Managers must ensure a free and open flow of up-and-down communication and information. They must make certain their people are well trained, highly motivated, and have the tools to do their jobs.

"Managers must also ensure that every individual is encouraged to take appropriate risks to achieve breakthroughs," according to the former director of education and management development. "In this free and open management system, managers and employees must trust one another and work together as partners to achieve mutual goals."

Managers should have documented plans, developed jointly with employees, showing how they and their teams are implementing IBM's overall commitment to market-driven quality.

With a shared purpose, common objectives, and commitment to the plans, all employees will be able to carry out their own responsibilities and be accountable for their actions.

Teamwork

In transforming IBM, more and more work is being accomplished by teams. While task forces, teams, and teamwork have long been a way of life in IBM, departmental, organizational, and hierarchical relationships have traditionally constituted the primary structure. In a market-driven quality organization, work may best be done through the creation of teams in which individuals come together and synergistically develop a result greater than the sum of their individual achievements. This emphasis on teams does not mean that IBM has forsaken its commitment to individual accomplishment or recognition. Not at all. Individuals continue to be encouraged to perform to the best of their abilities.

Only when the team succeeds, however, will all individual team members succeed, and only when all team members succeed individually will the team succeed. Trust is essential in teamwork.

Managing Teams

What is the role of the first-line manager in managing teams? On a specific project, people for whom the manager is responsible may be working in areas outside the manager's organizational responsibility, presenting new challenges.

Managers must develop and nurture an atmosphere that encourages open communication—the free flow of ideas and views.

To make certain teams work smoothly together, managers must find ways to motivate groups to achieve agreed-upon goals and must promote progress without intervening unnecessarily. When needed, the manager must support the team with ideas, resources, and other forms of assistance. Finally, the manager must evaluate the team's work products and give feedback in order to ensure positive business results.

A manager's responsibility in managing teams is distinguished from that of a team leader because the manager retains all the people-management responsibilities for an employee. We have adapted our practices to incorporate team initiatives and will continue to do so.

Management of Change

The role of the first-line manager in managing change is more critical in today's environment than ever before. There is no question that IBM must continue to change if it is to compete successfully globally.

First-line managers must create a climate in which their employees understand the reasons for change and "buy into" the process. There is a concurrent requirement to determine and decide what should remain the same. For example, every manager must have a commitment to the principles, values, and beliefs of IBM and, at the same time, show a willingness to change everything else.

KIMBERLY-CLARK CORPORATION, NEENAH, WISCONSIN
KENNETH D. PETERSON II, MANAGER, TRAINING AND DEVELOPMENT

In order to encourage and facilitate the development of supervisors and other salaried employees, Kimberly-Clark has initiated an organized program called the "Educational Opportunities Plan." This plan consists of three parts: Employee Self-Development ("KimEd"), Family Education ("FamEd"), and Extended Education Leaves.

The KimEd portion of the plan is an annual program (funds do not accumulate from year to year) for employee self-development. The purpose of KimEd is to offer employees the chance to explore activities that will help them become more knowledgeable, more skilled, and better able to realize their full potential.

With KimEd funds, employees can maintain and improve knowledge and skills that relate directly to their jobs. They may also broaden and acquire knowledge and skills not directly related to the job. With KimEd funds, employees may even pursue a cultural interest.

While the employee self-development part of the plan (KimEd) is an annual program, the family education savings portion (FamEd) is a long-range program under which funds can accumulate from year to year. The purpose of FamEd is to help employees set aside funds for employee education and the education of members of the family. FamEd is made up of three types of accounts: a basic account, an employee savings account, and a savings incentive account. All three accounts earn interest and grow from year to year.

KimEd: Eligibility

Salaried employees become eligible for plan benefits after completing six months of continuous service. The plan year is July 1 through June 30. Except during the first year of eligibility, KimEd allotments are made on July 1. For exempt salaried employees, the KimEd allotment will be $650. For nonexempt salaried employees, the KimEd allotment will be $525. On June 30 (the last day of the plan year), any portion of the KimEd allotment that has not been used or authorized for use will lapse. In other words, the KimEd allotments do not accumulate, but new allotments are made every July 1.

KimEd funds may be used to help meet the cost of academic, cultural, or job-related vocational courses. All courses of instruction must be offered by an institution or organization accredited by an approved accrediting association . . . or by an institution, organization, or individual approved by the Educational Opportunities Plan Committee. For employees within two years of eligibility for unreduced retirement benefits, KimEd funds may also be used to cover non-job-related vocational courses and avocational courses, such as hobbies and crafts.

KimEd funds can also be used to cover the cost of other job-related activities such as job-related educational seminars. In addition, KimEd funds can be used for special books and tapes that are job-related.

FamEd

FamEd, which provides educational funds for employees and their families, consists of three types of accounts:

1. *FamEd Company Basic Amount Account.* Except in the first year of eligibility, $150 will automatically be credited to a FamEd Company Basic Amount Account in the employee's name each time he or she receives a new KimEd allotment. In the first year of eligibility, the amount credited depends upon the date the employee becomes eligible.
2. *FamEd Employee Savings Account.* This is an optional savings account in which employees may set aside from $50 to $200 per plan year through payroll deduction.
3. *FamEd Company Savings Incentive Account.* If employees choose to contribute to their FamEd Employee Savings Account, Kimberly-Clark will credit their FamEd Company Savings Incentive Account with an amount equal to 20 percent of the employee's contribution.

Unlike the KimEd funds, which lapse at the end of each plan year, the FamEd accounts continue to accumulate from year to year. The money saved in the FamEd Employee Savings Account goes into a trust fund and earns income. FamEd money credited to the Basic Amount Account and Savings Incentive Account does not go into the trust fund but is credited to the employee's account on the plan's books and earns interest at the rate earned by the fund.

In other words, the combined FamEd funds earn income to help pay for future education expenses for employees and their families. While the amount credited to the FamEd Basic Amount Account will be less if an employee first becomes eligible during the second half of the plan year, the employee may still contribute up to $200 to the FamEd Employee Savings Account and receive the 20 percent Savings Incentive Credit.

FamEd funds are available for the employee and spouse as well as children or other dependents under age 25, who have either earned a high school diploma or reached age 18.

FamEd funds may be used to help pay the cost of all recognized educational courses of instruction. As with KimEd, these courses of instruction must be offered by an institution or organization accredited by an approved accrediting association . . . or by an institution, organization, or individual approved by the Educational Opportunities Plan Committee. Primary and secondary school courses, however, are covered only for the employee's spouse.

If employees choose to make savings contributions to the FamEd account, they may withdraw the savings (and any earnings on those savings) at any time by simply completing an Authorization/Payment Request Form and submitting it to the Education Plan Unit Coordinator. In other words, employees can use the optional savings portion of the FamEd account as they would a regular savings account. When withdrawing any savings from the FamEd account for other than a FamEd or KimEd activity, however, the Company Savings Incentive Account balance will be reduced by 20 percent of the amount withdrawn.

Extended Education Leaves

In some cases, extended education leaves of as much as one year with pay may be granted to employees who have shown a high level of performance and ability. These special leaves are granted to provide an opportunity for individuals to pursue special activities that could not otherwise be pursued . . . or would require a long period of time and serious inconvenience.

Administration

A Plan Committee is established to act on behalf of the company in certain matters regarding the plan. As part of their duties, the committee interprets the plan, adopts rules and procedures for operating the plan and handling claims, decides questions of eligibility for participation, and provides the plan administrator and trustee with facts and directions for making proper payments under the plan. A separate committee is established to act on behalf of the company in certain matters regarding extended education leaves.

MINNESOTA DEPARTMENT OF TRANSPORTATION, ST. PAUL, MINNESOTA
SUE MUEHLBACH, EMPLOYEE DEVELOPMENT PROGRAM MANAGER

The Office of Human Resources, looking forward to the twenty-first century, realizes the importance of being proactive in addressing the challenges of this decade. To meet these challenges, we have developed a strategic plan that identifies what changes are necessary for the office to be successful within the next five years.

Throughout the past year we have:

▸ Used a systematic participatory process to assess our strengths, limitations, threats, and opportunities.
▸ Evaluated and prioritized methods to ensure success in meeting our customers' needs.

While the Office of Human Resources serves a variety of customers, including our employees, staff of the Department of Employee Relations, exclusive representatives of the state associations/unions, and job applicants, the direct customers which are the focus of this plan are the managers and supervisors of Mn/DOT [Minnesota Department of Transportation]. It is by forming partnerships and sharing accountability with this group that we seek to improve and expand services to all who are served by Mn/DOT programs. It is this relationship which has guided us in determining the appropriate direction to accelerate changes necessary in our office.

The results of our effort are outlined in the following pages, which contain our vision for the future, our sense of mission, guiding core values, a grand strategy to describe the transition we see as the driving force for the years ahead, key result areas, and priority approaches that constitute our strategy.

In addition to this plan's being a framework for our future, we also will use its sense of direction to guide us in our day-to-day decisions and choices so there will be continuous progress toward the conditions and state of affairs we and our customers desire. . . .

Mission

The mission of the Office of Human Resources, in partnership with our customers, is to acquire and retain a diverse and effective work force; create a supportive and safe work environment; and provide progressive human resources management practices for present and future employees.

Vision

Someone looking at the Office of Human Resources in the future would find that we:

- ▶ Make comprehensive consultation and quality service to customers our top priorities.
- ▶ Anticipate staffing needs and respond to them in an innovative and progressive manner.
- ▶ Promote and encourage organizational effectiveness.
- ▶ Foster a dynamic and productive work force by improving worklife quality.
- ▶ Have a staff which provides leadership internally and externally and is recognized for excellence within the national transportation community.
- ▶ Facilitate the development of a work force which meets the needs of emerging technology and changing job requirements.
- ▶ Have earned the support, cooperation, and respect of internal and external customers.

Core Values

We embrace the core values expressed in our division philosophy as being indicative of the way we want to act in carrying out our mission and as we seek to make our vision a reality. The Mn/DOT Finance and Administration Division philosophy is as follows:

The Division seeks to provide quality and responsive leadership and service.

We seek to be innovative . . . thoughtful . . . analytical . . . ethical . . . open . . . fair

We seek to provide the best information we possess to our employees to enable them to make appropriate decisions.

We seek to have action taken by the employee closest to the situation and best suited to handle the responsibilities.

We will work to shape our future environment, rather than merely speculate on its content.

We will not overpromise. We ask our clients to realistically appraise our ability to respond to their needs.

We will offer alternatives to our clients when their specific requests cannot be met.

We will continually reevaluate the way we do things today, rather than defend the way we have always done things.

We will actively seek cooperation and coordination within our division, the department, with other governmental agencies and the public.

Grand Strategy

The Office of Human Resources is decentralizing authority for certain human resources actions within Mn/DOT and has requested and negotiated for additional responsibility from the Department of Employee Relations. Our dream is a leadership/service/consultative orientation which will put tactical human resources decisions and actions in the hands of our customers. Further, we are committed to the integration of our strategy with that of the Department of Transportation.

Strategy for Training and Development

With input from Mn/DOT managers, supervisors, and employees, the Office of Human Resources will create and implement innovative and alternative training and development plans to meet changing work force needs. Priority approaches in support of this strategy are:

- Integrate quality improvement philosophy in all components of training.
- Provide appropriate training curriculum to support Mn/DOT programs.
- Market the value of training and development.
- Advocate the need for adequate funding for training and development.
- Encourage managers/supervisors to accept their accountability for subordinate training and development.
- Increase employee accountability for self-development.
- Anticipate and prepare for future needs associated with new job and skill requirements.
- Foster innovation and the use of new technology in training delivery.
- Implement follow-up programs to ensure the knowledge, skills, and abilities learned from the training sessions are integrated into the employee's work environment.
- Look for alternative solutions to training needs to improve the probability of implementation.

SERVICEMASTER, DOWNERS GROVE, ILLINOIS
WILLIAM NEWELL, DIRECTOR OF TRAINING

The objective of the ServiceMaster Supervisory Development approach is much broader than simply improving "on-the-job skills." The emphasis and determination of this process is to have each unit or section of development for supervisors to have application in the many aspects of their own personal life as well. Instructors are encouraged to emphasize that "leadership" is a quality that will enhance a person's relationship with his or her family and increase his or her effectiveness in civic and possibly religious activities as well. More specific objectives of supervisory training at ServiceMaster are:

- To teach the basic elements of planning, which will provide a platform for both obtaining results and developing people.
- To demonstrate the necessity for follow-through on plans—to teach supervisors to act on and review plans in order to provide the best possible leadership to the people they lead.
- To demonstrate both the need for delegation and the basic techniques involved.
- To establish that giving good orders is one of the most crucial tasks a leader must accomplish to get things done through other people.
- To teach leaders (supervisors) to provide specific, measurable, challengeable, but achievable performance expectations for the people they lead (designing effective job descriptions and standards of performance).
- To teach the supervisor to communicate and implement performance expectation which will provide consistency and direction as well as improve productivity.
- To teach supervisors how to develop a successful communication climate of openness and trust.
- To teach supervisors the job skill training process for improving employee performance.

The specific content in the training and development of supervisors centers on the following concepts:

- Benefits of planning and the associated critical steps involved in the process.
- Project management by breaking projects down to small objectives and priorities.
- Effective delegation by using proved guidelines and how to use them.
- Teaching how to give good written and verbal orders.
- Teaching the basic skills of designing effective job descriptions and standards of performance.
- Demonstration of how to use standards to improve employee performance.
- Teaching supervisors the "how to's" for planning effective communications, how to eliminate communication killers, and how to clarify their communications process.

▸ Helping supervisors learn the process to identify initiative in those they lead and how to nurture it.
▸ Helping supervisors understand their role and responsibility to understand the positive aspects of effective training and the basic ways people learn.

Supervisors are developed by our managers who are placed at the facilities we serve in the health care, education, and industrial markets. The time frame for this development to occur varies by market and especially by facility served. The most effective way to teach, train, and develop supervisors would be monthly meetings with a time duration of $1\frac{1}{2}$–2 hours in length. The participants learn through a variety of methods such as:

▸ Overheads
▸ Case studies
▸ Videos
▸ Role playing
▸ Small group discussion
▸ Written assignments
▸ Accountability sessions
▸ Team assignments
▸ Review of recent articles

Participants receive a manual for each unit taught. They are asked to put their own name on their workbook and encouraged to write in it, which gives them ownership of not only the workbook but of the session.

Instructors for supervisory training and development are many times Service-Master personnel with the job title of "people development managers" who are trained and certified in this process. Many of our account managers and area operations managers also are qualified to teach this program. General information on ways to facilitate group discussion, such as classroom set-up/seating arrangements, encouraging participants to jot down key words and phrases in answer to questions throughout each unit, having participants break into small groups of three to four people to answer case study questions, are in an instructor's manual for each unit to be taught. A common practice of instructors is to send general information to participants well in advance to include the following:

▸ Advance assignment direction
▸ Session overview
▸ Type of format to meeting
▸ Materials they need to bring
▸ List of supplemental readings

In summary, at ServiceMaster there are essential aspects that must be developed within supervisors. These aspects or tasks are:

To inspect. A supervisor must know what to look for and how to interpret what is observed in terms of performance.

To motivate. This calls for skills in people handling. Motivation skills can be learned in order to turn "negatives" into "positives."

To train. One-on-one training. A teacher/learner experience. It fosters trust and confidence. The supervisor must be trained properly to train those who report to him or her.

To direct. As in any other leadership position, a supervisor must have the capability to "use" the work force as a team. The supervisor directs the how, the where, the when, and with what tools a job must be accomplished.

Summary

These six examples illustrate philosophy, strategy, and guiding principles that underlie the training and development of their supervisors. In each of the examples, emphasis has been placed on their concern for people and the belief that each one is important. Also, they consistently provide opportunity for people to grow and develop. A continuous emphasis is placed on managers as "leaders" who involve their subordinates in the decision-making process. "Empowerment" and "teamwork" are mentioned as means of getting maximum motivation and productivity from all employees.

Differences as well as similarities are evident in comparing these six organizations. Each has tailored philosophy, strategy, and guiding principles to coincide with corporate culture. Every organization should do the same.

4

Conditions for Maximum Learning by Supervisors

If training efforts are to be successful, consideration must be given to supervisors as learners. Some of the theories and principles of adult learning are described below. The eleven authors represented here are only examples of the many who have written articles and books on the subject.

STEPHEN D. BROOKFIELD

In his book, Understanding and Facilitating Adult Learning, *Brookfield refers to much research that has been done on "learning." He quotes W. B. James, who in 1983 "devised the following set of basic principles of adult learning after a team of researchers had undertaken a search of articles, research reports, dissertations, and textbooks on adult learning":*

1. Adults maintain the ability to learn.
2. Adults are a highly diversified group of individuals with widely differing preferences, needs, backgrounds, and skills.
3. Adults experience a gradual decline in physical/sensory capabilities.
4. Experience of the learner is a major resource in learning situations.
5. Self-concept moves from dependency to independency as individuals grow in responsibility, experience, and confidence.
6. Adults tend to be life-centered in their orientation to learning.
7. Adults are motivated to learn by a variety of factors.
8. Active learner participation in the learning process contributes to learning.
9. A comfortable, supportive climate is a key to successful learning.[1]

1. Stephen D. Brookfield, *Understanding and Facilitating Adult Learning* (San Francisco: Jossey-Bass Publishers, 1990).

NATHANIEL CANTOR

In his book The Learning Process for Managers, *Cantor states that "the average adult has learned how not to learn. He has learned how to avoid genuine, positive learning. His learning has come from anxiety, apprehensiveness, and fear of disapproval."*[2]

Genuine learning, according to Cantor, requires a change in behavior. Learners organize their attitudes, feelings, and understanding. No one ordinarily enjoys such experiences. Most of us have developed an involved system of defenses against the inevitable conflict between outward conformity and the independent need for self-expression. The ambivalence and conflict we experience over denying that at times our needs are different from the needs of others will not evaporate.

Individuals struggle to create their own syntheses or to resist creating anything of their own. The most important contribution that can be made by anyone close to the learner is to encourage the latter to create — to learn positively. The best way to do this is to remove the threat of recrimination, reprisal, or disapproval.

The popular idea that learning is a process of storing data and that the more data one has the more learning one possesses is false. Facts are integrated in relation to the ongoing experience of the learner. Seeing interrelationships and readjusting and modifying behavior is the essence of learning. To learn is to reshape, re-form, and remake one's experience.

ANDREW HENDRICKSON

In an article in Adult Leadership, *Hendrickson states nine principles for consideration by those who are called on to teach adults.*

1. Good teaching takes into account past negative school experiences, remoteness of past schooling, and the self-doubts of adults, and provides at the earliest possible time in the class for encouragement and for an experience of success.
2. Good teaching takes into account the relation between a pleasant social atmosphere and a satisfying educational experience.
3. Good training takes into account not only the need for an early experience of success but the need for frequently recurring experiences of success.
4. Good teaching takes into account the learning speed of learners.
5. Good teaching recognizes the validity of the principle of involvement.
6. Good teaching recognizes the adults themselves as a prime teaching resource.
7. Good teaching recognizes the concreteness and immediacy of most adult goals.

2. Nathaniel Cantor, *The Learning Process for Managers* (New York: Harper and Brothers, 1958).

8. Good teaching takes into account the key place which motivation holds in the learning process.
9. Good teaching recognizes physical and mental fatigue as a deterring factor in adult learning.[3]

J. R. KIDD

In his book How Adults Learn, *Kidd discusses theories of learning, as well as their application in the teaching situation. Some of his thoughts follow.*

1. The physical and sensory equipment of people of all ages is ample for most kinds of learning if it is used efficiently.
2. There is nothing about aging itself which prevents or seriously hampers learning.
3. A constellation of feelings associated with love (respect, admiration, generosity, sympathy, friendliness, encouragement) has much more "efficiency" for learning than have feelings associated with anger or with fear.
4. Of all the factors pertaining to success in learning, the most critical are those of motivation—how a person deeply engages himself in the learning transaction. Subject matter, environmental factors, methods, and techniques are also important, but they must be seen in the light of the key word, *engagement.*

There is no hierarchy of values in learning; every factor can be of critical importance—on occasion fresh air may be as important as fresh ideas. Environment, the place, shape, and character of the facilities—all affect the amount and quality of learning.

An astonishing variety of forms, methods, techniques, and devices is available to the agent in adult learning. But one of the chief skills of the teacher of adults is the ability to select. For example, it is possible to convey facts to very large groups of adults, but the sound pattern of languages is best learned in groups of no larger than six. Where skills are being taught, ample opportunity and facilities must be provided for practice.

The choice of participants, those who have had similar or very different previous experience, markedly affects the educational outcome. For some tasks, the best results are achieved when the participants are self-selected.

In every activity, arrangements must be made for the expression of a number of factors—for example, anticipating and dealing with apprehension or resistance to learning, gaining and holding attention, and providing for clear exposition, allowing for a two-way flow of communication, and ensuring that there is testing, application, and appraisal of the knowledge, skill, or attitude.

---

3. Andrew Hendrickson, "Adult Learning and the Adult Learner," *Adult Leadership* (February 1966). © Copyright 1965 The Sunday School Board of the Southern Baptist Convention. All rights reserved. Used by permission.

Among the most important developments in recent years have been many new applications of the "reality" principle—planning a learning experience that is concrete, vivid, and relevant. Examples of this are the use of actual machines, devices, or mock-ups in training, role playing, the "exercise," the case method, and the T-group.

Another noteworthy gain has been in the application and use of learning devices, such as motion picture films. Devices do not replace the teacher, but they can be an effective and economical means to good learning.

The key to learning is *engagement:* a relationship between the learner, the task or subject matter, the environment, and the teacher. Some of the factors within this relationship are already established by the nature and experience of the learner, but many of the factors are not fixed in any way; they can be modified and improved with planning and practice.[4]

MALCOLM S. KNOWLES

The best-known author concerning learning theory is Malcolm Knowles. Here, from The Training and Development Handbook, *are some assumptions he makes that he describes as the* andragological model:

1. Adults have a need to know why they should learn something.
2. Adults have a deep need to be self-directing.
3. Adults have a greater volume and different quality of experience than youth.
4. Adults become ready to learn when they experience in their life situation a need to know or be able to do in order to perform more effectively and satisfyingly.
5. Adults enter into a learning experience with a task-centered (or problem-centered or life-centered) orientation to learning.
6. Adults are motivated to learn by both extrinsic and intrinsic motivators.

Based on these assumptions, Knowles draws the following implications for practice:

1. Establish a climate that is conducive for learning. Two broad aspects of climate must be considered: institutional climate and the climate of the training situation.
2. Create a climate for mutual planning. It is critical that a planning committee or task force be used which is representative of all the constituencies that the program is designed to serve.

4. J. R. Kidd, *How Adults Learn* (New York: Associated Press, 1959).

3. Diagnose the participants' learning needs.
4. Translate learning needs into objectives.
5. Design and manage a pattern of learning experiences. Involve the participants in developing the plan.
6. Evaluate the extent to which the objectives have been accomplished. Develop procedures for involving the participants in the evaluation.[5]

GORDON LIPPITT

In an issue of Journal of ASTD, *Gordon Lippitt reminded training and development people of the following principles of learning:*

1. All human beings learn. Even older adults can learn. The old adage that "you can't teach an old dog new tricks" is wrong. It is just more difficult because the elderly have learned some wrong attitudes and skills.

2. Learning is an active process. People learn best when they are actively involved and interact with the teacher, boss, fellow students, environment, and learning stimulus. One does not learn by being passive. I believe in reflection, but for learning to be effective this must be an active process of synthesis and usually requires proper environmental conditions.

3. Learning is individualistic. Each person learns in accordance with his own personality, perception, expectation, and readiness. Persons attending a learning experience will go away with different things that they have learned.

4. Learning takes place at various levels. Learning experiences must be planned to fit the student's level of knowledge, skills, and attitude:

> *Knowledge level.* This level of learning may be achieved through managing, conditioning, one-way communication, or similar approaches. It should not be confused with *application* of the knowledge.
> *Skill level.* This level of learning requires adaptation and practice. Being able to convert intentions and knowledge into practical results requires learning in the "action" context and will utilize role playing, skill practices, videotape feedback plus practice, and other action-oriented methods of learning.
> *Attitude level.* At this level of learning we are dealing with perceptions, past experiences, and values. Learning which produces changes in attitude is much harder to achieve—it will require more sophisticated methods such as confrontation learning, laboratory training, or sensory experiencing.[6]

5. Malcolm S. Knowles, "Adult Learning" (Chapter 9), in *The Training and Development Handbook*, 3d ed. (New York: McGraw-Hill, Inc., 1987).
6. Gordon Lippitt, "Concepts of Learning and the Development Process," *Journal of ASTD* (May 1969).

These three levels of learning must be considered if we are to achieve and maintain *performance change* as a result of training and development activity. Those of us involved in the educational process should have performance improvement as a goal, rather than the mere acquisition of new words, gimmicks, or temporary responses that slip back into the same routine because change was not "fully" learned or reinforced. This is the challenge for all of us as we assess the needs of our organizations, design learning experiences, and evaluate the effect of our efforts.

ROBERT MAGER

In his book Developing Attitudes Toward Learning, *Robert Mager describes a number of factors that should be considered.*

1. Learning is for future; that is, the object of instruction is to facilitate some form of behavior at a point *after* the instruction has been completed.
2. The likelihood of the student putting his knowledge to use is influenced by his attitude for or against the subjects; things disliked have a way of being forgotten.
3. People influence people. Teachers, and others, do influence attitudes toward subject matter—and toward learning itself.
4. One objective toward which to strive is that of having the student leave your influence with as favorable an attitude toward your subject as possible. In this way, you will help to maximize the possibility that he will remember what he has been taught, and will willingly learn more about what he has been taught.[7]

GARRY MITCHELL

According to Mitchell: "There are ten recognized principles of adult learning" that should be considered in developing a training program:

1. People learn only when they are ready to learn.
2. People learn best what they actually perform.
3. People learn from their mistakes.
4. People learn easiest what is familiar to them.
5. People favor different senses for learning.
6. People learn methodically and, in our culture, systematically.
7. People cannot learn what they cannot understand.
8. People learn through practice.

7. Robert Mager, *Developing Attitudes Toward Learning* (Belmont, Calif.: Lake Publishing Co., 1984). © Copyright 1984 by Lake Publishing Company, Belmont, Calif. 94002.

9. People learn better when they can see their own progress.
10. People respond best when what they are to learn is presented uniquely to them. Each of us is different.

Mitchell quotes Thorndike's three laws of learning as a preface to his ten principles:

1. Law of Readiness
2. Law of Effect
3. Law of Exercise[8]

ROBERT W. PIKE

In his Creative Training Techniques Handbook, *Robert Pike sets out seven laws of learning.*

1. The Law of the TEACHER.

The teacher must know what is to be taught. You can't teach what you haven't learned. And you must teach from a prepared life as well as from a prepared lesson. The most effective instructors on any topic generally are those who have experienced what they are teaching.

2. The Law of the LEARNER.

The learner must attend with interest to the material being presented. If you are excited about what you are teaching, you can create a motivational environment. You can do that by answering the learner's question: "What's in it for me?" The learner has to see the benefits for himself or herself. What will they get out of it? How can they apply it? How can they use it?

3. The Law of the LANGUAGE.

The language you use must be comprehensible to the learner. Nobody likes experts; we want to knock them off their pedestals. But everybody loves the learner. Start where people are, and take them were they need to be. Go from the known to the unknown. When you use words or terms unfamiliar to the learners, define them immediately. Language should be a stepping stone, not a stumbling block.

4. The Law of the LESSON.

The truth or content taught must be learned through the truth or the content already known. Again, go from where the learners are. Build on what they already know.

5. The Law of the TEACHING PROCESS.

You must excite and direct your learners' self-motivation. People often learn best through self-discovery. I've frequently said that there are basically three ways people learn, and the first two of them don't work, so we don't use them.

8. Garry Mitchell, *The Trainer's Handbook Second Edition* (New York: AMACOM, 1993). Reprinted by permission of the publisher from *The Trainer's Handbook: The AMA Guide to Effective Training, Second Edition* by Garry Mitchell, © 1993 AMACOM, a division of American Management Association, New York. All rights reserved.

- You can tell people things.
- You can use statistics.
- We can put people in situations where they discover for themselves how effective or ineffective they are. People learn most effectively when they are actively involved in the learning process, not passively observing it.

6. The Law of the LEARNING PROCESS.

The learner must reproduce in his or her own life the content to be learned. Learning does not take place until behavior has changed. We're talking about being able to apply—not simply to know but also to do. Just because the instructor has rapport with the learners doesn't automatically guarantee that learning is going to occur. You want to involve as many senses as possible and use as many approaches as you can so that people grasp and apply the material you want them to learn.

7. The Law of REVIEW and APPLICATION.

You must confirm the completion of the content taught. And you do that by emphasizing practical application. Ask, "How can you use this in real life?" and "What do you expect if you apply what you've been learning?"[9]

RON ZEMKE AND SUSAN ZEMKE

Based on extensive research, Ron Zemke and Sue Zemke offer a number of ideas and recommendations.

Adult learners can't be threatened, coerced, or tricked into learning something new. Birch rods and gold stars have minimum impact. Adults *can* be ordered into a classroom and prodded into a seat, but they *cannot* be forced to learn. Though trainers are often faced with adults who have been sent to training, there are some insights to be garnered from the research on adults who seek out a structured learning experience on their own. It's something we all do at least twice a year, the research says. We begin our running tally from this base camp. Following are thirty things our research has taught us.

1. Adults seek out learning experiences in order to cope with specific life-change events. Marriage, divorce, a new job, a promotion, being fired, retiring, losing a loved one, and moving to a new city are examples.

2. The more life-change events an adult encounters, the more likely he or she is to seek out learning opportunities. Just as stress increases as life-change events accumulate, the motivation to cope with change through engagement in a learning experience increases. Since the people who most frequently seek out learning op-

9. Robert W. Pike, *Creative Training Techniques Handbook* (Minneapolis: Lakewood Publications, 1989). Distributed by Resources for Organizations, 7251 Flying Cloud Drive, Eden Prairie, Minn. 55344. 1-800-383-9210

portunities are people who have the most years of education, it is reasonable to guess that for many of us, learning is a coping response to significant change.

3. The learning experiences adults seek out on their own are directly related — at least in their own perceptions — to the life-change events that triggered the seeking. Therefore, if 80 percent of the change being encountered is work-related, then 80 percent of the learning experiences should be work-related.

4. Adults are generally willing to engage in learning experiences before, after, or even during the actual life-change event. Once convinced that the change is a certainty, adults will engage in any learning that promises to help them cope with the transition.

5. Although adults have been found to engage in learning for a variety of reasons — job advancement, pleasure, love of learning, and so on — it is equally true that for most adults learning is not its own reward. Adults who are motivated to seek out a learning experience do so primarily (80–90 percent of the time) because they have a use for the knowledge or skill being sought. Learning is a means to an end, not an end in itself.

6. Increasing or maintaining one's sense of self-esteem and pleasure are strong secondary motivators for engaging in learning experiences. Having a new skill or extending and enriching current knowledge can be both, depending on the individual's personal perceptions.

7. Adult learners tend to be less interested in, and enthralled by, survey courses. They tend to prefer single-concept, single-theory courses that focus heavily on the application of the concept to relevant problems. This tendency increases with age.

8. Adults need to be able to integrate new ideas with what they already know if they are going to keep — and use — the new information.

9. Information that conflicts sharply with what is already held to be true, and thus forces a re-evaluation of the old material, is integrated more slowly.

10. Information that has little "conceptual overlap" with what is already known is acquired slowly.

11. Fast-paced, complex, or unusual learning tasks interfere with the learning of the concepts or data they are intended to teach or illustrate.

12. Adults tend to compensate for being slower in some psychomotor learning tasks by being more accurate and making fewer trial-and-error ventures.

13. Adults tend to take errors personally and are more likely to let them affect self-esteem. Therefore, they tend to apply tried-and-true solutions and take fewer risks. There is even evidence that adults will misinterpret feedback and "mistake" errors for positive confirmation.

14. The curriculum designer must know whether the concepts and ideas will be in concert or in conflict with learner and organizational values. As trainers at AT&T have learned, moving from a service to a sales philosophy requires more than a change in words and titles. It requires a change in the way people think and value.

15. Programs need to be designed to accept viewpoints from people in different life stages and with different value "sets."

16. A concept needs to be "anchored" or explained from more than one value set and appeal to more than one developmental life stage.

17. Adults prefer self-directed and self-designed learning projects 7 to 1 over group-learning experiences led by a professional. Furthermore, the adult learner often selects more than one medium for the design. Reading and talking to a qualified peer are frequently cited as good resources. The desire to control pace and start/stop time strongly affects the self-directed preference.

18. Non-human media such as books, programmed instruction, and television have become popular in recent years. One piece of research found them very influential in the way adults plan self-directed learning projects.

19. Regardless of media, straightforward how-to is the preferred content orientation. As many as 80 percent of the polled adults in one study cited the need for applications and how-to information as the primary motivation for undertaking a learning project.

20. Self-direction does *not* mean isolation. In fact, studies of self-directed learning show self-directed projects involve an average of 10 other people as resources, guides, encouragers, and the like. The incompetence or inadequacy of these same people is often rated as a primary frustration. But even for the self-professed, self-directed learner, lectures and short seminars get positive ratings, especially when these events give the learner face-to-face, one-to-one access to an expert.

Apparently, the adult learner is a very efficiency-minded individual. Allen Tough suggests that the typical adult learner asks, "What is the cheapest, easiest, fastest way for me to learn to do *that?*" and then proceeds independently along this self-determined route. An obvious tip for the trainer is that the adult trainee has to have a hand in shaping the curriculum of the program.

21. The learning environment must be physically and psychologically comfortable. Adults report that long lectures, periods of interminable sitting, and the absence of practice opportunities are high on the irritation scale.

22. Adults have something real to lose in a classroom situation. Self-esteem and ego are on the line when they are asked to risk trying a new behavior in front of peers and cohorts. Bad experiences in traditional education, feelings about authority, and the preoccupation with events outside the classroom all affect in-class experience. These and other influencing factors are carried into class with the learners as surely as are their gold Cross pens and lined yellow pads.

23. Adults have expectations, and it is critical to take time up front to clarify and articulate *all* expectations before getting into content. Both trainees and the instructor/facilitator need to state their expectations. When they are at variance, the problem should be acknowledged and a resolution negotiated. In any case, the instructor can assume responsibility only for his or her expectations, not for those of trainees.

24. Adults bring a great deal of life experience into the classroom, an invalua-

ble asset to be acknowledged, tapped, and used. Adults can learn well—and much—from dialogue with respected peers.

25. Instructors who have a tendency to hold forth rather than facilitate can hold that tendency in check—or compensate for it—by concentrating on the use of open-ended questions to draw out relevant trainee knowledge and experience.

26. New knowledge has to be integrated with previous knowledge; that means active learner participation. Since only the learners can tell us how the new fits or fails to fit with the old, we have to ask them. Just as the learner is dependent on us for confirming feedback on skill practice, we are dependent on the learner for feedback about our curriculum and in-class performance.

27. The key to the instructor role is control. The instructor must balance the presentation of new material, debate and discussion, sharing of relevant trainee experiences, and the clock. Ironically, we seem best able to establish control when we risk giving it up. When we shelve our egos and stifle the tendency to be threatened by challenge to our plans and methods, we gain the kind of facilitative control we seem to need to affect adult learning.

28. The instructor has to protect minority opinion, keep disagreements civic and unheated, make connections between various opinions and ideas, and keep reminding the group of the variety of potential solutions to the problem. Just as in a good problem-solving meeting, the instructor is less advocate than orchestrator.

29. Integration of new knowledge and skill requires transition time and focused effort. Working on applications to specific back-on-the-job problems helps with the transfer. Action plans, accountability strategies, and follow-up after training all increase the likelihood of that transfer. Involving the trainees' supervisor in pre- and post-course activities helps with both in-class focus and transfer.

30. Learning and teaching theories function better as a resource than as a Rosetta stone. The four currently influential theories—humanistic, behavioral, cognitive, and developmental—all offer valuable guidance when matched with an appropriate learning task. A skill-training task can draw much from the behavioral approach, for example, while personal growth-centered subjects seem to draw gainfully from humanistic concepts. The trainer of adults needs to take an eclectic rather than a single theory–based approach to developing strategies and procedures.[10]

Summary and Recommendations

An analysis of the ideas of these eleven authors reveals some common threads, as well as some difference of opinion as to the most significant aspects of the learning process. To look at learning from the standpoint of supervisory training and development, it is important to consider the

10. Ron Zemke and Susan Zemke, "30 Things We Know for Sure About Adult Learning," *Training* (July 1988). Ron Zemke is president, Performance Research Associates, and senior editor of *Training* magazine. Susan Zemke is manager of management and professional development, the St. Paul Companies.

factors noted in Figure 4-1. One of the most important factors is the attitudes that supervisors bring to the training and development situation; these attitudes have an impact on the learning that will take place in the program. Supervisors may have negative attitudes toward the training program for a number of reasons:

- ▸ A poor attitude toward the job and toward the company in general—perhaps related to salary, pressures, or frustrations.
- ▸ A training schedule that may be inconvenient for them or may require them to take training on their own time.
- ▸ Subject content that has been determined by training and person-

Figure 4-1. Factors affecting learning.

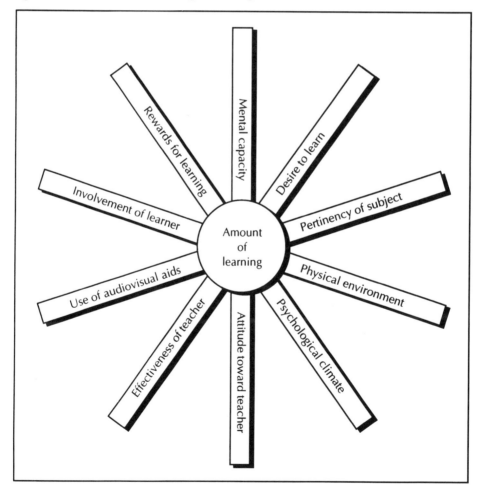

nel people or even by top management instead of by supervisors and middle management people.

▸ The instructor. Perhaps a young college graduate is teaching mature, experienced supervisors how to do the job better, or an outside psychologist has been called in to act as a teacher. The instructor may lack the respect of the supervisors who will be attending the meeting.

▸ A reaction to what they have heard about the training program. Perhaps they have been given insufficient information on the purpose of the training program and how it will help them, and they view the program as a complete waste of time and effort.

It is easy to see that a negative attitude on the part of the learner can have a detrimental effect on the effectiveness of the program. A learner who comes to the program with one or more of these negative attitudes is not going to put forth very much effort to learn. The teaching will probably be quite ineffective unless the attitude of the learner can be changed.

On the other hand, supervisors may come to a training program with a great deal of enthusiasm. They may be looking forward to it and recognize an opportunity for personal growth and development that will help them as well as the company. This is the kind of an attitude that can result in maximum learning. Those who plan supervisory and training programs should try to plan them and promote them in such a way that supervisors will come to the program with enthusiasm.

Consideration should be given to other classroom and on-the-job factors that affect learning. First, it must be recognized that learning is a process of change. The desired outcomes of a typical training program are changes in attitudes, knowledge, skill, and on-the-job behavior. Problems arise if supervisors resist the changes that are being encouraged by those who are teaching the programs. Perhaps they worry that their boss will not support the changes; perhaps they do not feel comfortable with the new ways; or if their old attitudes, habits, and behavior have proved to be successful, they may be reluctant to change because of the insecurity that would come with a new approach.

Another important factor related to the effectiveness of the teaching has to do with the anxieties and fears created in the classroom itself. If the climate is one in which participants do not feel free to speak up, they will not participate in the learning process. This kind of negative climate can be created by the instructor or by a top management person who may be in the meeting, either observing or as part of the group. The instructor can create a positive climate, and the presence of open-minded top management can encourage supervisors to say what they think.

One of the principles of learning that has been highlighted by several of the people who have been quoted in this chapter has to do with the learners' involvement and participation. All agree that active participation in the training sessions can improve the learning that takes place — not necessarily on the part of the one who participates but on the part of others in the group who can learn from the person who makes a contribution.

Another important principle that must be considered when planning and implementing a program is that it must be practical. As Knowles said, it should be "problem centered," and the people in the group should be able to apply it immediately. The closer the content is to this ideal, the more the participants will learn.

The facilities themselves should be conducive to effective learning. The comfort and relaxation of participants is important to effective learning. Consideration should be given to the room set-up, ventilation, schedule, breaks, and chairs and tables.

A final important factor is that learning should be a series of successes. People should like what they're learning; they should feel that it is beneficial to them and that they can use it on the job. If skills are being taught, opportunities must be provided for practice, because people do not learn skills just by listening and discussing.

As Mager put it, "If we are to look for changes in on-the-job behavior, we should have the student leave the classroom with as favorable an attitude toward the subject as possible. In this way, you will help to maximize the possibility that he or she will remember what has been taught and will willingly learn more about what has been taught."

The planners and implementers of supervisory training and development must maximize the learning possibilities on the part of the supervisors. They must:

- Create enthusiasm for the training activities in which they are engaged.
- Plan and implement training and development programs and activities so that supervisors maintain a high degree of enthusiasm and desire for them and thereby maximize the learning that takes place.
- Recognize that supervisors are adults who have feelings and emotions that must be considered. These supervisors probably want to be involved in the planning of the training program, perhaps identifying the subjects of greatest help to them, and in the training process itself, the supervisors will want to partcipate.

All of these principles and theories in learning can be put to good use in a carefully planned and conducted training and development program.

5

Determining Training Needs and Setting Objectives

Effective training programs are based on the needs of the supervisors to be trained—that is, the attitudes, knowledge, and skills the supervisors need in order to do their job effectively. The following questions must be answered in order to determine these needs:

1. Who should determine the needs?
2. Should the program focus on current needs or future needs?
3. How should the needs be determined?

From these needs, program objectives can be determined.

Who Determines Needs?

There are at least five different kinds of people who can help determine the needs for a supervisory and development program: (1) upper-level managers in the organization; (2) staff personnel in the organization such as human resources managers and training and development professionals; (3) the supervisors themselves; (4) subordinates of the supervisors to be trained; and (5) outsiders such as consultants, psychologists, and research specialists.

1. *Upper-level managers.* A common approach is for an organization's managers to decide what their supervisors need in the way of training and development. They base their recommendations on personal opinions, what other organizations are doing, the most pressing problems in the organization, and other subjective and objective criteria.

2. *Staff personnel.* Another common approach is for someone in the

human resources or training department to determine the supervisory training needs. This, too, can be done subjectively or objectively. These staff may look at what other companies are doing, see what kind of training is being offered by universities and professional or trade associations, analyze the jobs and performance of the supervisors, or simply decide what they think is best for the supervisors.

3. *Supervisors themselves.* Supervisors probably would like to establish their own needs. They feel they are in the best position to judge what will be helpful to them in the performance of their job. Some companies use this approach by interviewing the supervisors or by using a questionnaire to ask them what they need.

4. *Subordinates of the supervisors.* Even though the subordinates may be in the position to know the weaknesses and needs of their supervisors, they are not often asked to express those opinions. Many supervisors would not like the idea of their subordinates being asked for such information. And in many organizations, neither the top management nor the staff personnel feel that it's appropriate to ask hourly and clerical workers for the training needs of their bosses. An indirect approach is to use attitude surveys.

5. *Outsiders.* Larger companies, particularly, make use of outside consultants and psychologists to help them determine training needs for the supervisors in the organization. These consultants may use a very elaborate system of questionnaires and interviews to determine the needs. Or they may suggest personal experiences and ideas from other organizations and possibly sell them to the company for which they work at the moment.

It is difficult to judge which of these five approaches is the best. But the more important question is, Which is most practical? Information from several of these sources would be better than the information from any one alone. For example, the supervisors themselves could be asked to express their own needs. They understand their jobs, and they know what their current and future problems are likely to be. They also understand some of their own personal weaknesses and what might help them do their jobs most effectively. Therefore, those who will receive the training form one practical source of information concerning needs. Another important reason for asking them is that they are more likely to have a positive attitude toward learning the material if they have helped to develop it.

In addition to soliciting the opinions of the supervisors themselves, it is a good idea to ask upper-level managers for their opinions and recommendations on the needs of the supervisors who report to them. The immediate bosses of the supervisors are in a good position to see the problems that have occurred and may have in mind ways to improve efficiency, productivity, and general performance. Also, they will probably support the training program if they have helped to determine it.

Organizations with specialists in the field of training and development should certainly involve them in determining supervisory needs. Perhaps they can provide the most help by setting up questionnaires or interviews or approaches by which the opinions of supervisors as well as upper-level managers can be obtained and quantified. They also should have derived ideas from the techniques used by other organizations to determine needs.

Where the climate is right, subordinates can provide some helpful information about supervisory training needs. Great care should be taken in obtaining this information, however; subordinates should not be asked for their opinions unless their supervisors have given their permission.

Whether outsiders are used depends largely on the ability of—and time available for—the organization to determine its own supervisors' needs. Small companies as well as large can benefit from the use of outside consultants.

Should the Program Focus on Current or Future Needs?

The answer to this question of current versus future needs is that, in general, the focus should be on the current jobs. Improved knowledge, skills, and attitudes in this area result in the greatest payoff. Supervisors learn best when they can immediately use what they learn, and because most supervisors remain in their current job for many years, the main thrust of a training program should be on the present. As certain supervisors move into higher-level jobs or jobs that become more complicated, many of the approaches and techniques that they use on their current jobs will have direct application there.

Yet sometimes training programs regarding future needs are very important. For example, if a new computer or a new tape-controlled machine is being introduced into a company, supervisors should understand the basic principles and features of such equipment so that they may do their jobs better. Similarly, new management skills or knowledge should be taught to the supervisors as the need for them is anticipated— before they are actually needed on the job. For example, if a large number of employees are going to be hired in a department, supervisors should receive advanced training in how to induct and train these new employees to work effectively in that department.

Some organizations identify a few people as candidates for higher-level jobs. Special attention should be given to these people in training to prepare them for their future positions. In most cases, they will be sent to outside programs to receive training sponsored by organizations such as universities, but sometimes they may be trained in certain operations of the company by the department heads and other supervisors.

How Should Needs Be Determined?

There are many ways of determining the training needs of supervisors. Some of the more common and more effective methods are described below.

Job Analysis

One approach for determining training needs is to analyze the jobs of the supervisors. William Stewart made such an analysis of the tasks performed by industrial supervisors. His goal was to eliminate the "erroneous guessing in training needs, opportunities, or current whim on the part of those who control training [that] often underlies the weakness of many supervisory training programs."

Stewart surveyed 717 supervisors representing 110 industrial organizations in Ohio. He gave them a questionnaire listing 120 tasks that they might perform and asked them to select one of three categories to indicate their opinion of the importance attached to each task as representing an area of first-line supervisory training need:

Important	Of considerable value for training purposes. It is desirable that training be conducted in the area relating to the task.
Average	Of moderate value for training. Some consideration should be given to conducting training in the area related to the task.
Not important	Of little or no value for training purposes.

The second group of questions asked of these supervisors concerned the performance frequency of each task. They were required to indicate how often they actually performed the task. Possible responses to these questions were:

Often	The task is usually performed one or more times a week
Occasionally	The task is usually performed less than once a week but more than five times a year
Seldom	The task is performed fewer than five times a year
Never	The task is never performed

After collecting, tabulating, and analyzing the data to determine training needs of the supervisors in the study, Stewart concluded that that tasks concerned with human involvement and understanding were significant first-line supervisory training needs regardless of the type of work done in the department and that common needs existed in the personnel aspects of problem solving.[1] Stewart's approach can be used in other organizations. The results, however, could be entirely different.

Another approach to determining needs is to look, as Robert Mager has done, at descriptions of the jobs of a supervisor. The job description sketches the outlines and high spots of the job, but it isn't complete enough to be used to determine needs or develop a course, so the second step is to conduct a task analysis dealing with the specific tasks that might be included in the job.[2]

Mager believes that the job description and task analysis provide a picture of the kinds of knowledge, skills, and attitudes the supervisor must have to perform the job. These, then, could be considered training needs, particularly those of new supervisors, but they also could be considered the starting point for determining the needs of current supervisors. Obviously, the current knowledge, attitudes, and skills of supervisors have to be considered in relationship to what those supervisors need to have in order to do their job.

Analysis of the Problems

A look at records may reveal certain training needs. For example, an excessive turnover rate of new employees may pinpoint a supervisory training need. Or an excess amount of scrap in a certain department may indicate a need for training supervisors in quality control or other aspects of their job. Other indications of supervisory training needs may be the accident record or the absentee record of employees or an analysis of recent grievances.

---

1. William Stewart, "Determining First-Line Supervisory Training Needs," *Training and Development Journal* (April 1970).
2. Robert Mager, *Developing Vocational Instruction* (Belmont, Calif.: Lake Publishing Co., 1967).

Exit Interviews

Exit interviews, conducted with employees who are leaving the organization, are another technique for locating problem areas and possible supervisory training needs. The purpose of such interviews is to determine why the employee is leaving and any possible problem areas on the job that can be solved by supervisory training. To be objective, these interviews should be conducted by someone in the human resources department or someone other than the immediate supervisor.

Attitude Surveys

A common way of pinpointing training needs is to survey the attitudes of employees. Attitude surveys are usually prepared by outside organizations to measure employee attitudes toward working conditions, pay, supervisory practices, management policies, and other job-related items. The results of these surveys indicate some of the supervisory training needs that can help to improve attitudes of employees. These surveys should be conducted on a regular basis—perhaps once a year—to identify new needs as well as to see what improvement has taken place.

Following are case studies of approaches used by two organizations.

WISCONSIN GAS COMPANY

With the assistance of Jerry Kluza, an independent consultant, Wisconsin Gas Company (Milwaukee, Wisconsin) developed and implemented a program called "Supervisor Review: Improving Our Working Relationships." Here are details on the program.

▶ *What is the purpose of the supervisor review?*
The purpose of the review is to help us develop the best possible management skills and working relationships to make us stronger as a company. The management style team looked at various ways to increase management effectiveness. The team recommended using the supervisor review as a way to get people talking to one another. Those channels of communication may already be open. If they're not, this is a tool to begin a dialogue. It's also another way for managers to get an answer to the question, "How am I doing?"
▶ *When will it start?*
The review will be conducted this year on a division-by-division basis depending on each division's work load. Prior to the review, each division head will conduct meetings to discuss management practices and the supervisor review process.

▸ *Who will be reviewed?*

Everyone with supervisory responsibilities, from the president on down, will be reviewed. Right now there are approximately 200 people with supervisory responsibility.

▸ *How does the supervisor review work?*

You will be asked to review your supervisor by filling out a questionnaire organized around the four key characteristics—competence, integrity, participative leadership skills, and communications skills. The questionnaire will contain about thirty-five questions and will include room for comments. The responses will be anonymous.

▸ *Who will see the survey results?*

An outside company will tabulate the results and prepare the feedback report. The company that is working with us to prepare the questionnaire and will be tabulating the responses is Kluza Associates of Brookfield. A feedback report will be provided to the supervisor being reviewed. A one-page feedback summary will be provided to the supervisor's boss and the division vice-president. The one-page summary will also be added to the supervisor's personnel file. The person being reviewed and his or her supervisor will go over the feedback report and look for ways to build on strengths and work on areas that need improvement. The person being reviewed will also go over the results with the work group that filled out the questionnaire.

▸ *What happens after the review is completed?*

After the feedback report has been returned to the supervisor being reviewed, the supervisor and the supervisor's boss will work together to come up with a development plan that might include such things as additional training, etc. Supervisors and managers are also expected to share results and seek out feedback from the people in their work group who filled out the questionnaire.

▸ *Will this replace the performance review process that management uses now?*

No. The supervisor review is an additional tool we can use to improve performance by strengthening our management skills and improving our working relationships. It is intended to give managers and supervisors more information about how they are doing. It is another way for us to build on individual strengths and focus on areas that need improvement.

▸ *Is this an ongoing effort?*

Yes. We are committed to improving management practices. Change won't occur overnight; improvement will happen with time and teamwork. The survey is an important first step, but an ongoing effort and commitment on everyone's part is required to make sure that the results of the survey lead to improved management practices.

▸ *Will it affect pay?*

Yes, but not until you have had the opportunity to adjust to the process and work on achieving results. The pay tie-in will occur over three years. The first year we will find out where we are today as managers and supervisors. The second year we will implement individual development plans and work toward personal improvement.

The third year we will use the results along with other factors to evaluate employees on pay and promotion.

> ▸ *What other resources are available to develop management skills?*

The corporate library has reference materials (books, periodicals, and audio programs) and many independent-study courses that can help develop interpersonal skills. Many of these are described in the Professional Development and Training Catalog.

> ▸ *Where do I go if I have questions?*

If you have questions about how the supervisor review works or how it is administered, the human resources department can help.

[See illustration on page 49.]

Supervisor Review

All employees were asked to react to each item concerning their supervisor according to the following key:

1. *My supervisor almost never does this.*
2. *My supervisor seldom does this.*
3. *My supervisor sometimes does this.*
4. *My supervisor usually does this.*
5. *My supervisor does this most of the time.*

Competence

1. Is knowledgeable about his/her job.
2. Makes changes that result in improvements.
3. Plans and organizes work with clear priorities.
4. Makes appropriate and timely decisions.
5. Effectively deals with poor performance.
6. Is customer focused—both inside and outside "customers."
7. Is company minded and takes pride in doing his/her work.
8. Is helpful in working with me to develop measurable goals and objectives.
9. Encourages me to learn from my mistakes, develop, and grow.
10. Tries to keep me engaged and challenged by my responsibilities.
11. Measures results and progress toward goals.
12. Gives good guidance and advice.

Comments on this supervisor's Competence:

_____

_____

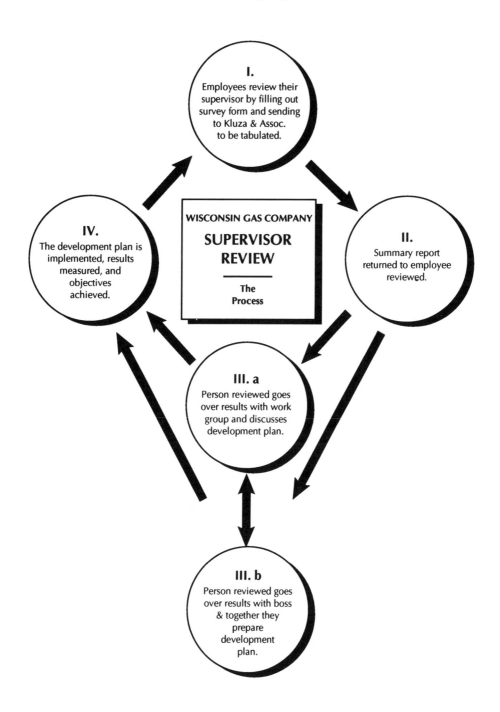

Communication

13. Keeps me informed of things I need to know to do my job effectively.
14. Encourages me to share ideas and concerns by being accessible and approachable.
15. Puts ideas across clearly.
16. Listens and considers what I have to say.
17. Is tactful when interacting with others.
18. Keeps me informed of how I'm doing.

Comments on this supervisor's Communication Skills:

_____

_____

Integrity and Fairness

19. Demonstrates openness and honesty in dealing with me.
20. Can be trusted to keep a confidence.
21. Treats all workers equally.
22. Is trustworthy.
23. Shows concern and respect for individuals.
24. Has work rules but knows when to exercise flexibility.
25. Is fair in dealing with people.

Comments on this supervisor's Integrity and Fairness:

_____

_____

Participative Leadership

26. Encourages innovation.
27. Involves others in decisions that affect them.
28. Sets guidelines that allow me to do my work independently.
29. Actively promotes cooperation between individuals, departments, and divisions.
30. Gives credit when credit is due others.
31. Delegates authority clearly and appropriately.
32. Encourages participation by asking for my opinions and ideas.
33. Allows for disagreement without becoming irritated.
34. Encourages me to uncover and solve problems.
35. Resolves conflicts constructively.

Comments on this supervisor's Participative Leadership:

_____

_____

According to Jody Zanton, coordinator of personnel and employee development, the feedback from this survey has been well accepted by the supervisors and helpful in determining training needs.

Advisory Committee

One of the best approaches to determing needs is to work with a carefully selected advisory committee of six to ten managers who are interested in supervisory development. They can represent different functions and levels in the organization. The committee can advise on subjects, schedules, group size and composition, and other aspects of the program. They can also be involved in implementing the program (introducing conference leaders, teaching certain topics) and can be good salespersons for it.

To get maximum use from the advisory committee, the training professional should provide them with data to be discussed. For example, the results of questionnaires should be given to the committee so that their interpretations and decisions can be based on data instead of off-the-cuff opinions.

Following is a description of how one company uses an advisory committee.

ALLEN-BRADLEY, MILWAUKEE, WISCONSIN
JOHN FLAGGE, PROGRAM SUPERVISOR, TECHNICAL TRAINING, HUMAN RESOURCES

Objective

To serve in an advisory capacity for the training and development function. Committee members will represent functional areas throughout the Company. The committee will provide feedback and evaluation of present and proposed training efforts. The evaluation will be based on constructive criticism and results evaluation.

Functions

1. Recommend changes in existing training programs to meet the changing needs.

2. Evaluate the need for new training programs based upon changes in technology, management theory, etc.
3. Recommend changes consistent with long-range strategies.
4. Make recommendations relative to course format, timing, facilities, content.
5. Communicate with department management within their function so as to represent a broad cross-section of viewpoints.
6. Serve as a communications link between the training and development function and all functions to improve and encourage two-way communications.

Organization

1. The advisory training committee will meet on a semiannual basis to evaluate progress and discuss mutual problems and suggestions.
2. The training advisory committee will consist of subcommittees whose focus will be dependent on current and strategic issues.
   A. Committee 1 will consist of at least two members from each functional area. These members will address current and strategic issues as they pertain to the Company. Each member of this cross-functional committee will be a permanent member of the training advisory committee.
   B. Committees 2–7 will consist of at least six members of their specific functional area. The members of each of the functional committees will address current and strategic issues as they pertain to their functional area. Each committee will appoint a chairperson and that chairperson will be a permanent member of the training advisory committee.
3. The Program Supervisor, Technical Training, will appoint a co-chairperson on an annual basis to assist in scheduling committee meetings and establishing an agenda.

Performance Review

In organizations with a formal performance review program, the completed forms can be analyzed to determine supervisory training needs. Performance reviews usually identify the weaknesses and the areas of improvement needed. These can be analyzed and quantified to determine which subject areas and which kinds of training activities can best help supervisors perform their jobs better. (Chapter 10 describes this approach in detail.)

Questionnaires

Probably the simplest method of determining needs is to prepare a questionnaire that can be administered to supervisors themselves and/or to higher-level managers. Figure 5-1 contains a sample form that any organization can use, although it should be adapted to include all possible

Figure 5-1. Questionnaire for determining subject content for training.

Please put an "X" after each topic to indicate your need for that topic:

	Great Need	Some Need	Little Need
1. The job of supervisor (objectives, functions, authority, responsibility)			
2. Leadership styles			
3. Interpersonal communication principles, barriers, approaches, methods			
4. Written communication			
5. Oral communication			
6. Listening			
7. Conducting productive meetings			
8. Interviewing			
9. Speed reading			
10. Understanding and motivating employees			
11. Orienting and training employees			
12. Supervising minority employees—diversity in the work force			
13. Appraising employee performance			
14. Preventing and handling complaints/grievances			
15. Planning			
16. Discipline			
17. Decision making			
18. Empowerment—self-directed work teams			
19. Managing change			
20. Delegation			
21. Managing my time			
22. Building teamwork			
23. Improving quality			
24. Resolving conflict			

(continues)

Figure 5-1. (*continued*)

	Great Need	Some Need	Little Need
25. Building morale among subordinates			

Other suggested topics:

topics for supervisory training that might apply to a particular organization. The use of three columns makes it easy to tabulate and quantify the needs as determined by the supervisors themselves.

Figure 5-2 shows a tabulation of the results of surveying twenty-one supervisors. In order to use the data in planning, a weight of "2" has been given to column 1 ("Great Need"), "1" to column 2 ("Some Need"), and "0" to the third column. The weighted scored—column 1 plus column 2—has been calculated and then converted to the rank order shown on the left side of the form.

The same process can be followed to get input from bosses. The topics would be the same, but the instructions at the top of the form would read instead, "Please put a check in the appropriate column after each topic to indicate your opinion of the need of supervisors who report to you." A comparison could then be made of the rank order of topics determined by the bosses with the rank order determined by the supervisors themselves. Other data should also be considered in deciding which needs are most important and urgent.

Interviews

A common way of determining supervisory training needs is to interview the supervisors themselves, their bosses, or both. To be an effective technique, a patterned interview should be used. This means that the same questions should be asked of different people so that responses can be quantified.

Following is a guide for a patterned interview with supervisors:

We are planning a training program to help you do your job better. You can help us determine subject content by answering the following questions:

1. What problems exist in your department?
2. What problems do you foresee in the near future?

Figure 5-2. A completed questionnaire.

Please put an "X" after each topic to indicate your need for that topic:

Rank Order		Weighted Score	(Weight) 2 Great Need	1 Some Need	0 Little Need
10	1. The job of supervisor (objectives, functions, authority, responsibility)	29	10	9	2
3	2. Leadership styles	34	13	8	0
17	3. Interpersonal communication principles, barriers, approaches, methods	25	7	11	3
15	4. Written communication	26	9	8	4
13	5. Oral communication	27	8	11	2
23	6. Listening	16	5	6	10
21	7. Conducting productive meetings	19	4	11	6
20	8. Interviewing	20	6	8	7
24	9. Speed reading	14	2	10	9
3	10. Understanding and motivating employees	34	13	8	0
2	11. Orienting and training employees	35	15	5	1
7	12. Supervising minority employees—diversity in the work force	32	12	8	1
18	13. Appraising employee performance	24	8	8	5
15	14. Preventing and handling complaints/grievances	26	10	6	5
25	15. Planning	10	2	6	13
7	16. Discipline	32	12	8	1
3	17. Decision making	34	13	8	0

(continues)

Figure 5-2. (*continued*)

Rank Order		Weighted Score	(Weight)		
			2 Great Need	1 Some Need	0 Little Need
13	18. Empowerment—self-directed work teams	27	9	9	3
3	19. Managing change	34	14	6	1
22	20. Delegation	18	6	6	9
10	21. Managing my time	29	11	7	3
1	22. Building teamwork	40	19	2	0
7	23. Improving quality	32	11	10	0
12	24. Resolving conflict	28	9	10	2
18	25. Building morale among subordinates	24	8	10	3

Other suggested topics:

_____

    3. What subjects should be included in a training program to help solve these problems?

    4. What other topics should be included in order to help you do your job better?

    5. When would be the best time for you to attend a classroom training program?

    6. When is the worst time?

A checklist of possible topics described in Figure 5-1 can be used in question 3 so that the tabulations can be quantified.

The same type of approach can be used in conducting interviews with the bosses of the supervisors to be trained. These interviews are more personal and can provide more detailed information than questionnaires, but they are much more time-consuming.

Tests and Inventories

Another way of determining supervisory training needs is to test the supervisors on their attitudes, knowledge, and skills that are important in doing their job. (This testing could be a supplement to the job analysis described above.)

Tests and inventories can be developed and tailored to the organization, or appropriate standardized tests can be used to assist in determining needs. I've developed standardized tests on the subjects of communications, human relations, safety, managing change, time management, performance appraisal and coaching, and leadership, motivation, and decision making. Items are to be answered "agree" or "disagree."[3] Samples from each of these inventories follow.

Supervisory Inventory on Communication

1. A good definition of communication is the sending of information from one person to another.
2. The misunderstanding of an order or instruction can have serious results on safety, production, and cost.
3. A sender has failed to communicate unless the receiver understands the message the way the sender intended it.
4. When it is important that a new policy be understood by all employees, the best way to communicate is through channels of authority in the organization.
5. If employees do not understand, they will usually indicate lack of understanding by asking questions or by saying they don't understand.
6. If a supervisor is busy, it is best to tell an employee who wants to talk, "I'm busy right now, contact me later."
7. The shorter a memo, the more clear it is likely to be.
8. "Verbal" means the same as "oral."
9. Oral communication is more effective than written.
10. A supervisor has failed to communicate unless the employee understands, accepts, and carries out the instruction.

Supervisory Inventory on Human Relations

1. Anyone is able to do almost any job if he or she tries hard enough.
2. Intelligence consists of what we've learned since we were born.
3. Everyone is either an introvert or an extrovert.
4. An employee's attitude has little effect on his production.
5. People will work faster and longer if they always have a little more work ahead of them than they can possibly do.
6. A good supervisor must be able to perform all the jobs in the department.
7. In training an employee, the first thing the supervisor should do is show in detail how the job is performed.

3. Donald L. Kirkpatrick, *Supervisory/Management Inventories* (Elm Grove, Wis.: Donald L. Kirkpatrick, 1992).

8. To correct a worker who has made a mistake, a good supervisor will begin by pointing out the mistake.
9. The supervisor is closer to management than to subordinates.
10. It is a good idea to praise an employee in front of other employees.

Supervisory Inventory on Safety

1. Part of a supervisor's job is to be constantly searching for safer ways of doing the work in the department.
2. Hidden accident costs are often higher than direct costs of compensation and medical payments.
3. A supervisor must choose between safety and production to keep things in proper balance.
4. The elimination of an unsafe condition is the most effective means of preventing an accident.
5. Top management and visitors should be required to obey the safety rules of any department they visit.
6. Employees who perform unsafe acts have a reason for doing so.
7. Disciplinary action is the most effective means of enforcing safe practices.
8. The big secret of making safety "work" is to get employees to take an active part in the program.
9. Under the Occupational Safety and Health Act (OSHA), employees may complain to the government about unsafe working conditions and are protected against discrimination for filing a complaint.
10. Exits from buildings may be blocked as long as the blockage is only partial and for short duration.

Management Inventory on Managing Change

1. Managers should constantly be looking for changes that will improve department efficiency.
2. Suggestion systems are good because the suggestion goes to a neutral party instead of to the person who is in a position to implement it.
3. Managers should freely suggest changes to managers in other departments.
4. People who don't understand the reasons for a change will always resist it.
5. If subordinates participate in the decision to make a change, they are usually more enthusiastic in carrying it out.
6. "You can't make a silk purse out of a sow's ear."
7. "Ne Stupefaciamus" is good advice.

8. If you were promoted to a management job, you should make the job different than it was under your predecessor.
9. Bosses and subordinates should have an understanding regarding the kinds of changes that can be implemented by the subordinate without getting prior approval from the boss.
10. You've decided on a change and announced it. You then receive more data and now know it's a mistake. You should retract the decision and apologize for the mistake.

Management Inventory on Time Management

1. A manager should maintain a proper balance between time spent on the job, with the family, on personal hobbies, and for outside church, professional, and community organizations.
2. More discretionary time should be the goal of a manager.
3. Managers should be judged and rewarded on the basis of the amount of time they devote to the organization.
4. It is desirable for every manager to spend some time doing jobs under his or her supervision in order to keep a hand on the pulse of the organization.
5. A manager should always do the most important things first.
6. Unwanted visitors should be treated "cooly" so they won't stay long.
7. All managers should know how to say "No" to bosses, subordinates, and all other members of management.
8. The best way to control a meeting is to prevent it from getting out of control.
9. Delegation means the same as job assignment.
10. Delegation always saves time for a manager.

Management Inventory on Performance Appraisal and Coaching

1. The same performance appraisal program (forms, procedures, interview) should be used for performance improvement as well as for salary adjustments.
2. An understanding by the subordinate of "what's expected by the boss" is an important prerequisite to the appraisal of performance.
3. A standard of performance should be challenging (requires stretch but can be reached).
4. A standard of performance must be specific and measurable (dollars, percentages, numbers, etc.).
5. In the appraisal interview, a specific Performance Improvement Plan (who will do what and when) should be jointly developed to improve the performance needing improvement.

6. An important part of the Performance Improvement Plan is to determine what the boss can do to help the subordinate improve performance.
7. Managers as well as coaches should treat everyone equally.
8. Getting the job done (winning) is more important than building good attitudes and high morale.
9. When subordinates have been trained to do a job a certain way, they should be given the freedom to do it differently if they wish.
10. Action should be taken to remove players/employees who can't meet the standards of performance.

Management Inventory on Leadership, Motivation, and Decision Making

1. There is a clear distinction between a "leader" and a "manager."
2. A person with leadership qualities can be successful as a manager in any kind of organization or department.
3. In order to be effective, a manager must be able to perform all the jobs in the department he/she supervises.
4. The popular saying, "If it ain't broke, don't fix it" is good advice for managers.
5. It is possible for a manager to "motivate" employees.
6. Employees will do what their manager *inspects* rather than what the manager *expects*.
7. MBWA (managing by walking/wandering around) is a sure way to improve employee attitudes and increase productivity.
8. Employees who are asked for their opinions regarding a decision to be made are usually more enthusiastic in implementing the decision than those who were not asked.
9. A group decision usually ends up with a "camel" while trying to create a "horse."
10. A manager who supervises an employee who is not able to do a job should remove him/her from the job or modify the job so it can be performed effectively.

The last inventory also includes a question on the amount of participation and empowerment that should be given to subordinates when making a decision. It asks for past practice as well as what should be done in the future

A tabulation of responses to these inventories will reveal attitudes and knowledge. Figure 5-3 is an example of a form that can be used to obtain this data. After scoring the test/inventory, individuals are asked to circle those items they answered incorrectly and to tabulate their score. These forms are then collected and tabulated. The participants keep their

Figure 5-3. Form for tabulating inventory responses.

Please circle the ones you answered incorrectly according to the scoring key.

1	2	3	4	5	6	7	8	9	10	11	12	13	14	15
16	17	18	19	20	21	22	23	24	25	26	27	28	29	30
31	32	33	34	35	36	37	38	39	40	41	42	43	44	45
46	47	48	49	50	51	52	53	54	55	56	57	58	59	60
61	62	63	64	65	66	67	68	69	70	71	72	73	74	75
76	77	78	79	80										

My score = 80 − _____ = [   ]
            (# wrong)

test. Training program objectives and content can be based on these data. The inventories can also be used to stimulate lively and practical discussions (see Chapter 7) and to evaluate the effectiveness of the program (see Chapter 8).

The eight inventories are concerned with concepts, principles, and techniques that relate to supervision in all organizations. Some content of the supervisory training programs should be added that relates to specific technical knowledge that is important for supervisors in that organization.

Training professionals at MGIC (Mortgage Guarantee Insurance Company) in Milwaukee developed a Product Knowledge Test consisting of forty questions. It is given to supervisors as a pretest at the beginning of a training program to determine needs and administered again at the end of the program as a posttest to evaluate the learning that has taken place. Following are some of the questions from that test.

MGIC, MILWAUKEE, WISCONSIN

1. _____ MGIC is the only private MI company to offer . . .
   a. Condo status and loan progress report
   b. Underwriting guideline and premium rate bulletin boards
   c. Auto-delegated and Auto-Premium Payment

2. _____ How many times will MGIC/FAX retry a document delivery, if a lender's FAX machine is busy?
   a. Once
   b. Twice

          c. Five times
          d. Ten times
          e. Indefinitely

3. _____ RDS III currently offers delivery of two basic documents other than commitments. What are they?
          a. Loan sale notices and endorsements
          b. Premium acknowledgements and endorsements
          c. Loan sale notices and premium acknowledgements
          d. Endorsements and loan sale notices

4. _____ Which of the following is NOT an RDS III bulletin board?
          a. The MGIC Resource Directory
          b. MGIC Premium Rates
          c. The MGIC Underwriting Guideline Summary
          d. The MGIC Mortgage Market Summary

5. _____ Which of the following is NOT a category in the Loan Progress Report?
          a. Loans approved
          b. Loans-in-suspense
          c. Loans denied
          d. Loans received

6. _____ MGIC/FAX offers high speed delivery for . . .
          a. Commitments
          b. Premium acknowledgements
          c. a + b

7. T or F RDS III can be offered on a "sometimes" basis.

8. _____ When selling in RDS III, it is best to target:
          a. Managers
          b. Processors
          c. Technical support people
          d. a + c
          e. All of the above

9. T or F To receive the underwriting guideline bulletin board that is appropriate for his area of the country, a lender must enter a five-digit zip code.

10. _____ Which private mortgage insurers are able to provide electronic loan status?
          a. MGIC and GE
          b. MGIC, GE, and PMI
          c. MGIC, GE, and CMAC

MGIC PLUS

11. T or F   In addition to enhancing MGIC's investment income opportunities, single premiums benefit the company because they are earned at a more accelerated pace than annual premiums.

12. T or F   The size of the ceding commission that MGIC receives from the reinsurers is determined by loan amount, not premium dollars.

13. _____   Which of the following do not affect the MGIC PLUS buying decision?
    a. Consumer
    b. Realtor
    c. MGIC Underwriter
    d. Secondary Market Manager
    e. Servicing Manager
    f. All of the above
    g. None of the above
    h. Both b + c
    i. Both c + e

14. T or F   When preparing a truth-in-lending disclosure for a loan with a financed single premium, mortgage insurance should always be disclosed for the life of the loan.

15. T or F   FNMA will allow a "no cash out" refinance loan to exceed 90% LTV by the amount of a financed mortgage insurance premium as long as the combined loan-to-value does not exceed 95%.

16. T or F   FNMA will allow a 4% seller contribution on a fixed rate loan with a financed annual premium. The base LTV is 90% with a combined LTV of 91%.

17. _____   The following is not a benefit of MGIC PLUS for the lender:
    a. Conventional program to compete with FHA
    b. Decreased servicing costs on single premium loans
    c. Increased investment income
    d. Increased origination and servicing fee income
    e. None of the above
    f. Both a + c

18. T or F   MGIC is the only mortgage insurer offering special single premium pricing on loans with temporary buydowns

19. T or F   MGIC, GE, and PMI are the only mortgage insurers offering a nonrefundable single premium.

20. T or F   GE and MGIC have the same refund policy for refundable single premiums.

Capital Markets

21. _____ Effective December 7, 1989, savings associations are required to maintain minimum risk-based capital of _____%.
    a. 3%
    b. 1.5%
    c. 8%
    d. 6.4%
    e. None of the above

22. _____ The new "risk-based capital" regulations for S&Ls have caused many of them to:
    a. Convert whole loans into securities
    b. Begin originating home equity loans
    c. Put MI on their uninsured 90s
    d. All of the above
    e. a + c
    f. b + c

23. _____ A healthy institution is acquiring a troubled S&L. Which MGIC Capital Markets Service are they most likely to need in order to successfully complete the acquisition?
    a. Portfolio analysis
    b. Quality control services
    c. Contract underwriting
    d. Conduit services

Assessing Performance Effectiveness

Needs can be determined by collecting information to determine gaps between desired and actual performance, as well as by identifying the relationship between desired operational results and the skills or knowledge required to accomplish them.[4] Either questionnaires or interviews (or both) can be used. Figure 5-4 lists the advantages and disadvantages of each.

Comparing Methods for Determining Needs

In his chapter in *The Training and Development Handbook*, Geary Rummler compares four methods for determining training needs: training needs survey, competency study, task analysis, and performance analysis. Figure 5-5 outlines the approaches and sets out the advantages and disad-

(text continues on page 70)

4. Dana Gaines Robinson and James C. Robinson, *Training for Impact* (San Francisco: Jossey-Bass, 1989).

Figure 5-4. Advantages and disadvantages of data collection methods.

Advantages	*Disadvantages*

Questionnaires

More people can be included in study, to meet considerations of time and cost.	It is difficult to create good questions and requires a high degree of knowledge regarding the situation to do so; potential answers must also be created.
Respondents can be in several locations and still be included in the study.	You cannot ensure that individual receiving the questionnaire will be the one responding to it.
Confidentiality is more protected.	Response rate may be poor.
Each question is consistently presented to the respondent.	Instrument must be piloted to ensure clarity, which requires additional time.
Results are easy to tabulate (if closed questions are used).	Respondent may not understand the survey (even though it was piloted), and a certain percentage of returned surveys may need to be discarded due to responding errors (such as marking two answers to the same question).
Cost per instrument is less than with other data collection methods.	

Interviews

Respondents have opportunity to give information openly and freely.	They are labor intensive, requiring more time to include enough respondents.
If question is unclear, interviewer can restate.	If more than one person conducts interviews, each person must present each question in a similar manner.
If response is unclear, interviewer can probe for clarity.	Confidentiality of respondents cannot be ensured.
They are easier to create than questionnaires, because only questions need to be created (not potential answers).	Cost per interview is higher than cost per questionnaire.
They provide increased control over high response rate.	Tabulation is time-consuming (must be done manually); if more than one individual analyzes data, inter-rater reliability must be ensured.
As new information is obtained, interview process can be adapted so that additional information, other than what was initially considered, can be collected.	

Figure 5-5. Comparison of four approaches to determining training needs.

	Training Needs Survey	Competency Study	Task Analysis	Performance Analysis
Starting Point	What knowledge and skill is required?	What competences are required?	What tasks are required?	What job performance is required?
General Approach	▸ Ask key people what knowledge and skills they think or feel the trainee-performers require to do their job (or "X" portion of their job). ▸ Prioritize the knowledge and skills recommended and summarize as a topical list, a training agenda, curriculum, etc.	▸ Ask key people what competencies they think or feel the trainee-performer requires to do the job (or "X" portion of the job). ▸ Determine the knowledge and skills required to attain the stated competences. ▸ Prioritize the knowledge and skills recommended and summarize as a training agenda or curriculum.	▸ Determine what tasks are required of the trainee-performer in order for the job to be performed correctly and successfully. ▸ Determine the knowledge and skills required to correctly perform the tasks identified. ▸ Prioritize the tasks, and thereby the knowledge and skills, and summarize as a training design document, training agenda, or a curriculum.	▸ Determine what performance is required. ▸ Determine the critical job outputs or "accomplishments." ▸ Determine what tasks are required of the trainee-performer to produce the job outputs or "accomplishments." ▸ Determine the knowledge and skills required to correctly perform the tasks identified. ▸ Determine what other factors (in addition to knowledge and

skills) influence job performance (such as job design, resources, consequences, and feedback). ▸ Prioritize the knowledge and skills required based on impact on job performance and summarize as a training design document, training agenda, or curriculum. ▸ Summarize recommendations to modify negative influences identified above.	▸ Precise identification of tasks and required knowledge and skills. ▸ Is a form of output and can be	▸ Links knowledge and skill requirements to job performance. ▸ Can validate, evaluate. ▸ Addresses other
Advantages of This Approach	▸ Fast, inexpensive. ▸ Broad involvement. ▸ Low risk ▸ Low visibility.	▸ Relatively fast, inexpensive. ▸ Broad involvement. ▸ Consensus. ▸ In addition to training needs, articulation and

(continues)

Figure 5-5. (continued)

	Training Needs Survey	Competency Study	Task Analysis	Performance Analysis
Starting Point	What knowledge and skill is required?	What competences are required?	What tasks are required?	What job performance is required?
		agreement on a success "profile" for the performer. ▸ Identify generic training needs covering a broad population (e.g., first-time supervisors, first-time managers).	measured. ▸ Broad involvement. ▸ Objective, validated by observation.	factors affecting performance. ▸ Impact of job output is established and therefore can prioritize knowlege and skills input.
Disadvantages of This Approach	▸ Not precise or specific. ▸ Based on opinion, albeit "expert." ▸ Difficult to validate.	▸ Difficult to relate to output, to evaluate training. ▸ Difficult to assess relatiave	▸ Takes time and skill. ▸ Visible. ▸ Difficult to assess relative importance	▸ Takes time and skill. ▸ Visible.

- Difficult to set priorities.
- Difficult to relate to output, to evaluate importance of training.
- Once you ask people what training they feel is important, there is an implicit expectation that you will deliver it.

importance of competences and therefore difficult to set priorities for knowledge and skills input.
- Consensus will not necessarily identify the critical difference between exemplary and average performance.
- Does not address other factors influencing performance.
- Can be highly visible.

of tasks and therefore difficult to set priorities for knowledge and skills input.
- Does not address other factors affecting performance.

Source: Reprinted with permission from McGraw-Hill from Geary A. Rummler, "Determining Needs," in *The Training and Development Handbook,* 3d ed. (New York: McGraw-Hill, 1987).

vantages of each one. Rummler believes that a professional trainer is likely to use all four approaches at some time.[5]

S. V. Steadham describes the advantages and disadvantages of nine basic needs assessment techniques (Figure 5-6).[6]

Converting Needs to Objectives

According to Martin Broadwell, "The most important single consideration in the teaching-learning process is the setting of objectives. Taken in proper perspective, the entire course from beginning to end should revolve around objectives. These statements should be readily accepted by any instructor who is trying to produce a specific quantity and quality of learning."[7] In other words, before we plan program content, select leaders, and determine techniques or aids, we should be sure that we have carefully determined and stated the objectives we are going to try to accomplish.

Robert Mager has done much to encourage the setting of proper objectives. In his two books, *Developing Vocational Instruction* and *Preparing Instructional Objectives,* he has outlined not only the need for objectives but also specific techniques for setting them. According to Mager, "Course objectives represent a clear statement of instructional intent, and are written in any form necessary to clarify that intent." Mager describes the characteristics that objectives should have, among them the following two:

1. An objective says something about the student. It does not describe subject content, instructor, or the kinds of classroom experience to which the student will be exposed.
2. An objective is about ends rather than means. It describes a product rather than a process. As such, it describes what students are expected to be like at the end of instruction rather than the means that will be used to get them there.[8]

(text continues on page 76)

5. Geary A. Rummler, "Determining Needs," in *The Training and Development Handbook,* 3d ed. (New York: McGraw-Hill, 1987).
6. S. V. Steadham, "Learning to Select a Needs Assessment Strategy," *Training and Development Journal* (January 1980). Copyright 1980, the American Society for Training and Development. Reprinted with permission. All rights reserved.
7. Martin Broadwell, *The Supervisor and On-the-Job Training,* 2d ed. (Reading, Mass.: Addison-Wesley, 1977).
8. Robert Mager, *Preparing Instructional Objectives* (Belmont, Calif.: Lake Publishing Co., 1962).

Figure 5-6. Advantages and disadvantages of nine basic needs assessment techniques.

Technique	Advantages	Disadvantages
Observation		
▸ Can be as technical as time-motion studies or as functionally or behaviorally specific as observing a new board or staff member interacting during a meeting. ▸ May be as unstructured as walking through an agency's offices on the lookout for evidence of communication barriers. ▸ Can be used normatively to distinguish between effective and ineffective behaviors, organizational structures, and/or processes.	▸ Minimizes interruption of routine work flow or group activity. ▸ Generates in data, highly relevant to the situation where response to identified training needs/interests will impact. ▸ (When combined with a feedback step) provides for important comparison checks between inferences of the observer and the respondent.	▸ Requires a highly skilled observer with both process and content knowledge (unlike an interviewer who needs, for the most part, only process skill). ▸ Carries limitations that derive from being able to collect data only within the work setting (the other side of the first advantage listed in the preceding column). ▸ Holds potential for respondents to perceive the observation activity as "spying."
Questionnaires		
▸ May be in the form of surveys or polls of a random or stratified sample of respondents, or an enumeration of an entire "population." ▸ Can use a variety of question formats: open-ended, projective, forced-	▸ Can reach a large number of people in a short time. ▸ Are relatively inexpensive. ▸ Give opportunity of expression without fear of embarrassment. ▸ Yield data easily summarized and	▸ Make little provision for free expression of unanticipated responses. ▸ Require substantial time (and technical skills, especially in survey model) for development of effective instruments.

(continues)

Figure 5-6. (*continued*)

Technique	Advantages	Disadvantages
choice, priority-ranking. ▸ Can take alternative forms such as Q-sorts, or slip-sorts, rating scales, either predesigned or self-generated by respondent(s). ▸ May be self-administered (by mail) under controlled or uncontrolled conditions, or may require the presence of an interpreter or assistant.	reported.	▸ Are of limited utility in getting at causes of problems or possible solutions. ▸ Suffer low return rates (mailed), grudging responses, or unintended and/or inappropriate respondents.

Key Consultation

▸ Secures information from those persons who, by virtue of their formal or informal standing, are in a good position to know what the training needs of a particular group are:
  a. board chairman
  b. related service providers
  c. members of professional associations
  d. individuals from the service population
▸ Once identified, data can be
	▸ Is relatively simple and inexpensive to conduct.
	▸ Permits input and interaction of a number of individuals, each with his or her own perspectives of the needs of the area, discipline, group, etc.
	▸ Establishes and strengthens lines of communication between participants in the process.
		▸ Carries a built-in bias, since it is based on views of those who tend to see training needs from their own individual or organizational perspective.
		▸ May result in only a partial picture of training needs due to the typically nonrepresentative nature (in a statistical sense) of a key informant group.

Technique	Advantages	Disadvantages
gathered from these consultants by using techniques such as interviews, group discussions, questionnaires.		

Print Media

▸ Can include professional journals, legislative news/notes, industry "rags," trade magazines, in-house publications.	▸ Is an excellent source of information for uncovering and clarifying normative needs. ▸ Provides information that is current, if not forward looking. ▸ Is readily available and is apt to have already been reviewed by the client group.	▸ Can be a problem when it comes to the data analysis and synthesis into a usable form (use of clipping service or key consultants can make this type of data more usable).

Interviews

▸ Can be formal or casual, structured or unstructured, or somewhere in between. ▸ May be used with a sample of a particular group (board, staff, committee) or conducted with everyone concerned. ▸ Can be done in person, by phone, at the work site, or	▸ Are adept at revealing feelings, causes of and possible solutions to problems which the client is facing (or anticipates); provide maximum opportunity for the client to represent himself spontaneously on his own terms (especially when conducted in an open-ended,	▸ Are usually time-consuming. ▸ Can be difficult to analyze and quantify results (especially from unstructured formats). ▸ Unless the interviewer is skilled, the client(s) can easily be made to feel self-conscious. ▸ Rely for success on a skillful interviewer who can generate

(continues)

Figure 5-6. (*continued*)

Technique	Advantages	Disadvantages
away from it.	nondirective manner).	data without making client(s) feel self-conscious, suspicious, etc.

Group Discussion

▸ Resembles face-to-face interview technique, e.g., structured or unstructured, formal or informal, or somewhere in between. ▸ Can be focused on job (role) analysis, group problem analysis, group goal setting, or any number of group tasks or themes, e.g., "leadership training needs of the board." ▸ Uses one or several of the familiar group facilitating techniques: brainstorming, nominal group process, force-fields, consensus rankings, organizational mirroring, simulation, and sculpting.	▸ Permits on-the-spot synthesis of different viewpoints. ▸ Builds support for the particular service response that is ultmately decided on. ▸ Decreases client's "dependence response" toward the service provider since data analysis is (or can be) a shared function. ▸ Helps participants to become better problem analysts, better listeners, etc.	▸ Is time-consuming (therefore initially expensive) both for the consultant and the agency. ▸ Can produce data that are difficult to synthesize and quantify (more a problem with the less structured techniques).

Tests

▸ Are a hybridized form of questionnaire.	▸ Can be especially helpful in determining	▸ The availability of a relatively small number of tests that

Technique	Advantages	Disadvantages
▸ Can be very functionally oriented (like observations) to test a board, staff, or committee member's proficiency. ▸ May be used to sample learned ideas and facts. ▸ Can be administered with or without the presence of an assistant.	whether the cause of a recognized problem is a deficiency in knowledge or skill or, by elimination, attitude. ▸ Results are easily quantifiable and comparable.	are validated for a specific situation. ▸ Do not indicate if measured knowledge and skills are actually being used in the on-the-job or "back home group" situation.

Records, Reports

▸ Can consist of organizational charts, planning documents, policy manuals, audits, and budget reports. ▸ Employee records (grievance, turnover, accidents, etc.). ▸ Includes minutes of meetings, weekly, monthly program reports, memoranda, agency service records, program evaluation studies.	▸ Provide excellent clues to trouble spots. ▸ Provide objective evidence of the results of problems within the agency or group. ▸ Can be collected with a minimum of effort and interruption of work flow since it already exists at the work site.	▸ Causes of problems or possible solutions often do not show up. ▸ Carries perspective that generally reflects the past situation rather than the current one (or recent changes). ▸ Need a skilled data analyst if clear patterns and trends are to emerge from such technical and diffuse raw data.

Work Samples

▸ Are similar to observation but in written form.	▸ Carry most of the advantages of records and reports	▸ Case study method will take time away from actual work of

(continues)

Figure 5-6. (*continued*)

Technique	Advantages	Disadvantages

Work Samples

▸ Can be products generated in the course of the organization's work, e.g., ad layouts, program proposals, market analyses, letters, training designs. ▸ Written responses to a hypothetical but relevant case study provided by the consultant.	data. ▸ Are the organization's data (its own output).	the organization. ▸ Need specialized content analysts. ▸ Analyst's assessment of strengths/ weaknesses disclosed by samples can be challenged as "too subjective."

Source: S.V. Steadham, "Learning to Select a Needs Assessment Strategy," In *Training and Development Journal,* January 1980, *30,* pp. 56–61. Copyright 1980 by the American Society for Training and Development, Inc. Reprinted with permission. All rights reserved.

The setting of objectives is an important part of the training process. Time and care should be used to be sure that the objectives are carefully determined before course content is developed.

Kinds of Objectives

There are five kinds of objectives that can be determined and stated. They are concerned with attitudes, knowledge, skills, job behavior, and results that are expected to be accomplished. The first three can be accomplished in the classroom. The last two must be accomplished on the job. Following are some examples of each:

Attitude Objectives

▸ Supervisors feel that most workers want to take pride in the work they do.
▸ Supervisors realize that the time they spend in inducting and training new employees is well spent.
▸ Supervisors realize that upward communication is important to the morale and performance of workers.
▸ Supervisors feel that they are an important part of management.

Knowledge Objectives

- Supervisors can list and describe Abraham Maslow's Hierarchy of Needs.
- Supervisors understand the new contract provisions that have been negotiated into the union labor agreement.
- Supervisors understand the new personnel policy on vacations.
- Supervisors can list in sequence the following four steps to use in training employees.

1. Prepare the worker.
2. Present the operation.
3. Try out performance.
4. Follow up.

Skill Objectives

- Supervisors know how to use the four-step method for training new employees.
- Supervisors know how to use the checklist when inducting new employees.
- Supervisors know how to conduct problem-solving conferences.
- Supervisors know how to complete a flow-process chart.
- Supervisors know how to conduct an effective performance appraisal interview.
- Supervisors can write effective memos and reports.
- Supervisors know how to present information effectively in front of a group.

Job Behavior Objectives

- Supervisors use the four-step method for training whenever they train a new employee.
- Supervisors handle 90 percent of grievances at the first level.
- Supervisors listen actively when subordinates come to them with problems.
- Supervisors use the induction checklist whenever a new employee comes into their department.
- Supervisors conduct effective problem-solving conferences.

Results Objectives

- Turnover of new employees will be reduced to 5 percent per month by June 1.
- Grievances will be reduced to three per month by May 1.

▸ Morale will be improved from a year ago as measured by the attitude survey to be conducted in September.
▸ Accident frequency will be reduced to 2 percent by September 1.
▸ Absenteeism will be reduced to 1 percent by July 1.

Characteristics of Objectives

Classroom objectives of knowledge and skills should be stated from the standpoint of the learner, not the trainer, and whenever possible, all objectives should be stated in specific and measurable terms.

Summary

The many principles and techniques for determining needs and setting objectives outlined in this chapter are important prerequisites for selecting subject content for in-house programs and approaches for meeting the needs and reaching the objectives. Other chapters will discuss the approaches that should be considered.

6

An Overview of Training and Development Techniques

A variety of methods are available to improve the knowledge, attitudes, and skills of supervisors. Selection of the appropriate technique or techniques depends on objectives, subject content, cost, availability of materials and instructors, and time considerations. Some of the most common methods include on-the-job development (see Chapters 10 and 11); internal classroom training (see Chapters 7 and 8); and outside institutes, conferences, and seminars (see Chapter 9). This chapter briefly describes several other popular methods and provides references for obtaining more information (see Figure 6-1).

On-the-Job Development

According to an extensive research study conducted by the General Electric Company, "Ninety percent of the development of people is done on-the-job by the man's boss."[1] This may not apply in all organizations, but it does emphasize that on-the-job training and development are important methods. Chapters 10 and 11 discuss this technique.

Internal Classroom Training

The most common off-the-job method for training supervisors is attendance and participation in internal courses. Chapters 7 and 8 provide details.

1. Moorhead Wright, *How Do People Grow in an Organization?* (New York: National Association of Manufacturers, 1949).

Figure 6-1. Methods for supervisory training and development.

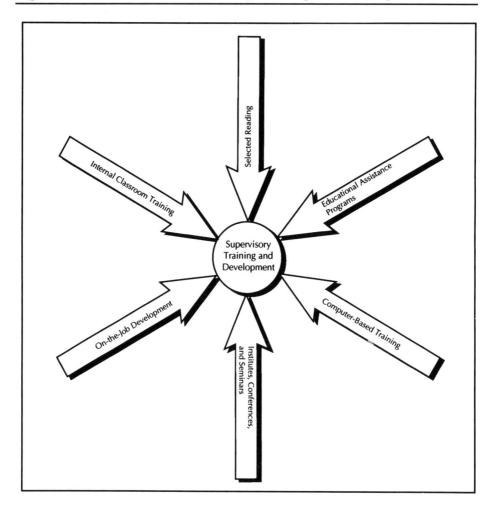

Outside Institutes, Conferences, and Seminars

Sending supervisors to outside programs on company time is another common way to train and develop them. Chapter 9 details this method.

Educational Assistance Programs

When supervisors attend daytime, outside management development programs, the organization nearly always pays all of the costs and provides company time. When supervisors attend evening programs on their personal time, educational assistance programs usually apply. Following are descriptions of the educational assistance programs of three organizations.

A LARGE OIL COMPANY

The purpose of the Educational Assistance Program is to provide substantial financial assistance to eligible employees who take, on their own time from an approved educational institution, approved courses of an educational or vocational nature which will benefit both them and the Company.

The Company will reimburse a participating employee for 85 percent of certain costs incurred in connection with the courses taken. There is no limit to the total reimbursement allowable for any one employee.

Participation in the program will not constitute a guarantee of advancement in earnings or job level.

Eligibility

A regular employee who (a) is not on a leave of absence or layoff and (b) is not receiving educational assistance from some other agency which would duplicate aid received under this program is eligible to participate. The educational assistance allowance which is payable under the Veteran's Readjustment Act, however, will not disqualify an employee for participation.

Temporary, casual, part-time, or dual-status employees are not eligible to participate.

Approved Courses

Courses may be approved if they (a) add to the employee's effectiveness in his or her present assignment or (b) contribute to the individual's overall development in such a manner as to be beneficial to both the employee and the Company. Courses may also be approved which do not meet the requirements of (a) or (b) but which are required in a curriculum that leads to a degree which does.

Correspondence courses may be approved when no classroom course is available locally in the particular subject desired, when the employee's work schedule interferes with enrollment in local educational institutions, or when such a course for some special reason would be more suitable for the employee.

Review courses may be approved when taken for the purpose of passing an examination to be licensed or certified, e.g., to be admitted to the practice of law or to qualify as a certified public accountant (CPA), certified life insurance underwriter (CLU), or a Fellow of the American Actuarial Society. Another type of review course which may also be approved is one taken for the purpose of achieving improved scores on enrollment tests such as the Graduate Management Admission Test or the Law School Admission Test. One course of each type may be approved for reimbursement.

Approved Educational Institutions

Educational institutions which will be approved are accredited schools, colleges, universities, trade schools, associations, professional societies, and organizations of a similar nature which may sponsor after-hours educational courses.

Reimbursement

An employee participating in the program will receive payment for 85 percent of the cost of reimbursable items provided the following conditions are met:

(a) The recipient is an employee of the Company at the time the course(s) are completed.
(b) The course(s) is completed with at least a passing grade as evidenced by a certification from the school on the refund application or a grade report.
(c) Receipted bills for all reimbursable items are submitted.
(d) Application for Refund is made within a reasonable time after completion of course work.

In the event an employee does not complete a course because of military service or as a result of Company action such as a transfer to a different location, night shift work, etc., course completion will be waived as a condition for reimbursement. If the course is not completed due to Company action, the employee will receive payment for 100 percent of the cost of reimbursable items, provided the following conditions are met:

(a) The recipient is an employee of the Company at the time the course(s) would otherwise have been completed.
(b) Receipted bills for all reimbursable items are submitted.
(c) Application for Refund is made within a reasonable time after cessation of course work.

Reimbursable items include tuition, required books, printed course materials required in lieu of textbooks, registration, laboratory, and other fees which the institution requires the student to pay, such as athletic, cap and gown, conference, enrollment, graduation (diploma), library or bookbinding, nonresident, matriculation, proficiency examination (if employee passes examination and receives credit for course not taken), student activity, tests such as enrollment or late examinations. If any of these items is not required by the institution and the employee elects to pay it, it will not be reimbursable. Also reimbursable are examination fees required for certification or licensing if the employee successfully completes the test.

Nonreimbursable items include equipment (such as radio parts, drafting equipment, and special laboratory equipment), application for entrance into college or university, class ring or pin, deferred payment or installment charges (including cash discount forfeited by late payment), fraternity or sorority dues or initiations, interest charged on loans from banks or credit associations to pay tuition, late registration fees, parking permit or parking fees, program changes at employee's request, room and board, transfer of credits from one institution to another, and transcript of credits.

Application for Participation

An Application for Participation should be submitted for approval before the course is started. If submission is delayed due to extenuating circumstances, the application may still be approved.

When a course requires more than one semester or one quarter for completion, the Application for Participation will cover the first such period, and a separate application will be submitted for each subsequent period of course work.

When a correspondence course requires more than one year to complete, the Application for Participation will cover the first year or any lesser period in which a definite part of the course will be completed, and a separate application will be submitted for subsequent parts of the course. The estimated completion date for the part of the course covered by the application must be shown on that form.

The Application for Participation will require approval by the supervisor, the department head (which for the purposes of this program will be any higher management level), and the program administrator. These approvals will be sufficient provided the total refunds to be paid, or previously paid, to the applicant in a calendar year will not exceed $2,000. In the event the total refunds will exceed $2,000, approval will also be required by the executive to whom authority to take such action has been delegated.

Tuition Advance

An employee may receive a cash advance for tuition expenses for a semester or quarter (or program requiring an annual upfront payment rather than a per course payment) which exceed 5 percent of the employee's annual salary. Request for a tuition cash advance should be submitted before the course is started, for approval by the appropriate member of the Management Committee of the Company or the executive to whom such authority is delegated. By receiving a tuition cash advance, the employee agrees to submit an Application for Refund immediately upon receipt of his or her grade at course completion. The employee also agrees to repay this advance to the Company if the employee fails to complete the course with a passing grade during his or her employment with the Company.

Application for Refund

An employee will pay the educational institution for expenses in connection with the courses taken, and when the course work is completed, submit an Application for Refund. Under ordinary circumstances the application should be submitted within a month.

To qualify for refund, all correspondence courses must be completed, except for unusual circumstances, within 60 days of the estimated completion date listed on the application.

Application for Refund must be made when each semester or quarter is completed in courses which require more than one semester or quarter for completion.

In the case of correspondence courses which require more than one year for completion, an Application for Refund must be made when the part of the course covered by each Application for Participation is completed. The refund will be calculated by proration of the total cost of the course. Verification of satisfactory progress for the part of the course completed must be obtained from the officers of the educational institution.

A refund will be approved for a review course the first time it is taken, even though the course is taken at a nonaccredited institution and no evidence of satisfactory completion is given at the conclusion of the course.

The refund will be mailed to the employees.

Program Administrators

Program administrators will review Applications for Participation with regard to course and institution to make sure that approvals are consistent with the terms of the program, will review such applications when they are considered unfavorably by either the supervisor or department head and express an opinion as to whether the application should receive further consideration, and will approve refunds up to a total of $2,000 per calendar year for an individual.

In the General Office, the Corporate Human Resources Department will act as program administrator.

In field locations which have a Human Resources staff, a staff member will act as program administrator. In field locations without a Human Resources staff, the role of program administrator will be performed by the Corporate Human Resources Department.

Questions pertaining to the interpretation and administration of the Program should be referred to the Corporate Human Resources Department.

A LARGE MIDWESTERN BANK

General

This plan is intended to provide for the educational development of qualified employees. Employees who receive tuition reimbursement are morally committed to remain in the service of the bank for reasonable lengths of time. It is also anticipated, but not assured, that better job performance will be realized, while enhancing an individual's advancement potential with the Corporation.

Eligibility

    A.   An individual must be a regular full-time employee or a part-time employee with a regularly scheduled work week of twenty hours or more.

    B.   The employee must be "satisfactorily" performing the duties and responsibilities of the present job.

    C.   The employee must have six months continuous service to be eligible for participation in this plan (i.e., before the course begins).

Courses

    A.   An educational course or program must be directly related to the employee's performance in his or her present position or enhance potential for advancement in the Corporation to a position which the individual has a reasonable expectation of achieving.

    B.   Courses or programs must be offered by an approved school, college, university, or correspondence school. The determination of approved institutions will be the responsibility of the Human Resources Department.

    C.   Courses or programs must be scheduled outside of the employee's regular working hours. All work in the course must be accomplished on the employee's own time.

    D.   This policy is not intended to cover professional seminars or conferences which an employee attends at the discretion of the Employer.

    E.   No commitment will be made to provide for all courses leading to a degree. Each course must be applied for separately and should be evaluated on its individual merits in accordance with the requirements of this policy.

    F.   Full-time employees may take up to six credits per semester/maximum twelve credits per calendar year.

    G.   Part-time employees may take up to three credits per semester/maximum six credits per calendar year.

    H.   Part-time employees are not eligible for graduate degree reimbursement.

Forms

    A.   Tuition reimbursement forms are available in Human Resources. Signatures of the applicant, supervisor, manager, and Human Resources are required for approval. This form is to be submitted to Human Resources prior to the start of classes.

Reimbursement

A. Employees are reimbursed for the cost of tuition and professional review courses which meet the requirements of this policy, with the following limitations:
  1. 100 percent reimbursement for qualified costs with a grade of "B" or better. 75 percent reimbursement for qualified costs with a grade of "C." Proof of payment and transcript is required.
  2. Reimbursement for schools outside of Metro Milwaukee is limited to the local cost per credit.
  3. If no grading system is used, the employee will submit evidence of having satisfactorily completed the course.
  4. Books are considered to be personal property, and their cost is the employee's responsibility.
  5. Lab fees, parking, mileage, etc., are not reimbursable.
B. Tuition reimbursements are processed through Benefits about the fifteenth of each month. A credit is issued to the applicant's checking account.
C. There will be no double payment under this policy. For instance, benefits under the G.I. Bill, an education grant, or a scholarship must be exhausted before reimbursement is made.
D. If an employee is terminated for reasons such as reduction in force or transfer to another assignment, reimbursement will be made for expenses authorized under this policy.
E. An employee who voluntarily leaves the bank or is terminated for cause prior to completing a course will be responsible for all expenses associated with that course and will not be reimbursed.

The Supervisor's Responsibility

A. The applicant's educational goals and the details of this Tuition Reimbursement Plan should be freely discussed with the employee. Additional information may be obtained from the Human Resources Department.
B. It is the responsibility of each supervisor to assure the eligibility of both the employee and the course before the application is approved.

A MAJOR INSURANCE COMPANY

A major U.S. insurance company supports continuing education and the Educational Assistance Program. However, the company does not guarantee career advancement based on course completion or graduation.

The Educational Assistance Program is administered by each department, subject to Company guidelines. Approval is not granted automatically. It is based on potential value of the course/degree to the applicant's career budgetary restrictions, and the criteria listed below. In addition, all employees working to receive reimbursement for courses covered by the Program should be encouraged to complete Courses I and II of the LOMA Insurance Education Program prior to applying.

Qualification Criteria

To qualify for tuition refund, an employee must meet the following qualifications:

1. Be employed by the company as a regular full-time or regular part-time employee for at least one full year. (Long-term and/or short-term temporary employees are not eligible.)
2. If a nonmanagement employee, have a performance rating of "Satisfactory," "Better," or "Best" for specific job-related courses; and "Better" or "Best" for degree programs. If a management employee, have a performance rating of "Capable," "Superior," or "Outstanding" for specific job-related courses; and "Superior" or "Outstanding" for a degree program.
3. Be employed by the company at the time the course is completed.
4. For graduate-level courses, be a management level employee or an NR on track to a management position.

Under special circumstances, exceptions to the above qualifications can be made only with department head approval after discussion with your department tuition refund coordinator.

Reimbursement Limits

If the above qualification criteria are met and the employee's application is approved, the employee is then eligible to receive reimbursement for tuition expenses, subject to the following limits:

1. A maximum of six credits per semester, if a full-time employee; and a maximum of three credits per semester, if a part-time employee.
2. For courses taken during the 1990–91 school year, a maximum of $195.00 per credit for undergraduate degree courses; and a maximum of $280.00 per credit for graduate degree courses.

Under special circumstances, exceptions can be made only with department head approval after discussion with your department tuition refund coordinator.

Application Procedures

To apply for the Educational Assistance Program an employee should:

1. Discuss the course/degree with immediate manager. Prior to beginning a

degree program, complete a Planning Chart for Degree Candidates with immediate manager.

2. Select a school which is accredited. (If uncertain about the accreditation of a particular college or university, check with the Training and Organizational Development Division of the Human Resources Department.)

3. Select a course/degree that is work related; that is, related to the current position or potential career opportunities as identified by department management.

4. Complete an Application for the company's Educational Assistance Program and obtain approval from and signatures of immediate manager, administrative officer, and departmental tuition refund coordinator. (Document receipt of other educational financial assistance on the application. The company will only reimburse the balance not covered by the other assistance.)

5. Submit the completed application for the company's Educational Assistance Program, with appropriate signatures, to the Training and Organizational Development Division of the Human Resources Department no later than one month after registering for a course. Late applications must be signed and approved by the department head.

The education and training coordinator of the Training and Organizational Development Division will notify the employee if the course/degree meets with Company policy.

Reimbursement Procedures

Upon successful completion of an approved course, complete the following for reimbursement:

1. Submit the final grade report to immediate manager for signature. The employee will be reimbursed only for courses for which he or she earned a final grade of C− (1.67 Grade Point Average) or above. (For courses in which a letter grade is not given, a "confirmation of attendance" must be submitted with manager's signature.)

2. Submit the following items to the Training and Organizational Development Division of the Human Resources Department:

   ▸ Copy of final grade report with manager's signature.
   ▸ Proof of tuition payment:
     —Copies of official school receipts *and*
     —Copies of cancelled checks (front and back to show they have been endorsed).

The reimbursement request will be processed by the Training and Organizational Development Division.

Information for Applicants

What's Covered?	*What's Not Covered?*
▸ Obtainment of a general equivalency diploma/high school diploma ▸ Required review courses ▸ Independent study courses ▸ Audit courses ▸ A basic computer knowledge course ▸ Associate degree courses* ▸ Undergraduate degree courses* ▸ Graduate degree courses* ▸ Books for vocational technical school courses only *These courses must be academic and part of a curriculum. If you receive assistance from other financial sources such as veterans' benefits, scholarships, or fellowships, NML will make up only the portion not covered.	▸ Application fees ▸ Assessment Center fees ▸ Books (unless attending technical school) ▸ Career counseling/placement services ▸ Compulsory activity fees ▸ Enrollment fees (e.g., Marquette and UWM application fees) ▸ Graduation fees ▸ Laboratory fees ▸ Professional licensing fees (e.g., state bar exam) ▸ Late fees ▸ Finance charges ▸ Fines ▸ Tools ▸ Equipment and supplies (e.g., calculator, notebooks, pens) ▸ Supplementary reading materials ▸ Suggested or recommended references ▸ Typing and clerical costs ▸ Postal charges ▸ Living and travel expenses ▸ Parking fees ▸ Data searches and research support Noncredit courses from a nonaccredited institution such as Dale Carnegie or Evelyn Wood Reading Dynamics are not covered under the Tuition Refund Program. Short courses which offer continuing education units are also not accepted under this tuition refund policy.

Selected Reading

Selected articles and books can be provided to supervisors as another way to train and develop them. Some supervisors (probably a small minority) are anxious to read material on supervision, but most supervisors are not and will not read if they can avoid it. If reading is to be an effective technique, three guidelines must be followed:

1. The reading material must be related to the supervisor's current job or a potential future one.
2. The material must be written so it can be easily understood by the supervisor.
3. The supervisor must be motivated to read it.

The first two guidelines are concerned with subject content. Someone must read available material and select articles, pamphlets, and booklets that relate to the supervisory job. Also, that person should seek material written in such a way as to be readily understood by the supervisor. Some material may be selected for one supervisor (with, say, an eighth-grade education) and a different kind of material selected for another supervisor (a college graduate). The content may be substantially the same, but the reading level may be entirely different.

The third guideline—that the supervisor must want to read it—may be a real challenge, particularly for supervisors who don't like to read. There are several ways to create interest:

1. Show supervisors they can benefit by reading the selected material.
2. Make it easy. Instead of suggesting that they go to the library to get a book or magazine, give the material to them.
3. Follow up by asking for a report or by discussing the material with them, either individually or in a group meeting.

A personal example will indicate the challenge of getting people to read. When I was responsible for supervisory training at International Minerals and Chemical Corporation (IMC), I initiated a selected reading program for supervisors and managers. First, I carefully selected one hundred management books that were pertinent to the management jobs at IMC. Then I wrote a summary of each and indicated the reading level, as well as the content and approach of the author. Next, I arranged for the books and summaries to be displayed in the IMC lounge. Each week books on a different phase of management (e.g., communication, delegation) were featured. Finally, a notice was sent to all supervisors encouraging them to look at the display and borrow any books that seemed helpful. Several weeks later, I checked with the library to see the extent of borrowing by supervisors and managers. Practically none of the books had been checked out—a disappointing result.

Stimulating supervisors to read is a real challenge. The supervisor's boss is in the best position to motivate because he is the boss, and encouragement and suggestions will probably be more effective than those of a staff training person.

One organization that makes extensive use of selected reading is Web Converting of Cedar Hill, Texas. All employees, managers and non-managers alike, read selected books on company time. The supervisor and subordinates then discuss the book and its application in the department. According to Web president Robert Fulton, "Books play maybe the major role in the change-of-thinking process going on here." Whenever he found a book that excited him, he sent copies to the twelve corporate and plant managers, who then discussed it at a managers' meeting. Web's key books for supervisors and managers are:

> William Byham and Jeff Cox, *Zapp! The Lightning of Empowerment* (New York: Harmony Books, 1988).
> Jan Carlson, *Moments of Truth* (New York: Harper & Row, 1989).
> Stephen R. Covey, *The Seven Habits of Highly-Effective People* (New York: Simon & Schuster, 1989).
> Peter M. Senge, *The Fifth Discipline* (Garden City, N.Y.: Doubleday, 1990).
> Max DePree, *Leadership Is an Art* (Garden City, N.Y.: Doubleday, 1989).
> Edgar H. Schein, *Organizational Culture and Leadership* (San Francisco: Jossey-Bass, 1985).

Computer-Based Training (CBT)

CBT involves the use of computers to deliver instructional materials to a central training facility or workplace. It can be effectively used to teach a variety of subject content as well as to develop skills. It was originally planned as a means of presenting single-topic, stand-alone training programs. Today, it is usually combined with other training delivery systems.

One of the main advantages of CBT is that a student can select the time to learn from it and can do it at his or her own pace. This makes it a "tailor-made" approach and saves time and money. It can, however, be a lonely way of learning and lacks the interaction and stimulation that classroom training provides. Unless a student is highly motivated to learn, CBT is not effective.

Some CBT packages can be purchased that are related to supervisory needs. Programs can also be developed for in-house use. Both approaches are costly and require many people to use the program in order to be cost-effective.

According to Mitchell,[2] "In the training/learning universe, computers have both wonderful power and major limitations. They can bring much involvement and interaction into the learning experience. On the other hand, they can easily become demotivational and counterproductive experiences. This is particularly true when they are forced into the uncomfortable role of linear progressive tutorial instruction."

In supervisory training, the subjects that best lend themselves to CBT are problem solving and decision making. The format would be to create a situation and ask the learner to make a decision or solve a problem. All of the necessary information would be available in the computer provided the learner asks for it. After the supervisor solves the problem or makes a decision, the computer provides feedback on the best solution. If the supervisor has not done well, the computer provides remedial action, and the learner can try again and again and again.

Summary

This chapter had identified six ways to train and develop supervisors. Most organizations use a combination of these. For example, most larger organizations have their own human resources trainers who plan, coordinate, and sometimes teach in-house programs for supervisors. They carefully select outside programs to meet the needs of certain individuals at all levels of management. Smaller companies that lack professional trainers often rely on outside programs for supervisory training and development.

Educational assistance programs exist in most organizations, regardless of size. Organizations that are located in cities usually take advantage of the many evening programs that local universities and colleges offer.

Many organizations, particularly the larger ones, have libraries, although most of the books and periodicals in them are of a technical nature. Management books are usually located instead in the offices of human resources professionals.

Computer-based training is quite new and is not widely used to train supervisors. It is more typically used for technical training.

Each organization should determine its needs for supervisory training and development, research the various ways it can be done, and use those approaches that are most cost-effective.

2. Garry Mitchell, *The Trainer's Handbook, Second Edition* (AMACOM, 1993). Reprinted by permission of the publisher from *The Trainer's Handbook: The AMA Guide to Effective Training, Second Edition* by Garry Mitchell, © 1993 AMACOM, a division of American Mangement Association, New York. All rights reserved.

7

Planning and Implementing Internal Classroom Training

Most organizations offer classroom courses to train and develop supervisors. They can be effective or ineffective, depending on a variety of factors. This chapter describes concepts, principles, and techniques to maximize the effectiveness of the courses. The next chapter offers specific advice on how to evaluate the programs.

Setting Objectives

Most classroom training programs are run for one purpose—to stimulate and teach proper supervisory behavior so that improved organization results will be achieved: improved profitability, reduction of turnover, reduction of accidents, reduction of cost, improved quality, and improved employee morale and satisfaction.

To accomplish change in behavior and to improve results, the following specific objectives should be considered:

> ▸ *Knowledge.* To improve supervisors' understanding of company policy rules, procedures, and the labor agreement if there is a union; theories, principles, and techniques of management; technical information related to the supervisor's job; and the backgrounds, attitudes, needs, and other characteristics of subordinates, typically referred to as "diversity of the work force."
> ▸ *Skills.* To improve the supervisor's skill in such areas as inducting and training new employees; effective communication, including listening, reading, speaking, and writing; team building; decision making; disciplining employees; delegating; motivating; planning;

conducting performance appraisal interviews; and managing change.

▸ *Attitudes.* To create proper attitudes of supervisors toward the company, their job, supervisors and staff people in other departments, and the employees who work for and with them.

The objectives of classroom training should be clearly set at the beginning. They should be oriented to the supervisors who will be in the class and related to the attitudes, knowledge, skills, and the behavior that those attending should have after the course. Robert Mager's book, *Preparing Instructional Objectives,* provides suggestions for determining needs and stating objectives.[1]

Determining Subject Content

Once the objectives have been arrived at, it becomes relatively simple to determine the subject content of the course. Each objective indicates the kind of subject that needs to be taught if the objective is to be accomplished. For example, objectives that describe attitudes, knowledge, and skills of the trainees directly indicate the kind of topics, forms, and procedures that must be taught in the course. In the case of objectives dealing with behavior, however, there are some complicating factors that make it more difficult to determine subject content.

For example, let us assume we are teaching the supervisors the four-step method for effective on-the-job training. One of the objectives is to be sure that they know how to use this method when training employees. They will be taught how to do it in the classroom and demonstrate in the classroom that they know how to do it. But if one of the objectives is to be sure that supervisors *use* the four-step method when training new employees who come into their department, the job becomes more difficult. In addition to teaching supervisors the skill of the four-step method, we must also teach them an attitude that will make them want to use it on the job.

Even these two objectives are not sufficient to be sure they will use the four-step method on the job; we must also be concerned with what takes place from the time they leave the classroom until a new employee comes into the department. Perhaps the supervisor is tied up doing something vital when a new employee comes into the department. He feels that the task he is in the midst of is more important than applying

1. Robert Mager, *Preparing Instructional Objectives* (Belmont, Calif.: Lake Publishing Co., 1962).

the four-step method and may rationalize that the old way of training a new employee is good enough. To prevent such occurrences, the training program should not only (1) teach knowledge and (2) skills but should also (3) stimulate the supervisor to apply the skills on the job and (4) be sure that the boss of the supervisor provides a positive climate for implementation.

An important consideration in transforming objectives into subject content has to do with the length of the program. A good approach for determining specific subject content is to list the possible subjects and topics, consider them in relation to the specific objectives to be accomplished, and, finally, analyze and screen them in the light of the amount of time available for the training. This sorting-out process will help to determine the specific subject content for each session. Additionally, the advisory committee can be very helpful in making these decisions.

Some topics are appropriate in nearly any organization, particularly as a basic program—for example:

▸ *The Supervisor's Job.* This topic emphasizes that the supervisor is part of management and clarifies the objectives he is expected to accomplish, including contributing to the profitability and effectiveness of the organization and maintaining high morale among subordinates.

For the first objective, emphasis would be placed on quantity of work, quality, low cost, schedules, safety, housekeeping, and satisfied customers.

In addition to clarifying objectives, the session should describe the following functions that a supervisor performs in order to meet the objectives:

1. Plan
2. Organize
3. Communicate
4. Train
5. Motivate
6. Delegate
7. Coach
8. Innovate
9. Manage paperwork
10. Control

▸ *Styles of Leadership.* This subject describes different styles and the pros and cons of each and stresses the need for tailoring the style to the culture of the organization and the specific situation.

▸ *Understanding and Motivating Employees.* Here, the need for developing empathy—the ability to put oneself in the situation of subordinates—is stressed. Possible topics are the need for understanding employees, techniques for getting to know them better, recent research and theory in motivation, and application to the job of supervisor.

▸ *Effective Communication.* Areas important here are a definition of communication, barriers to effective communication, communication problems in the organization, principles for effective communication—such as empathy and planning—and specific skills in listening, oral, and written communication.

▸ *Decision Making.* The emphasis is on the amount of involvement and empowerment that is appropriate for the decision to be made, as well as the steps to follow in making a decision.

▸ *Orienting and Training New Employees.* The subjects to cover include the need for proper orientation and training of new employees, the development of an orientation and induction checklist, principles of training new employees, and practice in how to induct and train new employees.

▸ *How to Manage Change.* The need for empathy, communication, and participation in deciding on changes and seeing that they are accepted and implemented is the focus.

▸ *Total Quality Improvement.* Because of increased competition and customer demands, this has become one of the most popular subjects for supervisory training and development. It teaches the attitudes, knowledge, and skills needed to obtain maximum quality.

A LARGE MIDWESTERN BANK

The following list of subjects chosen by a midwestern bank should be considered for an internal training program.

1. *Developing Effective Leadership Skills*—16 hours. Provides the new or soon-to-be supervisor with essential policy and procedure information as well as a foundation for positive supervisory skill development. A prerequisite for "FrontLine Leadership."
2. *Effective Interviewing and Selection Techniques*—4 hours. An understanding of current equal employment opportunity legislation, how to develop a strategy for choosing among applicants for interviews, a behavior-based strategy for the actual interview that allows the interviewer to go well beyond the typical "hypothetical interview," and how to choose the best probable candidate among those interviewed.
3. *FrontLine Leadership—Series One*—4 hours each session. A curriculum-based supervisory skill program where each session builds upon those sessions preceding it. The approach to each topic allows supervisors to establish action plans using their own actual supervisory situations. Each of the following represents one session. Additional units are added each year:

    —Basic Principles of Supervision
    —Recognizing Positive Results
    —Giving Constructive Feedback
    —Getting Good Information from Others/Getting Your Ideas Across
    —Dealing with Emotional Behavior

4. *Performance Evaluation and Goal Setting*— 3 hours. Identifying critical job elements for evaluation, determining and communicating expected standards of performance, properly conducting the performance appraisal meeting, and formulating an action plan for future development.

5. *Successful Business Writing*— 2 hours. Fundamental guidelines covering the most common business writing situations.

6. *FrontLine Leadership—Series Two*— Prerequisite: "FrontLine Leadership— Series One."
    —Establishing Performance Expectations
    —Taking Corrective Action
    —Coaching for Optimal Performance
    —Clarifying Team Roles and Responsibilities

7. *Achieving Team Excellence—Part One*— 8 hours. To open communication lines, establish performance expectations, and develop specific departmental goal plans, derived from the input of all members of the individual team.

8. *Running Effective Meetings*— 4 hours. Explores strategies to maximize meeting effectiveness, understand meeting participant styles, develop effective meeting agendas, and using the appropriate leadership style based on the type of meeting being conducted.

9. *Valuing Diversity*— 8 hours. Develops a heightened awareness of the impact and value of the multicultural, multiracial work force. Explodes stereotypes and provides a forum for developing a work environment where cultural, ethnic, and gender differences can be appreciated rather than as a source of potential conflict.

10. *FrontLine Leadership—Series Three*— Prerequisite: "FrontLine Leadership— Series Two."
    —Delegating Responsibility
    —Fostering Creativity
    —Managing Change in the Organization

11. *Achieving Team Excellence—Part Two*— 8 hours. As an extension of the above, this program utilizes the Myers-Briggs Type Indicator to allow team members a better understanding of their personality preferences and its impact on how they handle their job responsibilities and how their preferences (and relative nonpreferences) impact the team's ability to accomplish departmental goals. Prerequisite: "Achieving Team Excellence—Part One."

12. *FrontLine Leadership—Series Four*— Prerequisite: "FrontLine Leadership— Series Three."
    —Ethical Business Decisions
    —Developing a Value-Driven Leadership Strategy for the Future

The list presented in this case study is only a suggestion. Each organization should select its own subject content based on needs.

Establishing the Schedule

The establishment of a proper schedule can be important to the effectiveness of the program. Schedules should be convenient for the participants so they feel that the time selected is a good one for them to attend. There are other considerations, of course, including the best time for them to be off their jobs so that their bosses do not have negative attitudes toward the program.

    ▸ *Should programs be held on company time?* The main consideration here is the attitude of participants toward attendance. If they feel that the company owes it to them or if they consider it an imposition to attend on their own time, then the program should probably be offered on company time. If the program is offered on employees' personal time and they are expected to attend, then they should be rewarded for attending. For instance, a Saturday program could be scheduled from 8:00 A.M. to 2:00 P.M. with breakfast, morning coffee break, and lunch provided. This can lessen the feeling that the individuals are contributing too much and the company too little. In general, if the participants can be spared, the program should be offered on company time. However, if it is important for them to be on the job all the time or if their bosses feel that they should not be taken off their job, consideration should be given to having it on their own time. A combination of the two is possible. For example, a number of companies offer programs late in the afternoon so that part of the time is company time and part of it is the participants' own time.

    ▸ *How long should sessions be?* It depends. They can vary from one-hour sessions held periodically (once a week, once a month) to a program that runs for a full week. One consideration is the amount of learning that occurs. Some educators believe that spaced learning is better and that sessions conducted periodically are better than one solid week of meetings. Others think that it is better to conduct a program in a continuous time period. Distance is another factor. If people gather from different locations, the sessions should be longer than if all people are located in the same place. That said, there is a most common length of a session—from one and one-half to three hours—and a general rule—the more participation from the learners, the longer the session should be.

    ▸ *How often should sessions be held?* Supervisory training meetings are typically conducted once every two weeks or once every month to allow time between them for on-the-job application. In addition, sessions are not held so frequently as to interfere with production. Each organization must determine length and frequency to fit its own circumstances. An important factor is that supervisory training and development is a continuous process and not a one-shot approach.

Choosing Facilities

The facilities for classroom supervisory training must be large enough and comfortable enough so that the participants are in a proper climate for learning. If there are adequate facilities on the premises, this is probably the best location. Otherwise meetings should be held at a nearby restaurant, hotel, or other location with satisfactory facilities. One advantage of holding meetings away from the workplace is to reduce interruptions and increase the level of concentration of the participants. A disadvantage is travel time. If the session is short (less than a half-day), it is probably better to use in-house facilities.

Deciding on a Room Setup

Every conference leader has a favorite room setup. Many prefer a U shape, with participants seated at the outside of the U (Figure 7-1). Others prefer a more traditional classroom (Figure 7-2). If supervisors are going to be involved in small group activities, a herringbone shape is probably best (Figure 7-3). The setup depends on the size of the group and the size of the room, as well as the leader's preferences.

Selecting the Participants

The size and the composition of the group must be determined before meetings start. Generally there should not be more than twenty-five persons in a class in supervisory training, and some companies limit size to fifteen. The optimum size depends on room size, as well as on the approach and conference skills of the leaders.

In most organizations, the group consists of participants at the same level in the organization. For example, supervisory training meetings are limited to first-level supervisors; higher management should not be in attendance. Some companies, however, have taken a different approach and have purposely included several levels of management. The American Telephone and Telegraph Company (AT&T), for example, frequently conducts sessions with "family groups": groups in which several levels

Figure 7-1. U-shape room setup for training.

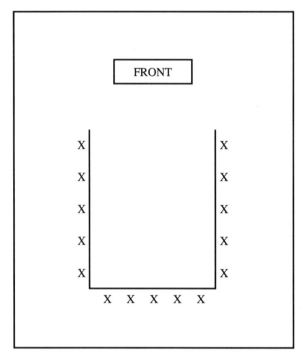

of management from the same department attend at the same time. Generally, however, if the attendance of higher-level management people in supervisory training meetings inhibits the participation and learning that is taking place, it is better to restrict the attendance to first-level supervisors. If the presence of higher-level management people enhances the involvement and learning of supervisors, several levels should be included.

Another consideration regarding group composition is whether a meeting should be attended by all supervisors or only by those who can benefit from the subject matter. Most companies do not single out those persons who need the training most. They include all supervisors so that no stigma is attached to those who attend and so that those who are better supervisors can help in the teaching process. And some organizations make a number of courses available to supervisors on a voluntary basis.

Selecting Instructors

Careful attention should be given to the selection of the program teachers. Among the qualifications that should be considered are these:

Figure 7-2. Traditional classroom setup for training.

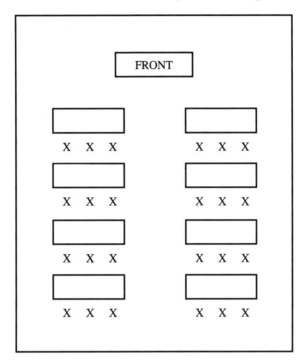

- subject knowledge
- a desire to teach
- a positive attitude toward the students
- time for preparation
- skills in presenting information and controlling discussion
- tact, patience, and open-mindedness
- respect from the participants

Whether to use persons within the organization or to hire consultants and teachers from the outside depends on the qualifications of those inside. If persons inside have the qualifications just listed, there is no need to hire anyone from the outside. If this is not so, outside trainers should be hired. One caution is that outsiders should be carefully screened for effectiveness. For example, they may have most of the qualifications listed, but if they are weak in presenting information and leading discussion, the program is sure to be a failure. Therefore, when references about outside people as possible leaders for internal company programs are checked, specific information should be obtained regarding their previous experience and teaching effectiveness.

A number of years ago I was asked by Allis-Chalmers Corp. to develop a lesson plan for a basic training program for supervisors, with

Figure 7-3. Herringbone-shape setup for training.

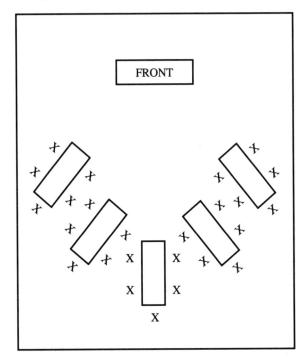

emphasis on human relations, communication, and discipline. The plan was to select only line managers to do the teaching. I was surprised and concerned that my lesson plan might not be properly implemented by line managers and suggested that I conduct a short course with them to teach them how to teach.

I think it was a mistake to insist that only line managers do the training. One or more of the eight qualifications might be absent, and the program would not be effective in terms of improving knowledge, developing skills, and creating positive attitudes on the part of those attending. In addition, if the line manager is not effective as a teacher, negative attitudes toward him might be created, which could adversely affect the job relationship. If line managers have all eight qualifications, use them. If not, select a leader who has them.

Determining Classroom Techniques and Aids

Supervisory training classes should be enjoyable as well as beneficial. The first consideration for use of any technique is that it helps accomplish the objectives. Many different techniques and methods meet this criterion, and some of them the participants will enjoy more than others. Therefore, a variety of techniques should be used to accomplish the objectives and to make the sessions interesting and enjoyable. The participants' reactions can have an impact not only on what they learn at the meeting but also on how they apply it on the job. The teaching methods and techniques we will explore here are presentation, guided discussion, films and videotapes, case studies, role playing, the incident process, tests and inventories, and management games and exercises.

Presentation

The most basic technique used in a supervisory training course is presentation on the part of a leader to impart knowledge to the participants. This should be used whenever the leader has information that the group does not have. Barriers and practical tips are listed in detail in my book *No-Nonsense Communication.*[2] The tips include a number of ideas to make the presentation interesting and enjoyable, as well as beneficial:

1. Present the information in a way that is easily understood.

2. Show the practical application of the information for the participants. Research and theory can be presented, but the connection between them and practical application should always be clear. In other words, the question "So what?" must be answered to the satisfaction of the participants.

3. Be enthusiastic. Speakers are salespersons of ideas.

4. Use visual aids to communicate effectively. Visual aids hold the participants' attention and help to convey ideas. They make use of the seeing sense in addition to hearing. Effective visual aids should be simple, pertinent to the subject content and objectives, easy to see and read, and attractive. The most common forms of visual aids are films and videotapes, overhead transparencies, slides, charts, illustrations on a chalkboard or easel, handouts, and specific objects. An additional aid that can be used effectively is the Hook 'n Loop board, in which cards can be prepared and stuck to the board.[3]

Questions and answers are usually a part of the presentation technique. When questions are raised, the leader should assess each one:

2. Donald L. Kirkpatrick, *No-Nonsense Communication*, 3d ed. (Elm Grove, Wis.: Donald L. Kirkpatrick, 1991).
3. Hook 'n Loop Board, Charles Mayer Studios, 776 Comming St., Akron, Ohio 44307.

1. Is this question on the subject we are discussing?
2. Is it pertinent to others in the group?

If the answer to either of these is no, the leader can indicate politely that it can be answered after the class is over. If the question is of general interest, time should be spent in answering it. Meetings should not end with a question-and-answer period. A summary of the major points instead of an answer to a question is a better ending.

The presentation technique is basic to effective supervisory training meetings. Presenters must maintain interest and attention, as well as communicate if the session is going to accomplish the objectives.

An informative manual is Info-Line's *How to Make a Large Group Presentation.*[4]

Guided Discussion

In guided discussion, the supervisors participate under the guidance and control of the leader. It can be effective when participants have ideas to contribute.

There are two approaches to the use of guided discussion in the classroom: (1) an open discussion in which the leader suggests a question or problem and volunteers or selected people from the group answer it and (2) small groups that allow for participation from everyone. The term *buzz groups* describes the situation in which subgroups of four to seven people are assigned a topic. To be sure that the buzz groups operate effectively, the meeting leader should see that:

1. Participants understand exactly what they are supposed to do and how much time they have to do it.
2. Each buzz group has a chairperson who is responsible for the performance and reporting of the group. The chairperson can be appointed by the meeting leader, selected by buzz group members, or selected by a criterion suggested by the leader (perhaps the tallest person; person who has on the brightest clothes; person whose birthday is closest to Ides of March).
3. Each chairperson understands that this role includes:

   ‣ Being sure that all members of the group understand the assignment
   ‣ Getting everyone to participate

4. Info-Line, *How to Make a Large Group Presentation* (Alexandria, Va.: American Society for Training and Development, 1991).

> ‣ Keeping discussions moving toward the objective
> ‣ Taking notes or delegating this role to another member of the group
> ‣ Reporting or delegating this role to another member of the group

For effective guided discussion, the meeting leader must prepare questions and assignments that will help to accomplish the objectives of the meeting. Getting people to participate is the first requirement. The second requirement is to control the meeting. A manual, *How to Plan and Conduct Productive Business Meetings,* provides principles and methods for meeting these two requirements.[5]

Scott Parry of Training House in Princeton, New Jersey, has described sixteen techniques for getting responses from participants in a training program:

1. After asking a question, pause for ten seconds before selecting a respondent. Look around the group. Restate the question. Give all trainees time to formulate responses in their heads. Then select a respondent.

2. Some questions are easy; everyone can answer out loud simultaneously. For example, "What color do we get when we mix red and yellow?" Orange. "When we mix yellow and blue?" Green. "When we mix red and blue?" Purple. "Which colors are called the primary colors?" Red, yellow, and blue. "Which are the secondary colors?" Orange, green, and purple.

3. With questions that require only a few words or numbers, have participants write the answers. You can circulate around the room to read some of the answers, thereby seeing whether everyone got them right. That may also help you decide on whom to call.

4. From time to time, ask learners to take a guess on something you're about to give them.

5. Distribute a handout that contains a half-dozen questions and space for the answers. After each major stimulus (say every five minutes on the average), have learners respond to the next question. Then give them feedback before proceeding. This breaks a forty-five-minute lecture into eight or nine S-R-F links in an instructional chain.

6. Use a preprinted response sheet for trainees to complete throughout the lesson (perhaps a flowchart, checklist, schematic diagram, or list of pros and cons on which they must fill in words). Direct learners to the response sheet each time you cover a new item on it.

7. Distribute a self-assessment. This should be a self-scoring, quickly admin-

5. Donald L. Kirkpatrick, *How to Plan and Conduct Productive Business Meetings,* 2d ed. (New York: AMACOM, 1987).

istered exercise that lets you and the learner know where she or he stands. It can tap knowledge, attitude, or skills, and serves to establish the "entering behavior" of your learners, on which you will build.

8. Ask for a show of hands. This is especially useful when you want to polarize the group on a dichotomous issue. For example, "How many of you think that preparing an inductive lesson is harder? How many think that a deductive lesson is harder to prepare?"

9. Have participants respond to each other, working in groups of two or three. For example, in a course on time management, you could say, "Turn to your neighbor and tell him or her what percentage of your time you think *is* and *is not* under your control."

10. When the group is large (say, more than thirty trainees), give each participant four colored, cardboard squares: red, yellow, blue, and green. Then pose a multiple-choice question from time to time; the four alternatives are color-coded. Trainees answer by holding up the corresponding cards, with the colors facing you. This gives you feedback and lets you know whom to call on and whether learners need more explanation.

11. When teaching interaction and communication skills (such as in sales, interviewing, counseling, training, and supervising), prepare a script of the interaction. Number each line and distribute copies to trainees.

Elicit responses in a "notes" column by referring trainees to specific lines that illustrate concepts or techniques you've just dealt with. Ask whether they are good or poor examples, and why.

12. After every new topic, lesson, module, or sequence, have participants get out their action plan sheets. Ask them to write down what they plan to do back on the job to apply the things they've just learned. Have learners read the entries of the people sitting on each side of them. Have them give one another feedback.

13. If you're teaching a whole job, have each participant create a job description by making a new entry after you go over each duty, responsibility, and procedure. They should include criteria for performance. Have each trainee take this back to work to share with her or his supervisor.

14. Prepare mini role plays. You play the "foil" role and place trainees in the "critical" role. Have them make their responses to one another and evaluate each other after each interaction.

15. Allow time for silent decision making or reflection on questions that don't require overt responses. For example, "When did you last write a note commending one of your workers for a job well done? When did you last ask your boss to send such a letter to one of your subordinates?"

16. At times, responses will be confidential. For example, they may cover topics such as how much trainees earned in commissions last year, how they scored on the management style assessment, or how much time they spend with their bosses in a typical week.

In such cases, have learners respond on pieces of scrap paper, without giving their names. Collect the scraps in a box, shake them up, and draw them out for posting on a flip chart or chalkboard. Then you can discuss and process the data.[6]

Videotapes and Films

Both videotapes and films are available for older productions, but 16-mm films are no longer produced by most film organizations.

These aids come in several forms. Some are animated and tell a story that can be used for discussing supervisory principles and techniques. Some use live actors to provide a case study for discussion. Others feature an expert who makes a presentation, usually supplemented and illustrated by vignettes or case studies of situations that are pertinent to the subject.

The person who will be using the videotape should view it before showing it to the class. In most cases, a leader's guide is available to suggest ways in which it can be used effectively. So that it will be of maximum benefit, the leader should prepare an introduction that will relate the videotape to the subject being studied, conduct a discussion or use some other way to summarize the benefits from the videotape, and consider stopping the videotape partway through to discuss a dramatized case study before proceeding with the rest of it.

Following are some sources for films and videotapes to be considered for supervisory training and development programs:

> American Management Association
> 9 Galen Street
> Watertown, Massachusetts 02172
> 617/926-4600

> American Media, Inc.
> 1454 30th Street
> West Des Moines, Iowa 50265-1390
> 800/262-2557

> Cally Curtis Co.
> 1111 North Las Palmas Avenue
> Hollywood, California 90038
> 213/467-1101

> Copeland Griggs Productions
> 302 Twenty-third Avenue
> San Francisco, California 94121
> 415/668-4200

6. Scott Parry, "An Equal Opportunity to Learn," *Training and Development Journal* (January 1991).

CRM Films
2215 Faraday Avenue
Carlsbad, California 92008
800/421-0833

Films, Inc.
5547 North Ravenswood Avenue
Chicago, Illinois 60640-1199
312/878-2600

Menninger Management Institute
5800 Southwest Sixth
Topeka, Kansas 66601-0829
800/288-0318

Salenger Films and Videos
1635 Twelfth Street
Santa Monica, California 90404
310/450-1300

Case Studies

Case studies assume a number of forms. Some are a five- to ten-page detailed description of an industrial or business situation. This type of case study requires a great deal of reading and study by participants and much time to discuss it and benefit from it. Case studies can also be short—not more than one page—and describe a particular situation for the group to discuss. Some case studies are presented on videotape or film instead of on paper. Usually dramatized case studies are more effective than written ones because the participants are better able to understand the situation.

Bradford Boyd has set out six steps in writing a case study for use in supervisory training:

▸ *Define the principles you are trying to bring a group to understand.* This first step is essential for it provides the foundation upon which the case is to be built. A good instructor does not use a case simply to stir up activity; he uses the case to bring his group to the recognition of a principle he is trying to teach. In this first step, then, the trainer sets forth the direction for his plan. . . .

Examples of a defined principle: Managers have a responsibility to keep others informed and cannot afford the attitude that communication is a one-way street leading to them

and/or

Awareness of the need to communicate is the key factor in how well we communicate with one another.

▸ *Establish a situation that illustrates the principle.* This step begins to give the plans for writing some substance. It creates the setting in which the case is to take place. Here is where [instructors] call upon our knowledge and experience of typical problems and problem individuals around us.

Example: How about a manager whose attitude is that people around him create an endless array of problems because they can't or won't communicate with him.

▸ *Develop the symptoms.* Identify the symptoms that illustrate positively, negatively, or both the principles to be taught. Consider what incidents and situations create or relate to the attitude defined in step 2 and illustrate the principle identified in step 1.

Examples: a. The attitude expressed in the common complaint, "Nobody tells me anything."
b. The attitude expressed in the feeling that people everywhere have to cooperate with me if I'm going to do my job.
c. A subordinate goes over the supervisor's head to ask a favor of the department head.
d. People misunderstand "simple" instructions and create disturbing foul-ups in the daily routine.
e. We don't get cooperation when we ask for special effort.

▸ *Develop the characters.* These might be "do-righters," or "do-wrongers." Either can be true to life and provide realism for the case. Developing the characters is somewhat like assembling the finishing materials for the construction job. Listen to trainees describe their bosses, employees, peers, and associates. We live in a world of case-study characters.

Example: a. Let's give the key person a name—Bill Newman is as good as any unless we are working with a group where names reflect a predominate nationality group. Then he might be a Stan Dombrowski or a Jose Martinez.
b. Place him in the management hierarchy. For this situation we might make Bill Newman a department head.
c. What is his attitude or outlook? Make him a "do-wronger"—impatient, wrapped up in himself, looks for others to blame when a problem arises, typical of "the guy upstairs who needs this training."

▸ *Write the case.* From here on it's simple. . . . Build in the essentials. Describe the situation, the attitudes, the symptoms, and the characters but don't overburden the case with detail. If the preparation outlined in the first four steps has been carefully done, the writing is almost automatic.

▸ *Conclude with questions.* They give direction to your group's thinking and provide your discussion a pathway to the principle. Questions should state specifically what we want considered and discussed so that trainees approach the problem along the lines the instructor intends to direct the discussion.[7]

Following are some case studies I developed:

The Case of the Late Deliveries

You are Jim Marshall, general manager of a lumber yard employing twenty-five people. Harry Brown, your yard foreman, supervises four truck drivers. He has worked for you for six years and does an excellent job.

It has come to your attention that deliveries are not always made as promised to customers. This morning, you received telephone calls from two angry customers, Tom Gibson from Allied Construction and Bill Bailey who is building a new home. Both told you that yesterday's deliveries arrived more than two hours late. Tom said that this has happened before and that he was thinking of changing suppliers.

  1. What are your objectives in solving this problem?
  2. What are you going to do?

This type of case study can be used in a training meeting on such subjects as interpersonal relations and problem solving. It could be discussed in open discussion or assigned to buzz groups. Each group could then report on its solution. This type of case also lends itself very well to role playing.

The following four case studies can be used in a training program on how to manage change.

The Case of the New Equipment

You are the supervisor in the accounting department. A new computer is going to be installed to replace some of the manual opera-

7. Bradford B. Boyd, *Supervisory Training: Approaches and Methods* (a collection of articles from the *Training and Development Journal*) (Alexandria, Va: American Society for Training and Development, 1976).

tions in your department in order to reduce costs. You have looked at new equipment and are still considering two different types. You have not yet decided which one to buy.

Your department now consists of fifteen clerical and professional workers. When the new computer is in operation, you will need only seven people. You expect the new equipment to be installed in about six months.

You will find other jobs in your company for the eight people who will not be needed.

The Case of the New Method

You are supervisor of a department that assembles small radios. There are six stations in the assembly line; the worker at each station performs one part of the assembly and passes it to the next station.

You have decided that the use of job enrichment will improve the challenge of each job and will create more satisfaction on the part of the employees. Also, you feel that it will result in higher productivity.

You are going to have each worker assemble the entire radio instead of doing only one part. Each radio will have a number attached to it to identify the worker who assembled it.

The Case of the New Policy

You are the foreman of a machine shop. Recently, your workers have been taking varying amounts of time to wash up and get ready to go home at the end of the shift. Some have taken as much as thirty minutes; others have taken as little as five. You have had no specific rules covering the amount of time they should take and have never told anyone that he was taking too long.

To increase productivity, top management and you have agreed to implement a new policy that workers will be allowed a maximum of ten minutes to wash up before their shift ends.

The Case of the Loss-Producing Product

You are a supervisor in an assembly department. When you received an order for a new product, you quoted a price that was based on assembling 130 units per day, a figure that had been arrived at in order to get the bid. Also, your engineers and top manufacturing management had agreed that it could be done. You, the supervisor, were not consulted on the number of units your people could assemble.

You have a long-term contract and you are losing money every day. You cannot change the price to the customer and you must increase productivity to stay in business.

If you have four subgroups in the meeting, one of these cases could be assigned to each. Or you could ask each person to volunteer to participate in the case in which she is most interested. Each group would then be given the following assignment:

1. Select a chairperson for your group who will be responsible for leading and controlling the discussion and reaching the assigned objectives.
2. Appoint a secretary who will be responsible for taking notes and summarizing the discussion that takes place.
3. Your specific objectives will be:

   ‣ To discuss and agree on how employees in your department would react to the specific change described in your case.
   ‣ To discuss and decide how you would communicate the change to the employees in your department.
   ‣ To discuss and decide how you would see that the change is effectively implemented in your department with emphasis on participation and teamwork.

This type of case study and approach can be readily adapted to any organization. Cases can be written to describe a typical situation that supervisors have faced or will face, with each group given from thirty to forty-five minutes to analyze a case. The chairperson or another member of the group then reports to the entire group on the case. Next, the case study is opened to discussion by the entire group, after which the leader has the key role of supplementing and commenting on the principles, approaches, and techniques that have been elucidated and tying the case study into the objectives of that particular session.

Role Playing

Role playing is a training technique in which one or more members of the supervisory training group assumes a role that is assigned. For example, in "The Case of the New Policy" described above, one of the group members will be asked to play the part of a foreman. The conference leader can take the part of an employee who feels that ten minutes is not enough time to wash up before the shift ends. In front of the group, the foreman then conducts a discussion with the employee. The rest of the supervisors observe the role playing and comment on it after it is finished.

In multiple role playing, all members of the supervisory training class participate at the same time. Half of them take the role of foreman and the other half the role of employee. They will all be buzzing at the same time. After a period of multiple role playing, open discussions will analyze the situation from the standpoint of both the foreman and the employee. The multiple role playing can be repeated, with each individual taking the opposite role. A modification of this approach is to divide the group into subgroups of three persons each, with the third person as an observer. After each role play, they change roles.

Role playing can be very effective in supervisory training. It involves the group, maintains high interest and enjoyment on the part of participants, and can be helpful in learning. By participating in role playing, persons may learn better than by merely listening to someone discuss a case. Also, by observing a role-playing situation, supervisors can see what happens and can discuss these events as a case study.

The Incident Process

A unique approach to the case study,[8] developed by Paul Pigors, formerly of the Massachusetts Institute of Technology, is the incident process, a method by which a group of supervisors can study problems and reach decisions by a systematic approach. When possible, the case selected is an actual one that has already been solved, so the group decision can be compared with the real solution. If a real case is used, Pigors suggests that it be unrelated to the jobs and problems of the participants. This facilitates the learning of principles, because the participants are not relating real people and problems to the case. Actual cases from their own organization can be effectively used after problem-solving principles and techniques have been learned.

In the incident process, participants receive a short written account of the problem (called the *incident*). Their assignment is to search for facts, weigh them in view of the circumstances, and decide what action should be taken. An example is given below.

8. Paul Pigors, *The Incident Process* (Rockville, Md.: BNA Communication, 1961).

The Incident

Joe Grimm, one of your employees, complains to you that Tom Jones is cheating the company. Joe claims that Tom often has someone else punch the time clock for him in the morning when he comes in late. Also, according to Joe, Tom abuses the company rules on break periods and wash-up time. You supervise both Joe and Tom. What would you do?

The method of analysis is divided into five phases:

1. *Studying the incident.* Individual members take time to discuss what approach they will take in progressing toward the decision.

2. *Fact finding.* Questions are directed to the leader (the person with the facts) in an attempt to reconstruct the sequence of events. The leader answers all questions but does not provide any additional information. When the group feels that it has sufficient information to make a decision, a participant summarizes the key facts that have been brought out.

3. *Stating the issue.* The group decides what questions it must answer in making a decision—for example, "Is discipline indicated under the circumstances, and, if so, to whom and to what degree?"

4. *Making a decision.* Each participant writes an answer to the issue with supporting reasons. The decisions are divided into pros and cons. Participants who think alike get together, appoint a spokesman, and consolidate their thinking for a short debate. As soon as each side has debated the reasons for its position, the conference leader summarizes the actual decision.

5. *Learning from the case.* The conference leader moderates a discussion on what the case has taught and how effective the participants were in analyzing the problems.

The incident process can provide several benefits in supervisory training classes. Supervisors in the classes:

- Have an opportunity to analyze actual problems by a practical method.
- Share a group's accumulated experience in working with people.
- Test their own decision-making and reasoning capabilities by comparing them with those made by other group members and the historical (actual) decision (if a real case was used).
- Develop an appreciation of different viewpoints in approaching and solving problems.

‣ Develop their abilities as leaders in the individual roles of team leader, observer, and discussion member.

Tests and Inventories

Tests and inventories can be used in determining needs as well as specific subject content for supervisory training programs. They can also be used effectively as a teaching tool. I have used the following technique in teaching principles and methods of effective communication to supervisors in many organizations:

‣ Administer the Supervisory Inventory on Communication (SIC) to the participants.[9] Eighty items are to be answered "A" (agree) or "DA" (disagree).
‣ Select ten to twenty pertinent items from the SIC.

For example, the following items could be selected:

1. A good definition of communication is the sending of information from one person to another.   A   DA
19. A sender has failed to communicate unless the receiver understands the message the way the sender intended it.   A   DA

‣ Ask each buzz group of four to six people to reach consensus on each item. (This is done before they have scored their test.)
‣ Have the reporter from each group give the results to the leader, who records them on a flipchart.
‣ Tell them their score—the number "correct" according to the scoring key.
‣ Tell them to score their own tests.

This technique allows the participants to challenge and learn from each other. After they do this, they are very interested in the scoring key answers and in voicing their opinions. The ensuing discussion becomes interesting and practical. This technique also can be used to precede presentation and guided discussion on any subject and makes for a meeting that is interesting, enjoyable, and helpful.

Four sources for a variety of tests, inventories, and other learning instruments are:

9. Donald L. Kirkpatrick, *Supervisory Inventory on Communication* (Elm Grove, Wis.: Donald L. Kirkpatrick, 1987).

Dr. Donald Kirkpatrick
1920 Hawthorne Drive
Elm Grove, Wisconsin 53122
414/784-8348

Organization Design and Development, Inc.
2425 West Loop South
Suite 855
Houston, Texas 77027
800/648-1480

Resources for Organization
7251 Flying Cloud Drive
Eden Prairie, Minnesota 55344
612/829-1954

Training House
Box 3090
Princeton, New Jersey 08543-3090
609/452-1505

The following suggestions for using tests and inventories will help make
supervisory training meetings interesting as well as beneficial:

- Be sure the test content is related to the subject content and objectives of the session.
- Administer the test at the start of the program.
- Score the test and return it to participants, or allow participants to score their own and tell the leader how many items were wrong.
- Select items for discussion that will be of greatest interest and benefit to the group.
- During the discussion, encourage both sides of the question to be argued by participants.
- Provide the participants with the author's rationale for the correct answer.
- Summarize the discussion and the principle or technique that was illustrated by the test item.

Management Games and Exercises

When management games and exercises, commonly called *simulation* are
used, the supervisors are divided into small groups and given a realistic
situation to deal with. They compete with each other and are judged on
their effectiveness (usually in terms of productivity, profits, sales, or similar criteria).

Some management games are simple and require less than an hour of meeting time; others are complicated and use a computer. They can be created for a particular session or purchased from:

Allen Communication
5225 Wiley Post Way
Salt Lake City, Utah 84116
800/537-7800

AMS Courseware Developers
300 Chapel Road
Manchester, Connecticut 06040
203/646-3264

Associated Training Systems
Suite 104, 2560 First Avenue
San Diego, California 92103
619/239-3577

CES Training Corp.
10 Forest Avenue
Paramus, New Jersey 07652
201/843-6444

Creative Training Techniques
7251 Flying Cloud Drive
Eden Prairie, Minnesota 55344
612/829-1954

Training Advantage
88 Rock Ridge
Stamford, Connecticut 06903
203/322-2246

Training and Development Resources
401 Washington Avenue
Bridgeville, Pennsylvania 15017-2340
412/221-4411

Vector Strategic Resources
425 Madison Avenue
New York, New York 10017
212/644-6200

The following books and manuals describe exercises and games that can make supervisory training programs interesting and enjoyable, as well as practical:

Ken Jones, *ICEBREAKERS: A Sourcebook of Games, Exercises and Simulations* (San Diego: Pfeiffer & Co., 1991).

Ed Scannell and John Newstrom, *Games Trainers Play* (1981), *More Games Trainers Play* (1983), *Still More Games Trainers Play* (1991) (New York: McGraw-Hill).

Arthur B. VanGundy, *Idea Power: Techniques and Resources to Unleash the Creativity in Your Organization* (New York: AMACOM, 1992).

Packaged Training Programs

There are two basic approaches to supervisory training and development. One is to develop a tailor-made program consisting of subject content, aids, and techniques developed by the human resources professionals in the organization. Previous sections of this chapter provide suggestions. The other approach is to purchase a program and implement it, with or without modifications by those planning and teaching the course. Some of the organizations that develop and market these programs are:

Aldrich Associates
265 East Village Road
Shelton, Connecticut 06484
203/929-6234

Blanchard Training and Development, Inc.
125 State Place
Escondido, California 92029
619/489-5005

Butler Learning Systems
1325 West Dorothy Lane
Dayton, Ohio 45409
513/298-7462

Development Dimensions International
1225 Washington Pike
Bridgeville, Pennsylvania 15017-2838
412/257-2277

HRD Press
22 Amherst Road
Amherst, Massachusetts 01002
800/822-2801

Talico, Inc.
2320 South Third Street
Jacksonville Beach, Florida 32250
904/241-1721

Teleometrics International
1755 Woodstead Court
The Woodlands, Texas 77380
800/527-0406

Training House
P.O. Box 3090
Princeton, New Jersey 08543-3090
609/452-1505

Zenger-Miller
1735 Technology Drive
San Jose, California 95110-1313
408/452-1244

Summary

Internal classroom training courses are developed and implemented by nearly every organization large enough to have ten or more supervisors. They take all kinds of approaches. Some are continuous and others are one-shot programs; some are required, while others are voluntary; some use inside instructors, while others call on outside consultants to do the training; some develop their own content and aids, while others purchase programs. Some are effective, and others are ineffective. There is no one best way to develop and implement training courses. The training professional and line managers in each organization must make their own decisions.

This chapter has described some principles and techniques that should be carefully considered so that internal courses have positive results in terms of reaction, learning, change in job behavior, and final results in improved productivity and morale.

Some of the case studies in Part II of this book describe successful in-house programs. An analysis of these can provide practical ideas for your program. In determining subject content, consider the topics described in the case studies in Chapters 13, 14, 15, and 17.

8
Evaluating Internal Classroom Training

Training programs should be evaluated to determine their effectiveness so that future programs can be improved, to decide if the program should be repeated, and to justify the value of the training department to top management. At a recent conference of the National Society for Sales Training Executives (NSSTE), a representative of Hobart Corporation presented this thought:

> All managers, not just those in training, are concerned over their own and their department's credibility: They want to be accepted by their company. They want to be trusted by their company. They want to be respected by their company. They want their company and fellow managers to say, "We need you!"
>
> When you are accepted, trusted, respected, and needed, lots and lots of wonderful things happen.
>
> - Your budget requests are granted.
> - You keep your job. (You might even be promoted!)
> - Your staff keeps their jobs.
> - The quality of your work improves.
> - Senior management listens to your advice.
> - You are given more control.
> - You sleep better, worry less, and enjoy life more.
>
> In short, it makes you happy!
> Wonderful! But just how do we trainers become accepted, trusted, respected, and needed? We do so by proving we *deserve* to be accepted, trusted, respected, and needed. And this means we evaluate our training and communicate its worth.

Many different evaluation methods have been suggested and used. Some say that the only real evaluation measures the change in behavior that takes place on the job. Others claim that measuring changes in behavior is not sufficient; it's the results that count. Both of these groups usually view questionnaires and comment sheets as nothing more than "happiness" ratings. But other trainers and educators—and I am among them—feel that questionnaires and comment sheets can be helpful in evaluating training programs.

Evaluation can take many forms. Each can be helpful as long as the objectives and guidelines are understood. This chapter discusses areas to consider: reaction, learning, behavior, and results.

Reaction

The first stage of the evaluation process is to measure the trainees' reactions to the training program—that is, how well they liked it. Evaluating reaction is the same as measuring the feelings of the conferee: it is a measure of customer satisfaction. It does not include a measurement of any learning that takes place. Because reaction is so easy to measure, it is the most common type of evaluation.

There are two important reasons for measuring reaction. In most instances, favorable reaction means that the learner is paying attention, enjoying the experience, and thus probably making an effort to learn. When reaction is unfavorable, probably the learner is not putting forth much effort to learn.

The other reason for measuring reaction is to determine satisfaction. The participants are really customers. Favorable reaction means that the customer is happy and will probably "buy the product" again if it is offered. Additionally, a satisfied customer will tell other potential customers about the training program and will encourage those others to "buy the product." If the reaction is negative, the customer will probably tell others about the ineffective program and probably will not attend future meetings unless required to do so.

Favorable customer reaction is critical to organizations such as universities and to consultants that offer public institutes, seminars, and conferences. It is not quite as obvious that it is also important to training professionals who offer in-house programs. But the situations are similar; unfavorable reaction in either case can mean that the people offering the program are out of business.

Guidelines for Measuring Reaction

1. Determine what you want to find out.
2. Design a form that will quantify reactions.

3. Encourage written comments.
4. Get 100 percent immediate response.
5. Get honest responses.
6. If desirable, get delayed reactions.
7. Develop an acceptable standard.
8. Measure reactions against the standard.
9. Take appropriate action.

A reaction sheet (Figure 8-1) was used to measure reaction at a national institute of the American Society for Training and Development. The planners of this program were interested in reactions to subjects, conference techniques, and the performance of each conference leader, and the form was designed accordingly. The conferees were asked to place a check in the appropriate spaces so that the reactions could be readily tabulated and quantified. In question 3, the designers of the form felt that a more meaningful rating could be given the leader if the conferees considered items A through G before checking the overall rating. This question was designed to prevent a conference leader's personality from dominating group reaction. Question 4 encourages the conferees to suggest improvements. The optional signature was used so that follow-up discussions with conferees could be held. In this case, about half of the conferees signed their names. In all probability, the optional signature did not affect the honesty of the answers in this type of group. It is strongly suggested, however, that unsigned sheets be used in meetings held within a company to ensure truthful answers.

Figure 8-2 illustrates a simpler form that can be used for internal sessions. It should be completed by those attending at the end of each meeting unless the same leader is conducting a series of meetings on the same subject. In that case, the comment sheet should be given at the end of the second or third session, with the comments and suggestions taken into consideration to make the last sessions more effective. A final reaction sheet, such as that in Figure 8-3, should be used to obtain reactions to the total program.

Other types of reaction sheets can also be used to obtain valuable information. A form such as that in Figure 8-4 should be used where there are a variety of leaders who appear for a short time on a program. This form obtains the important separation of reactions to subjects from the reactions to the leaders. It also provides space for comments and suggestions.

Figure 8-5 illustrates a practical approach used by chapters of the American Society for Training and Development. One part of the form is a simple reaction sheet. The other part is for participants to use for taking

Figure 8-1. A conference reaction sheet.

Leader _____ Subject _____

Date _____

1. Was the subject pertinent to your needs and interests?
   ☐ No   ☐ To some extent   ☐ Very much so

2. How was the ratio of lecture to discussion?
   ☐ Too much lecture   ☐ OK   ☐ Too much discussion

3. How about the leader?

	Excellent	Very Good	Good	Fair	Poor
A. How well did he/she state objectives?					
B. How well did he/she keep the session alive and interesting?					
C. How well did he/she use the blackboard, charts, and other aids?					
D. How well did he/she summarize during the session?					
E. How well did he/she maintain a friendly and helpful manner?					
F. How well did he/she illustrate and clarify the points?					
G. How was his/her summary at the close of the session?					

What is your overall rating of the leader?
   ☐ Excellent   ☐ Very Good   ☐ Good   ☐ Fair   ☐ Poor

4. What would have made the session more effective?

_____

_____

_____

_____

Signature _____

Figure 8-2. A simple reaction sheet for internal sessions.

Please give us your frank reactions and comments. They will help us evaluate this program for possible improvement in future programs.

Leader _____ Subject _____ Date _____

1. How do you rate the subject content?
   - ☐ Excellent   Comments:
   - ☐ Very Good
   - ☐ Good
   - ☐ Fair
   - ☐ Poor

2. How do you rate the conference leader?
   - ☐ Excellent   Comments:
   - ☐ Very Good
   - ☐ Good
   - ☐ Fair
   - ☐ Poor

3. What benefits do you feel you got from this session?
   - ☐ New knowledge that is pertinent.
   - ☐ Specific approaches, skills, or techniques that I can apply on the job.
   - ☐ Change of attitude that will help me in my job.
   - Other:

4. How was the lunch?
   - ☐ Excellent   ☐ Very Good   ☐ Good   ☐ Fair   ☐ Poor

5. How were the meeting facilities?
   - ☐ Excellent   ☐ Very Good   ☐ Good   ☐ Fair   ☐ Poor

6. What would have made this session better?

notes. At the close of the program, participants complete the reaction part and turn it in to the program coordinator. They keep their notes.

All of these forms provide data that can be tabulated and quantified so that program leaders and coordinators can measure the effectiveness of the program. At the Management Institute (MI), University of Wisconsin, acceptable standards of performance were established so that leaders

Figure 8-3. A final reaction sheet for the entire program.

Name of program ————————————————— Date ——————

1. How would you rate the overall program as an educational experience?
   - ☐ Excellent   Comments:
   - ☐ Very Good
   - ☐ Good
   - ☐ Fair
   - ☐ Poor

2. To what extent will it help you do a better job for your organization?
   - ☐ To a large extent   Comments:
   - ☐ To some extent
   - ☐ Very little

3. What were the major benefits you received? (Check as many as you wish.)
   - ☐ Helped confirm some of my ideas.
   - ☐ Presented new ideas and approaches.
   - ☐ Acquainted me with problems and solutions from other companies.
   - ☐ Gave me a good chance to look objectively at myself and my job.
     Comments:

4. How were the meeting facilities?
   - ☐ Excellent   Comments:
   - ☐ Very Good
   - ☐ Good
   - ☐ Fair
   - ☐ Poor

5. How would you rate the luncheon(s)?
   - ☐ Excellent   Comments:
   - ☐ Very Good
   - ☐ Good
   - ☐ Fair
   - ☐ Poor

6. Would you like to attend future programs of a similar nature?
   - ☐ Yes
   - ☐ No
   - ☐ Not sure

7. Other comments and suggestions.

Figure 8-4. A reaction sheet for multiple leaders.

The purpose of this training program is to help you. Therefore, we need your reactions and comments to help us evaluate the program. It will help us decide the approach and content for future programs. Please use the following scale for your ratings.

5 = Excellent   4 = Very Good   3 = Good   2 = Fair   1 = Poor

I. Subjects and Leaders

Subject	Rating	Leader	Rating	Comments
A. Manpower Planning		Mason		
B. Technical Training Programs		Deady		
		Horwitz		
C. Pattern for Instruction		Fetteroll		
D. Audiovisual Materials		Thomas		
E. Supervisory Training		Morgan		
F. Trainee Involvement		O'Brien		
G. Evaluation		Kirkpatrick		

II. Other Aspects of Program

	Rating	Comments
A. Schedule		
B. Location		
C. Meeting Facilities		
D. Food		
E. Room		
F.		

III. How do you rate the overall program?

Rating

a. What did you find most valuable?

_____

_____

b. Suggested improvements

_____

_____

IV. Your suggestions for future programs (subjects, location, schedule, etc.).

_____

_____

_____

---

and subjects could be measured against these standards. On a five-point scale:

Excellent   = 5
Very good = 4
Good   = 3
Fair   = 2
Poor   = 1

The established MI standard is **4.7**; a lower rating is considered unacceptable. The standard was established by gathering data from past performance of MI leaders and effective outside leaders. Each organization should gather such data and establish its own standards of performance. Leaders who do not meet these standards can be coached so that they can meet standards or otherwise be tactfully eliminated from conducting future meetings.

The planner and coordinator of a meeting may be able to give reactions that can be a helpful supplement to the reactions of conferees. Figure 8-6 illustrates the kind of form this person can complete after observing the meeting from the back of the room.

The combined reactions of the conferees and the coordinator should be communicated to the conference leader or speaker to help in understanding the feelings of the conferees and to improve conference leadership performance at future sessions. Care should be taken to communicate negative reactions in a constructive manner so that they will be accepted and considered in future sessions.

(text continues on page 133)

Figure 8-5. A combined form for evaluating reaction and taking notes.

Subject _____   Date _____

Speaker/Leader _____

Your reactions and comments will help us determine whether our programs meet your needs and interests. They will also provide a basis for program improvement.

1. Reaction to **Subject:**

    ☐ Excellent   Comments:
    ☐ Very Good
    ☐ Good
    ☐ Fair
    ☐ Poor

2. Reaction to **Speaker/Leader:** (if more than one, insert name next to rating)

    ☐ Excellent   Comments:
    ☐ Very Good
    ☐ Good
    ☐ Fair
    ☐ Poor

3. What did you find most valuable?

4. Suggested improvements:

REACTION SHEET (continued)

5. Suggestions for future programs: (subjects, speakers, locations, approaches, etc.)

(continues)

Figure 8-5. (*continued*)

NOTES

Subject _____   Date _____

Speaker/Leader _____

NOTES (continued)

The American Society for Training and Development
"dedicated to the development of human potential"

_____

Name (optional)

Reprinted with permission from the American Society for Training and Development (ASTD), Alexandria, Virginia.

Figure 8-6. A trained observer's reaction sheet.

Rating _____   Date _____   Rater's initial _____

Name of leader _____   Subject _____

	Very much so	To some extent	No
A. Preparation 1. Did he/she prepare for the meeting?			
2. Was his/her preparation geared to the group?			
B. Conducting 1. Did he/she read the material?			
2. Did he/she hold the interest of the group?			
3. Was he/she enthusiastic/dynamic?			
4. Did he/she use visual aids? If yes, what aids?			
5. Did he/she present the material clearly?			
6. Did he/she help the group apply the material?			
7. Did he/she adequately cover the subject?			
8. Did he/she summarize during conference and at end?			
9. Did he/she involve the group? If yes, how?			

C. Constructive Comments
   1. What would you suggest to improve future sessions?

   _____

   _____

D. Potential
   1. With proper coaching, what would be the highest rating he/she could
      achieve? _____

E. Additional Comments:

   _____

   _____

It is important to determine how people feel about the programs they attend. Decisions by top management are frequently made from one or two comments they receive from people who have attended. A supervisory training program may be cancelled if even one manager tells the vice-president that a program was "a waste of time." A quantitative tabulation of the comments from all supervisors can help to avoid decisions based on insufficient data.

Also, supervisors who like a training program are more apt to obtain maximum benefits from it. According to a noted educator: "For maximum learning you must have interest and enthusiasm." A past president of the American Society for Training and Development said: "It is not enough to say, 'Supervisors, here is the information, take it.' We must make it interesting and motivate them to want to take it."

Learning

Enthusiastic reactions do not guarantee that learning has taken place, so the second stage of evaluation is to determine what knowledge, attitudes, and skills were learned in the training program.

Guidelines for Measuring Learning

1. Measure before-and-after attitudes, knowledge, and/or skills. Use a paper-and-pencil test for knowledge and attitudes and a performance test for skills.
2. Get a 100 percent response.
3. Statistically analyze the data.
4. Use a control group if practical.
5. Take appropriate action based on evaluation data.

These guidelines indicate that evaluation in terms of learning is more difficult than evaluation in terms of reaction. Because some knowledge of statistics is necessary, the evaluation should be designed by a person well acquainted with research design. Two methods of the many available to measure learning are classroom performance and paper-and-pencil tests.

Classroom Performance

It is relatively easy to measure the learning that takes place in training programs that teach skills—those, for example, in job instruction training, conducting performance appraisal interviews, work simplification, employment interviewing skills, reading improvement, effective speaking, and effective writing. Classroom activities such as demonstrations, individual performance of the skill being taught, and discussions following role playing can be used as evaluation. The training coordinator can organize these so as to obtain a fairly objective evaluation of the learning that is taking place.

In a course that is teaching effective training methods to supervisors, for example, each supervisor will demonstrate the skills in front of the class. From the performance, the training coordinator can ascertain if the supervisor has learned the principles and can use them, at least in the classroom. In a work simplification program, each conferee can be required to fill out a flow-process chart, and the training coordinator can determine if the conferee knows how to go about this task. In a reading improvement program, the reading speed and comprehension of each participant can be readily determined by classroom performance. And in an effective speaking course, each conferee can be required to give a number of talks, which can be recorded on videotape and played back. A training coordinator and other participants can evaluate the amount of learning that is taking place by observing successive performances.

In these programs, an evaluation of the learning can be built into the course. If the evaluation is organized and implemented properly, the training coordinator can obtain a fairly objective measure of the amount of learning that has taken place and can set up before-and-after situations in which each conferee demonstrates the principles and techniques being taught.

Paper-and-Pencil Tests

When principles and facts, rather than skills, are taught, a paper-and-pencil test can be used. In some cases, standardized tests can be purchased to measure learning, but in others each organization must construct its own.

To measure the learning in human relations programs, for example, the Supervisory Inventory on Human Relations can be used.[1] (See Chapter 5 for sample items.) Standardized tests are also available to evaluate training programs that are designed to teach communication, safety, leadership, motivation, managing change, time management, decision making, performance appraisal, and coaching.

These inventories should be used as follows:

1. They should be given to all conferees before the program as a

---

1. Donald L. Kirkpatrick, *Supervisory Inventory on Human Relations* (Elm Grove, Wis.: Donald L. Kirkpatrick, 1990).

pretest. If practical, they should also be given to a control group that is comparable to the experimental group.

2. The pretests should be analyzed by the total score of each person as well as the responses to each item of the test. A form can be used to get this information (Figure 8-7). There is no need to identify the person. The second tabulation (responses to each item) assists in evaluating the program and provides some knowledge and understanding of the group before the program.

3. After the program is over, the same test or its equivalent should be given to the conferees (as well as the control group if there is one). The total scores and individual responses of this posttest are then compared with those of the pretest to see what changes have taken place. Any changes in the responses of the control group must be deducted from those of the experimental group (those receiving the training). A statistical analysis will reveal the level of significance of the changes that have taken place because of the program.

Example 1 of Figure 8-8 shows that a positive gain of 9 was achieved by the experimental group, while the control group averaged a gain of

Figure 8-7. A form for analyzing inventories.

Name of inventory _____ Date _____

1. Please circle items that are "wrong" (different than the scoring key).

| 1 | 2 | 3 | 4 | 5 | 6 | 7 | 8 | 9 | 10 | 11 | 12 | 13 | 14 | 15 |

| 16 | 17 | 18 | 19 | 20 | 21 | 22 | 23 | 24 | 25 | 26 | 27 | 28 | 29 | 30 |

| 31 | 32 | 33 | 34 | 35 | 36 | 37 | 38 | 39 | 40 | 41 | 42 | 43 | 44 | 45 |

| 46 | 47 | 48 | 49 | 50 | 51 | 52 | 53 | 54 | 55 | 56 | 57 | 58 | 59 | 60 |

| 61 | 62 | 63 | 64 | 65 | 66 | 67 | 68 | 69 | 70 | 71 | 72 | 73 | 74 | 75 |

| 76 | 77 | 78 | 79 | 80 |

2. Tabulate your *raw score* (number right), which is 80 minus the number wrong.

80 − _____ = [   ]

Figure 8-8. A comparison of the scores of two groups on an inventory.

Experimental Group: 25 supervisors who completed the training program

Control Group: 25 supervisors who did not attend the training program

		Experimental Group	Control Group
Example 1	Pretest	61	60
	Posttest	70	62
	Gain	9	2
	Net Gain	7	
Example 2	Pretest	61	60
	Posttest	70	68
	Gain	9	8
	Net gain	1	

only 2. The net gain was significant: 7. Example 2 shows a positive gain of 9 by the experimental group and a gain of 8 by the control group. The net gain was not significant: 1.

Figure 8-9 shows two examples of the change in responses on individual items. Example 1 shows that on item 5, four people answered it correctly on the pretest, while 21 answered it correctly on the posttest, for a significant gain of 17. Example 2 shows that on item 10 of the test, the gain was only 2 from pretest to posttest. This would not be significant and would clearly indicate to the instructor a failure to teach the principle, fact, or technique covered by that item.

Unless the test or inventory covers the material presented, it will not be a valid measure of the effectiveness of the learning. Frequently, a standardized test covers only part of the material presented in the course, so only that part of the course covered is being evaluated. If certain items on the test are not being covered, no change in these items can be expected.

Some persons responsible for training programs have developed their own paper-and-pencil tests to measure learning in their programs. Training professionals at MGIC in Milwaukee developed a Product Knowledge Test consisting of forty questions important to the job of supervisor. (See Chapter 5 for the test items.) The results of the pretest

Figure 8-9. A comparison of the change in responses on the pretest and posttest.

Item 5	Correct	Incorrect	
	4	21	Pretest
	21	4	Posttest
	17		Gain
Item 10	Correct	Incorrect	
	6	19	Pretest
	8	17	Posttest
	2		Gain

revealed the preprogram knowledge of participants. A comparison of pretest and posttest scores revealed what learning took place.

A pretest versus posttest design with a control group is very effective in training evaluation, although it does not completely eradicate the possible impact of factors other than training.[2] Taking a pretest may sensitize the supervisors to do better on a posttest measure. Additionally, many organizations are not static, so events in an organization may have differential effects on the posttraining behavior of the experimental and control groups.

In summary, a paper-and-pencil test can be used effectively to measure the learning of attitudes and knowledge, while performance tests can measure skills. The evaluation should be systematic and statistically oriented. A comparison of before-and-after scores and performance should be made to measure how much learning has taken place.

Behavior

When I joined the Management Institute of the University of Wisconsin, my first assignment was to attend a one-week course on human relations for foremen and supervisors. During the week, I was particularly impressed by Herman, a foreman from a Milwaukee company. Whenever a conference leader asked a question requiring a good understanding of human relations principles and techniques, Herman was the first to raise his hand. He had all the answers in terms of good human relations. I was

2. David A. Grove and Cheri Ostroff, "Program Evaluation," in *Developing Human Resources* (Alexandria, Va.: Society for Human Resource Management, 1991).

impressed and said to myself, "If I were in industry, I would like to work for a man like that." A cousin of mine was working for that company, and, coincidentally, Herman was his boss. At the first opportunity, I asked my cousin about him and found that while Herman might have known all the principles and techniques of human relations, he didn't practice them on the job. He performed as the typical bull-of-the-woods who had little consideration for the feelings and ideas of his subordinates. I thus realized that there can be a big difference between knowing principles and techniques and using them on the job.

Even if supervisors learn, there is no assurance that they will change their behavior. Five basic requirements must exist to ensure a changed behavior:

1. Desire to improve
2. Required knowledge and skills
3. The right climate
4. Encouragement and help
5. Rewards for improvement

Items 1 and 2 can be accomplished in the classroom. The "right climate" in item 3 refers to the situation that exists on the job—in other words, the climate for change that is created by the supervisor's immediate boss. Five possible climates exist:

1. *Preventive.* The boss does not permit any change in behavior that has been taught and encouraged in the classroom.
2. *Discouraging.* The boss doesn't say, "You can't do it," but discourages any change unless he approves it.
3. *Neutral.* The boss doesn't seem to care. His attitude allows supervisors to do as they see fit, as long as it doesn't interfere with production.
4. *Encouraging.* The boss takes an interest in what was learned and offers to assist in the implementation.
5. *Requiring.* The boss is informed of the behavior changes that are taught and insists on their implementation.

It is obvious that little, if any, change in behavior will occur if the climate is preventive or discouraging. Trainers should be aware of the existence of these climates and try to change them to "neutral" or better. One way to do this is to provide the bosses with similar training before the supervisors are trained. Another is to involve them in the planning and implementation of the program. Malcolm Knowles has stated, "Create a climate that is conducive for neutral planning. It is critical that a planning committee or task force be used which is representative of all the constituencies that the program is designed to serve."[3]

Items 4 and 5 are also important. Encouragement and help can come from the boss, human resources professionals, or both. And the most positive way to encourage change in behavior is a "requiring" climate established by the manager. One form of this is learning contracts recommended by Thomas Quick. He suggests three contracts:

1. Between the trainer and the manager whose subordinate supervisors attend the training
2. Between the trainer and the supervisors who attend
3. Between the manager and the supervisors[4]

The first two contracts require a careful determination of needs by considering the suggestions of the trainees (supervisors) and those of the managers of the departments that the supervisors represent. The third contract should consist of agreement between supervisor and manager of what will happen as a result of the training. Discussions should focus on the department's needs and the supervisor's needs. These discussions and agreements should take place prior to the training program. Unfortunately, this kind of contract or even a brief premeeting discussion of the program is usually absent.

Knowles suggests that learners answer the following questions:

"What are you going to learn?" [*Objectives*]
"How are you going to learn it?" [*Resources and strategies*]
"What is your target date for completion?"
"How are you going to know that you learned it?" [*Evidence*]
"How are you going to prove that you learned it?" [*Verification*][5]

In a requiring climate, the boss of the learner would be involved in answering all five of the questions.

Guidelines for Measuring Behavior

1. Measure on a before-and-after basis if practical.
2. Allow time for behavior changes to take place.
3. Survey and/or interview one or more of the following:
   a. The trainees

3. Malcolm Knowles, *Using Learning Contracts* (San Francisco: Jossey-Bass Publishers, 1986).
4. Thomas Quick, *Training Managers So They Can Really Manage* (San Francisco: Jossey-Bass, 1991).
5. Knowles, *Using Learning Contracts*.

    b. The bosses of the trainees
    c. The subordinates of the trainees (use caution!)
    d. Others who know the behavior of the trainees
 4. Get a 100 percent response or a sampling.
 5. Use a control group (not receiving the training) if practical.
 6. Statistically analyze data.
 7. Repeat the evaluation at appropriate times (in three months, six months, twelve months).
 8. Consider cost versus benefits.

The application of these guidelines requires knowledge of research design, as well as time and effort.

Tom Newman, the international training manager for Johnson Wax, regularly evaluates the effectiveness of all the programs he conducts. In order to measure changes in behavior that resulted from a two-day seminar on leadership and influence (L&I), four areas were considered:

1. Training skills used
2. Changes in behavior
3. Obstacles to use of the skills learned
4. Benefits from the program

A follow-up questionnaire completed by 80 participants yielded these responses to the questions:

1. Which training skills have you used two or more times since the program?

Planned L&I tactics in advance	87%
Used the "Interaction Guide"	72%
Used the meeting checklist	57%
Completed the Interaction Planning Sheet	32%

2. What significant changes have occurred in your interaction with others?

Better organized, prepared	28%
Improved communication skills	20%
More receptive to others	17%
More self-confident	11%
Changes in behavior were positive	86%

3. To what extent has L&I training helped on the job?

A high degree	3%
Substantially	56%
Somewhat	31%
None	10%

Alexander Braun described an evaluation approach that asked each trainee, at the conclusion of each day, to write at least one realistic objective of how she would implement the day's learnings. The goal was to get participants committed to on-the-job changes in behavior and provide a basis for boss-subordinate discussion and implementation.[6]

T. K. Meier and Joseph P. Pulichene evaluated changes in behavior resulting from a course on assertiveness. The managers of those attending the course were given the questionnaire shown in Figure 8-10 before the course and again six weeks after the completion of the fifteen-hour course presented over a six-week period. The results were statistically significant in accomplishing three objectives: decreased passiveness, decreased aggressiveness, and increased assertiveness.[7]

George Morrisey and William Wellstead evaluated a supervisory training program at McDonnell-Douglas. The supervisors who attended the program were required to commit themselves to specific objectives on how they would apply the learning on the job. In addition, they had to send in a progress report sixty days later in order to earn a certificate of completion. Getting the supervisors to make a written commitment to improvement action is a key element in the course. It resulted in "a tremendous return for a very modest investment," according to the authors.[8]

Frederic Swierczek and Lynne Carmichael described their approach to evaluating learning and behavior changes. The program was the "Planning and Organization for Effective Supervision" workshops offered to public agencies in Florida by the University of South Florida Institute of Government. At the end of the workshop, participants were asked:

1. What skills did you learn in the workshop?
2. How will you apply these skills back at work?

In addition to question 1, pretests and posttests based on a Likert scale were used to measure learning, and in addition to question 2, a questionnaire was mailed to participants six months after the program. Some of the responses from ninety-one participants were:

6. Alexander Braun, "Assessing Supervisory Training Needs and Evaluating Effectiveness," in American Society for Training and Development (ASTD), *More Evaluating Training Programs* (Alexandria, Va.: ASTD, 1987).
7. T. K. Meier and Joseph P. Pulichene, "Evaluating the Effectiveness of Assertiveness Training," in *More Evaluating Training Programs*.
8. George L. Morrisey and William R. Wellstead, "Supervisory Training Can Be Measured," in *More Evaluating Training Programs*.

Figure 8-10. Manager's questionnaire for evaluating a course on assertiveness.

Characterize your impression of the employee's behavior in various situations by using the following number scale:

Never or Rarely	Seldom	Sometimes	Usually	Almost Always or Always
-1-	-2-	-3-	-4-	-5-

_____ 1. Others may take advantage of him/her because he/she finds it difficult to refuse requests.

_____ 2. A reluctance to express his/her ideas hampers effectiveness on the job.

_____ 3. Downgrades his/her own work or attempts to offer excuses for his/her work even though it hasn't been criticized.

_____ 4. Seems to prefer giving other people the upper hand in a discussion rather than challenging their opinions or data.

_____ 5. During a performance review, he/she receives criticism without comment.

_____ 6. If he/she were genuinely overloaded with work in comparison to peers, he/she would try to complete the assignments alone regardless of the sacrifices required.

_____ 7. If you were treating him/her unfairly, he/she would do nothing, but wait for you to explain your intention.

_____ 8. Able to discuss someone's criticism of him/her openly and constructively.

_____ 9. If a friend made an unreasonable request, he/she would refuse in a manner that would allow him/her to retain the person's full friendship.

_____ 10. Actively seeks more information about an assignment if he/she did not completely understand original instructions.

_____ 11. If informed of declining performance during a performance review, he/she would ask for more specific information or examples of how his/her performance had declined and seek suggestions for improvement.

_____ 12. Asks favors of other people when necessary but does not "wear out his/her welcome."

_____ 13. If he/she had a "personality conflict" with his/her office mates, he/she may suggest a meeting between them and perhaps with their supervisor to iron out their differences and solve the conflict.

_____ 14. In group meetings, he/she expresses ideas freely without dominating others.

_____ 15. May "fly off the handle" if he/she loses an argument.

_____ 16. Complains when he/she is unhappy in a work situation, before seeking ways to improve the situation.

Never or Rarely	Seldom	Sometimes	Usually	Almost Always or Always
-1-	-2-	-3-	-4-	-5-

_____ 17. Steps in and makes decisions for others, without consulting them, even if the principal person is available for consultation.

_____ 18. Reluctant to admit an error, regardless of how small the mistake may be.

_____ 19. If informed of a perceived decline in performance, he/she offers a series of excuses or tries to blame others.

_____ 20. Acts as if he/she "knows it all."

_____ 21. Once he/she has drafted a letter or memo, he/she firmly resists making significant changes and acts as if he/she resents the suggestions for change.

Do my job better	43%
Delegate more	31%
Use skills with employees	26%
Communicate better	13%[9]

Terance Jackson suggests that changes in attitude are an important benefit that can result from a supervisory training program.[10] The following attitudes should be measured on a before-and-after basis, using the scale suggested:

Attitudes to Self (Self-Confidence, Drive, Ambition)

Has no self-confidence, drive, or ambition	0
Requires more self-confidence to do the job and more ambition to get on in the organization	.5
Has sufficient self-confidence to do a competent job; may progress through overambition	1.0
Has a certain self-confidence, drive, and ambition, which is shown much of the time	1.5
Has a great deal of self-confidence, drive, and ambition, which is shown all of the time	2.0

Attitudes to Task/Job (Motivated by Current Job)

Is not motivated by current job	0
Is motivated a little by current job, which sometimes provides a small degree of satisfaction	.5

9. Frederic William Swierczek and Lynne Carmichael, "The Quantity and Quality of Evaluating Training," in *More Evaluating Training Programs*.

10. Terance Jackson, *Evaluation: Relating Training to Business Performance* (San Diego: University Associates, 1989).

Derives a moderate amount of satisfaction from current job,
   which motivates from time to time   **1.0**
Mostly motivated by current job, which often provides
   satisfaction   **1.5**
Current job motivates very highly and provides a high
   degree of satisfaction most of the time   **2.0**

The attitude to self can be modified in classroom training, while changes in attitude toward the job probably require a positive job climate and possibly a change in job content, responsibility, and authority. Pretest and posttest measures of attitude should probably be done at a later date also to measure changes that could have occurred after the training program was completed.

Dana Robinson and James Robinson advise that the following scale be used on a questionnaire to measure changes in behavior:[11]

This is a behavior I never use.   1
This is a behavior I rarely use (less than 15% of the time).   2
This is a behavior I use very infrequently (less than 33% of
   the time).   3
This is a behavior I use infrequently (less than 50% of the
   time).   4
This is a behavior I use frequently (more than 50% of the
   time).   5
This is a behavior I use very frequently (more than 67% of the
   time).   6
This is a behavior I almost always use (about 90% of the
   time).   7
This is a behavior I always use.   8

Each behavior is described, and participants are asked to rate each one before the training program and again three months after the program is completed. A comparison of the response indicates the change in behavior as the trainee sees it.

Results

The objectives of most training programs can be stated in terms of results to accomplish improved profits, reduced costs, improved quality, re-

11. Dana Gaines Robinson and James C. Robinson, *Training for Impact: How to Link Training to Business Needs and Measure the Results* (San Francisco: Jossey-Bass, 1989).

duced accidents, improved customer relations, reduction in turnover, and improved moral.

Guidelines for Measuring Results

1. Measure on a before-and-after basis if possible.
2. Allow time for possible results to take place.
3. Use a control group (not receiving the training) if practical.
4. Statistically analyze data.
5. Repeat at appropriate time.
6. Consider cost versus benefits.
7. Look for "evidence" if "proof" is not possible.

The results of certain kinds of training programs are relatively easy to evaluate. For example, in teaching clerical personnel to be more effective in keyboarding, the measurement can be the number of words per minute before and after. Or if the goal is to reduce grievances in a plant, the number of grievances before and after a training program on how to prevent grievances can be counted.

In most programs, however, it is difficult, if not impossible, to evaluate results because of the problem called the *separation of variables*. That is, many factors can affect results, and it may not be possible to isolate the effect caused by the training program. For example, a supervisory training course may be given to train foremen to induct and train new employees properly, with the objective being the reduction in the high rate of turnover among new employees. After the training program has been completed, a reduction in turnover may occur, but it must be proved that the training program caused the reduction in turnover. Other causes might be new employment practices, the tightness of the labor market, the season of the year, or recent wage increases.

Two graduate students at the University of Wisconsin used two techniques to measure the results of a Cost Reduction Institute conducted by the university's Management Institute. The first was to conduct in-depth interviews with some of the supervisors who had attended the course and with their immediate superiors. The other was to mail questionnaires to the remaining enrollees and to their supervisors.

Questions Used in Interviews With Trainees

1. Have you been able to reduce costs in the few weeks that you have been back on the job?

Yes	No	Noncommittal or Evasive	Did Not Answer
13	3	2	1

2. How?

The thirteen trainers who answered yes said they made their cost reductions in different areas but with ideas that stemmed directly from the program.

Interviews With the Superiors of the Trainees

Eight of the cost-reduction actions described by the trainees were confirmed by the immediate superior, and these superiors estimated total savings to be from $15,000 to $21,000 per year. The specific ideas used were described by superiors and trainees.

Questionnaires Mailed to Trainees Not Interviewed

Questionnaires were mailed to those trainees who were not contacted personally. The results on the questionnaire were not as specific or useful as those obtained by personal interview, leading to the conclusion that a personal interview is better than a questionnaire to measure this kind of program.

One way to measure financial benefits versus costs is to use a formula:

$$TV = (T \times N \times I \times M) - (N \times C)$$

where:

TV = training value
T = duration of training effect
N = number of supervisors trained
I = impact of the training program
M = monetary value of the impact
C = cost of the training program

One large company used the formula to evaluate one of their programs. The results were:

$$TV = (1 \times 100 \times .67 \times \$30,000) - (100 \times \$7,200) = \$1,290,000$$

From this they determined a payback period of three to four months and a return on investment of 179 percent.

Linn Coffman's article, "An Easy Way to Effectively Evaluate Program Results," details an approach that consists of a series of follow-up meetings with those who have been trained. They are asked for their input on what results have been accomplished because of attending the training program. In addition, their managers also provide input on what results they have seen.[12]

James Cullen and associates used an evaluation approach to assess the training investment in terms of cost-effectiveness by comparing training costs with benefits measured in monetary terms. They found the calculation of training costs and returns to be complex, with no single formula. Their model combined the economic reasoning of three cost-effectiveness models that have been used.[13]

Ann I. Kelley, Robert Orgel, and Donald Baer stated, "The bottom line is closer than you think!" They used before-and-after sales figures, as did Hahne.[14] They also used productivity improvement among production lines receiving various supervisory training.

Robinson and Robinson suggest the following measures for evaluating results from a supervisory training program:

- Decreased rejection rate*
- Increased output*
- Reduced absenteeism*
- Reduced tardiness*
- Reduced number of grievances
- Reduced turnover
- Decreased waste*
- Increased number of employees' suggestions adopted
- Decrease in production costs*
- Reduced costs of new hires*
- Reduced overtime*
- Climate-survey data[15]

Those marked with an asterisk can easily be measured in dollars. The others require some effort to interpret in terms of dollars.

Figures 8-11 and 8-12 describe a case study of an organization that

(text continues on page 151)

12. Linn Coffman, "An Easy Way to Effectively Evaluate Program Results," in *More Evaluating Training Programs.*
13. James G. Cullen, Stephen A. Sawzin, Gary R. Sisson, and Richard A. Swanson, "Cost Effectiveness: A Model for Assessing the Training Investment," in *More Evaluating Training Programs.*
14. Ann I. Kelley, Robert F. Orgel, and Donald M. Baer, "Evaluation: The Bottom Line Is Closer Than You Think," and C. E. Hahne, "How to Measure Results of Sales Training," both in *More Evaluating Training Programs.*
15. Robinson and Robinson, *Training for Impact.*

Figure 8-11. Training cost analysis.

Direct costs: The travel and per-diem cost is zero, because training took place adjacent to the plant. There is a cost for classroom space and audiovisual equipment, because these were rented from a local hotel. Refreshments were purchased at the same hotel. Because different supervisors attended the morning and afternoon sessions, lunch was not provided.

Indirect costs: The clerical and administrative costs reflect the amount of clerical time spent on making arrangements for the workshop facilities, sending out notices to all participants, and preparing class rosters and other miscellaneous materials.

Direct Costs

Outside instructor	0
In-house instructor—12 days × $125	$1,500.00
Fringe benefits @ 25% of salary	$ 375.00
Travel and per-diem expenses	0
Materials—56 × $60/participant	$3,360.00
Classroom space and audiovisual equipment—12 days @ $50	$ 600.00
Food; refreshments—$4/day × 3 days × 56 participants	$ 672.00
Total direct costs	$6,507.00

Indirect Costs

Training management	0
Clerical/administrative	$ 750.00
Fringe benefits—25% of clerical/administrative salary	$ 187.00
Postage, shipping, telephone	0
Pre- and postlearning materials—$4 × 56 participants	$ 224.00
Total indirect costs (rounded to nearest dollar)	$1,161.00

Development costs: These costs represent the purchase of the training program from a vendor. Included are instructional aids, an instructor manual, videotapes, and a licensing fee. The instructor training costs pertain to the one-week workshop that the instructor attended to become prepared to facilitate the training. Front-end assessment costs were covered by the corporate training budget.

Overhead costs: These represent the services that the general organization provides to the training unit. Because figures were not available, we used 10 percent of the direct, indirect, and program development costs.

Compensation for participants: This figure represents the salaries and benefits paid to all participants while they attended the workshop.

Development Costs

Fee to purchase program	$3,800.00
Instructor training	
Registration fee	$1,400.00
Travel and lodging	$ 975.00
Salary	$ 625.00
Benefits (25% of salary)	$ 156.00
Total development costs	$6,756.00

Overhead Costs

General organization support	10% of direct, indirect,
Top management's time	and development costs
Total overhead costs	$1,443.00

Compensation for Participants

Participants' salary and benefits (time away from the job)

Total compensation	$16,696.00
Total training costs	$32,564.00
Cost per participant	$ 581.50

Source: Dana Gaines Robinson and James C. Robinson, *Training for Impact: How to Link Training to Business Needs and Measure the Results* (San Francisco: Jossey-Bass Publishers, 1989).

Figure 8-12. Operational results analysis.

Operational Results Area	How Measured	Results Before Training	Results After Training	Differences (+ or −)	Expressed in $
Quality of panels	% rejected	2% rejected 1,440 panels per day	1.5% rejected 1,080 panels per day	.5% 360 panels	$720 per day $172,800 per year
Housekeeping	Visual inspection using 20-item checklist	10 defects (average)	2 defects (average)	8 defects	Not measurable in $
Preventable accidents	Number of accidents	24 per year	16 per year	8 per year	
	Direct cost of each accident	$144,000 per year	$96,000 per year	$48,000	$48,000 per year
				Total savings:	$220,800.00

$$\text{ROI} = \frac{\text{Return}}{\text{Investment}} = \frac{\text{Operational Results}}{\text{Training Costs}} = \frac{\$220,800}{\$32,564} = 6.8$$

Source: Dana Gaines Robinson and James C. Robinson, *Training for Impact: How to Link Training to Business Needs and Measure the Results* (San Francisco: Jossey-Bass Publishers, 1989).

makes wood panels. Figure 8-11 shows how costs of training were determined (figures are from 1980), and Figure 8-12 represents the operational results twelve months after the training. The Return on Investment (ROI) of 6.8 was determined by dividing the operational results by the training costs.

It's obvious to most training professionals that results are relatively easy to measure for some kinds of programs and difficult in others. In sales, production, and safety, for example, specific figures can be readily compared on a before-and-after basis. When subjects like leadership, communication, motivation, decision making, and time management are offered, evaluation in terms of financial benefits is difficult, and maybe impossible, to measure. "Proof" is sometimes impossible to achieve. Evidence is much easier to obtain, and most top executives will be more than satisfied when this is presented.[16]

One word of caution: Be sure that the cost of evaluating is worth the possible benefits. If programs are expensive and will be offered many times, it is worthwhile to spend time and money to evaluate them. If they are offered only once or twice or they are economical to present, attempted evaluation of results may not be practical.

Summary

Evaluation of internal classroom programs may include all of the four stages: reaction, learning, behavior, and results. All programs should be evaluated in terms of reaction. This is easy to do and is important because it is a measure of customer satisfaction. If the supervisors (customers) are unhappy with the program (product), they will tell others (perhaps their boss and even higher-level managers), and the program will be eliminated. Also, the very process of asking for participant reaction tells the supervisors, "We want to help meet your needs, and we want you to tell us if we are doing it."

Evaluation of reaction has its limitations. It doesn't prove that learning has taken place and says nothing about changes in behavior and improved results. Therefore, as time, money, and skill permit, professional trainers should progress to evaluation in the other three stages.

Grove and Ostroff described the training evaluation strategy of one company as follows:

- Be determined by the overall strategic plan.
- Require specific training objectives.

16. Donald L. Kirkpatrick, "Evaluating Training Programs: Evidence vs. Proof," in *More Evaluating Training Programs.*

► Obtain trainee reactions to every course.
► Evaluate behavior changes in "flagship" programs (high-volume, high-expense programs)
► Remember that some courses will not be evaluated beyond trainee reactions (it isn't worth it).[17]

This chapter has offered guidelines and examples. Design, forms, and techniques can be borrowed and adapted to other organizations; results of the evaluation of other programs cannot.

REFERENCES

Fisk, Catherine N., *Evaluation Instruments*. Alexandria, Va.: American Society for Training and Development, 1991.
This tool kit contains several articles and instruments used by various organizations to evaluate their training programs.
Kirkpatrick, Donald L., ed. *Evaluating Training Programs*. Alexandria, Va.: American Society for Training and Development, 1975.
Contains all the articles on evaluation that appeared in *Training and Development Journal* from 1965 to 1975.
Kirkpatrick, Donald L., ed. *More Evaluating Training Programs*. Alexandria, Va.: American Society for Training and Development, 1987.
Contains all the articles on evaluation that appeared in *Training and Development Journal* from 1976 to 1986. "Judging From the Feds" by Ruth Salinger is of special interest; it describes a number of evaluation studies conducted by federal agencies.

17. Grove and Ostroff, "Program Evaluation."

9

Getting Maximum Benefits From Outside Supervisory Development Programs

An effective way to train and develop supervisors is to send them to programs sponsored by outside organizations, such as universities, trade associations, professional groups, and consultants. Many benefits may result from participating in these programs. Those attending gain increased knowledge of the latest and best management philosophies and principles, improved management skills, and increased chances of promotion, salary increases, and other rewards. The organization also reaps benefits: improved attitudes, knowledge, and skills of individuals, resulting in better management; improved profitability because of better management; and an improved image of the organization as being progressive, which can be important in attracting the best candidates for positions at all levels.

Selecting Programs

The first step in selecting the best programs is to find out what programs are available. The bulletins sent to human resources managers and training directors are the best source of this information.

The second step is to evaluate programs and pick the best. The careful reading of program bulletins will provide some indication of the program content, quality of leaders, and other pertinent information on cost and possible benefits. Remember, though, that subject content, qualifications of the leaders, and benefits may be exaggerated by some organizations in order to sell enrollments.

Probably the best way to judge the relative merits of different programs is to use a systematic method of evaluating participation. After each program, the participant should be required to fill out an evaluation

Figure 9-1. Form for evaluating outside supervisory training programs.

Name _____ Title _____ Date _____

Program attended:

Name of program _____ Dates _____

Location _____ Fee _____

Organization presenting program _____

1. How accurately did the program announcement describe what was covered at the program?

   ☐ Very accurately   ☐ Fairly accurately   ☐ Inaccurately

2. To what extent did the subject content meet your needs and interests?

   ☐ Very well   ☐ To some extent   ☐ Very little

3. How effective were the speakers and conference leaders?

   ☐ Excellent   ☐ Very good   ☐ Good   ☐ Fair
   ☐ Poor

4. How were the facilities, meals, etc.?

   ☐ Excellent   ☐ Very good   ☐ Good   ☐ Fair
   ☐ Poor

5. What benefits do you feel you gained?

   ☐ Knowledge of what other companies were doing.
   ☐ New theory and principles that are pertinent.
   ☐ Ideas and techniques that can be applied on the job.
   ☐ Other (please explain).

6. How would you rate the entire program in relation to time and cost?

   ☐ Excellent   ☐ Very good   ☐ Good   ☐ Fair
   ☐ Poor

7. Would you like to attend a future program presented by the same organization?

   ☐ Definitely   ☐ Possibly   ☐ No

8. Would you recommend that others from our company attend programs presented by the same organization?

☐ Yes ☐ No ☐ Not sure. . . . If yes, who should attend?

9. Other comments.

---

form, such as that shown in Figure 9-1. Future participation can be based on an analysis of these forms.

One of the most extensive and best quality programs for training and developing supervisors is offered by the Management Institute, University of Wisconsin. The program was initiated in 1944 and has continued to grow in scope and quality. Currently it is being offered in both Madison and Milwaukee. Chapters 15 and 16 provide details.

Selecting Participants

The human resources manager, training director, or other development person can determine which management development organizations offer high-quality programs at the least cost. The selection of the participants, however, should be a line decision, probably made with the assistance of a staff professional. In the selection process, the individual and/or the boss should study the program announcement and determine if the subject content is pertinent to the current or future job of the individual.

An organization should plan its participation for the entire year instead of waiting until the last minute to make a decision so that the participants can plan ahead, and fees and expenses can be budgeted.

Preprogram Discussion

Those selected for an outside development program should be counseled before they attend. The participants' managers should be involved; someone from the human resources department may assist. The following checklist is a guide for this discussion.

1. Discuss the program with the supervisors. Show them you are

interested in their development, and see if they want to attend. If they are not enthusiastic, sell them on the benefits. (This discussion may be part of the process of selecting the programs to attend.)

2. Review the program details, including where and when.
3. Be sure all necessary arrangements have been made in the department during the supervisors' absence.
4. Encourage supervisors to participate in the discussions during the sessions and in the off-hours.
5. If attending the program will necessitate being away from home one or more nights, show interest in the arrangements for their family.
6. If expenses are involved, discuss expense account arrangements.
7. Encourage supervisors to relax and enjoy the experience.
8. Explain what you expect on their return. This may include one or more of the following:
   a. A written report (evaluation plus content)
   b. An oral report (to the boss or to a group)
   c. Discussion with the boss
   d. On-the-job implementation of ideas learned
   e. Presentation to other interested supervisors
9. Answer any questions.

Postprogram Discussion and Implementation

To obtain maximum benefits from attendance, it is necessary to approach postprogram discussion and implementation systematically. The following checklist suggests items to be used; most of them should be handled by the supervisor's manager and some by the human resources department.

1. Obtain a written evaluation of the program. Use the same form for all participants (Figure 9-1).
2. Obtain a written and/or oral summary of what the supervisors learned, such as principles, approaches, and techniques.
3. Show an interest in the materials brought back.
4. Discuss any ideas that might be implemented on the job.
5. Give supervisors an opportunity to discuss the program at a meeting of interested persons.
6. Discuss possible follow-up (other programs or reading).

Keeping Records

It may seem obvious that records should be kept that show participation in supervisory development programs; however, it is common to find organizations in which no one knows what programs the supervisors have attended. These records are important to the supervisor as well as to the organization and should be kept in the human resources office or in some other place where they will be accurately maintained and readily available.

Summary

All types of business, industry, and government organizations can benefit from participating in outside supervisory development programs. To maximize these benefits, a systematic approach is needed with the following steps:

1. Careful selection of quality programs
2. Careful selection of participants
3. Discussion with participants before they attend
4. Discussion with participants after they return
5. Encouraging and assisting participants in on-the-job application of what they have learned

This chapter has listed some specific factors to consider. If a systematic approach is to be used, someone in the organization should be selected as the coordinator. This person should:

- Screen bulletins and announcements to select high-quality programs.
- Work with line management to select participants.
- Handle necessary arrangements for enrollment, payment of fees, travel, and expense accounts.
- Coordinate preprogram discussion.
- Coordinate postprogram discussion and implementation.

Organizations that participate in outside supervisory development programs should realize that the time and money spent are an investment in the future of the individual and the organization and thus should try to get the best possible return. A systematic approach can maximize the return.

10

On-the-Job Performance Appraisal

Middle and upper-level managers are constantly training first-line supervisors by the example they set. They are also coaching them by appraising their performance formally or informally and telling them what they should do and what they should quit doing. Training professionals can provide guidance and assistance by planning and implementing a performance appraisal program. This chapter provides guidelines for doing it effectively. Chapter 11 provides principles and techniques for effective coaching.

In developing a supervisor, the manager should:

▸ *Let the supervisor know what is expected.* Before subordinates can do an effective job, they must understand what they are expected to do. They should know their job duties, the standards of performance they are expected to achieve, the objectives, goals, and targets, and what level of authority they have been given by the boss.

▸ *Let the supervisor know how well he is doing.* Supervisors must know what they are doing well and not doing well. Appraisal and communication of performance should be related to duties, standards, objectives, and goals.

▸ *Provide encouragement and help.* It isn't enough for managers to say to subordinates, "You're doing a poor job of quality control, and I expect you to do better." Bosses must provide assistance and help on how the supervisor can do better. They should explore with the supervisor specific ways to improve the quality of work.

▸ *Reward the supervisor for performance.* Bosses should emphasize accomplishments and contributions rather than activities and energies expended. If subordinates are to be motivated to do their best, appropriate rewards, both monetary and nonmonetary, must be given.

This chapter appeared in slightly different form in Donald L. Kirkpatrick, *How to Improve Performance Through Appraisal and Coaching* (New York: AMACOM, 1982).

Performance Appraisal and Review

To ensure that on-the-job development will be effective, a formal program of performance appraisal and review is probably needed. Four requirements must be met if this program is to be successful.

1. *The program must be well designed.* The program must fit the organization. It must consider the amount of paperwork and time required and the amount of staff help that is available for line managers to do the job. Well-designed programs are job oriented; they are concerned with the job to be done and how well it's being done, not with the personality traits of the person being appraised and developed.

2. *The program must be understood and accepted by managers.* This seems obvious, but in many cases it is not understood. Further, the managers should be enthusiastic about the program. If they believe that it is effective, they will act accordingly. If they understand it but do not accept it, they will probably do a poor job of implementation. Therefore, the program must be sold to managers as well as communicated to them.

3. *Managers must be properly trained to implement the program.* They must have the knowledge and the skills required to implement the program. For example, the program includes an appraisal interview, so managers must be trained in conducting it effectively. A well-written manual will not accomplish the necessary training. Live training sessions, including role playing and critique, are needed.

4. *Proper administration and controls must be established.* If managers are required to complete the performance appraisal form on a regular basis, then administrative procedures must ensure that it will be done. In many organizations, managers who do not complete their performance appraisals discover that there are no serious consequences. They may not even receive a reminder, to say nothing about warnings or penalties. The program then becomes a "should do" instead of a "must do" part of their job. When this happens, many managers do not find the time to complete their appraisals and conduct the appraisal interviews.

One example of a control is the following policy: "Managers who do not complete their performance reviews as scheduled will not receive salary increases for themselves or their subordinates." This helps to give performance reviews a "must do" priority.

Another administrative control is constant reevaluation of the program—its approach, forms, and results. In addition, if information is provided for the personnel department, this information should be used in decisions such as salary increases, training, and promotion. Proper administration should also include the performance review training of new managers and the constant effort to keep the program sold. To accomplish all of these administrative controls, one person should be in charge. This person, usually in the human resources department, should report to a high executive in the organization who can take necessary action if the program is not operating in the way it was designed.

Program Design

Nearly every large company has designed and tried to implement some kind of performance appraisal and review program. Most of them have been quite unsuccessful in accomplishing their objectives. Persons in the human resources department as well as line managers are generally unhappy with the programs and do not consider them a success. The problem may be in the design. The following steps should provide the basis for the forms and procedures in order for the performance appraisal program to be effective:

1. Manager and supervisor clarify the significant job segments that the supervisor performs. This is the "what" of the job.

2. Manager and supervisor jointly develop standards of performance that the supervisor is expected to achieve in performing the job. This is the "how well" of the job.

3. Manager and supervisor independently appraise the performance of the supervisor against the standards of performance that have been established. The following ratings can be used: "does not meet standards," "meets standards," "exceeds standards," and "outstanding."

4. An appraisal interview is conducted in which the manager and supervisor discuss the performance appraisals that each has completed. The interview has three goals:
   a. They reach agreement on a fair appraisal of performance for each standard established.
   b. The final appraisal is jointly analyzed to determine the strengths of the supervisor.
   c. The appraisal is jointly analyzed to determine the areas of weakness of the supervisor. These areas to be improved are ranked in order of priority, with top priority given to the one that most needs to be improved.

5. A written performance improvement plan (PIP) is jointly worked out by the manager and supervisor in order to improve performance on the item with top priority. A personnel and/or training professional can

assist in developing this plan. The plan includes on-the-job activities, as well as courses, books, and other approaches for improving knowledge, skills, attitudes, and behavior. The PIP should include what the manager can do as well as what the supervisor can do to improve the performance of the supervisor.

Human resources and training professionals usually spend considerable time deciding what forms to use in performance appraisal and review. Some forms are simple, and others are complicated, but all try to accomplish the same objective: to measure the performance of subordinates so that the boss can discuss performance with each one to help improve performance. The forms and procedures must fit the individual organization. If there is a shortage of clerical staff to help line management people, the forms and procedures should be simple. If clerical help is available, the forms can be more complicated, more extensive, and perhaps more useful to the organization.

Following are specific areas to consider when implementing the five steps.

Clarifying Significant Job Segments

In developing significant job segments, job descriptions can be helpful. Approximately six to eight segments should be selected. Figure 10-1 contains some examples from different types of organizations where the job description was used as the basis for selecting the significant job segments.

Developing Standards of Performance

There are eight characteristics of standards of performance:

1. *They are based on the job, not the person(s) in the job.* Standards of performance should be established for the job itself regardless of who occupies it. For example, the job of administrative secretary or production foreman may be one that a number of people perform. There should be one set of standards for the job, not one set for every person doing that particular job.

Standards of performance are different from objectives. Objectives should be set for an individual rather than for a job, and a typical characteristic of an objective or goal is that it should be challenging. Therefore, a manager who has several subordinates doing the same job will have one set of standards for the job but may have different objectives for

(text continues on page 164)

Figure 10-1. Examples of job descriptions.

Position Title: Payroll Supervisor

Duties and Responsibilities

1. Supervises the following:
    a. Compiling of data.
    b. Tabulation of data.
    c. Computing of detail.
    d. Preparation of summaries and control figures.
    e. Preparation of tax reports.
2. Assigns work to subordinates.
3. Interviews, selects, and trains employees.
4. Evaluates and counsels subordinates.
5. Recommends people for promotion.
6. Recommends salary increases.

Significant Job Segments

1. Data compilation, tabulation, and computing
2. Preparation of reports
3. Work assignment
4. Personnel
5. Promotions and salary increases

Position Title: Machine Shop Supervisor

Duties and Responsibilities

1. Plans and coordinates precision machining of standardized components involving diversified operations and machine setups.
2. Interprets and directs compliance with the union contract and labor relations policies.
3. Enforces compliance with administrative practices and procedures.
4. Establishes budgets.
5. Maintains surveillance to ensure timely production that meets quality standards.
6. Keeps costs within established budget.
7. Interviews, selects, trains, counsels, promotes, evaluates, and assigns work to nonsalaried personnel.
8. Acts as liaison with other divisions.

Significant Job Segments

1. Planning
2. Union contract and policies
3. Practices and procedures
4. Budgets
5. Schedules
6. Quality
7. Personnel

Position Title: Head Nurse

Duties and Responsibilities

To Patients

1. Plan safe, economical, and efficient nursing care.
2. See that quality patient care is given to each patient in accordance with quality standards.
3. Formulate and utilize patient care plan to assist in resolving patient problems.
4. Act as liaison between patient, physician, and family.

To Medical Staff

5. Act as liaison between physician and patient care team.

To Own Nurse Manager

6. Share appropriate communications with unit personnel.
7. Ensure adequate staffing.
8. Make out patient care assignments.
9. Help with budget planning; operate unit within budget.

To Department Personnel

10. Hold regular unit personnel meetings.
11. Promote an environment in which the patient care team can work cooperatively toward objectives.
12. Provide an opportunity for personnel staff development.
13. Counsel personnel when necessary.

To Committees

14. Participate actively in selected committee activities.

To Other Organizations

15. Maintain membership in appropriate professional organizations.

To Self

16. Participate in continuing education programs.

Significant Job Segments

1. Patient care
2. Medical staff
3. Staffing
4. Budget
5. Meetings
6. Subordinate development
7. Self-development

each person, based on that person's experience, skills, and past performance. For example, the objective for a mediocre performer may be the same as the standard, while the objective for an outstanding employee may be much higher than standard.

2. *They are achievable.* Practically all employees on the job should be able to reach the standard. (An exception is a new employee who is learning the job. The standard may not apply until the employee has passed the probationary period.) Most production standards are set so that practically everyone can meet the standard, and many employees can reach 125 percent of standard.

3. *They are understood.* The standard should be clear to boss and subordinate alike. Unfortunately, there is often confusion between the two parties on the exact meaning of a standard.

4. *They are agreed on.* Both boss and subordinate should agree that the standard is fair. This is very important for two reasons: it motivates the employee, and it becomes the basis for evaluation.

5. *They are as specific and measurable as possible.* Some people believe that standards must be specific and measurable; they insist that they must be stated in numbers, percentages, dollars, or some other form that can be quantifiably measured. Every effort should be made to do this, but if it can't be done, the standard should be stated as specifically as possible even if subjective judgment must be used to evaluate performance against it. Early in a performance review program, it might seem impossible to state standards in measurable terms. With practice and experience, it may be possible to be specific on all or nearly all standards.

6. *They are time oriented.* It should be clear whether the standard is to be accomplished by a specific date or whether it is ongoing.

7. *They are written.* Both boss and subordinate should have a written copy of the standards that are agreed on. In this way, they won't have to rely on memory, and the standard can be a constant reminder to both parties.

8. *They are subject to change.* Because standards should be achievable and agreed on, they should be periodically evaluated and changed if necessary. Perhaps there are new methods, new equipment, new materials, or changes in other significant job factors. They should not be changed just because a performer is not meeting the standard.

Determining How Many Standards to Develop

There is no magic number to the number of standards, and there is no rule of thumb that says it all depends on the job. The main factor that determines the number of standards is the boss: How many standards does the boss feel are needed to clarify what is expected of a subordinate? If two standards will do it (say, quantity and quality), then that should be sufficient. If it takes ten to twenty pages to do it, then that's how many there should be. There is an advantage to having many rather than few: It gives a subordinate a clearer understanding of the total job and allows the boss to appraise many different facets of the job and pinpoint an employee's areas of strength as well as those needing improvement. Therefore, an organization should not put a limit on the number of standards that should be developed for a job.

Figure 10-2 contains samples of standards of performance that have been developed for segments of different jobs in a variety of organizations.

Standards of performance are defined as conditions that will exist when the job has been done in an acceptable manner. They have two purposes. First, they guide the behavior of subordinates in accomplishing the standards that have been established. According to James L. Hayes, former president of the American Management Association and an internationally known expert on standards of performance, "If you go through the exercise of establishing standards of performance with your subordinates and clarify what your expectations are, it is a worthwhile exercise even if you never appraise their performance. This is because most people want to do an acceptable job."

The second purpose of standards of performance is to provide a basis against which the performance of an individual can be effectively and fairly appraised. Unless clear standards of performance are established, appraisals may be biased by feelings and subjective evaluation. Regardless of the approach and forms that are used in a program on performance appraisal and review, the process of clarifying what is expected is essential if the program is going to be effective. Standards of performance are the best way to do this.

Effective standards of performance are based on the job and are achievable, understood, agreed on, specific and measurable, time oriented, written, and subject to change. So that they can be properly set and subordinates are motivated to meet or exceed them, subordinates should be involved in setting their own standards. In case of disagreement, the boss must make the final decision.

There is no minimum or maximum number of standards that should be set for a job, although having many standards helps the subordinate understand more clearly what is expected and helps the boss pinpoint specific strengths and areas needing improvement. The boss and subordinate should decide how many are appropriate and practical.

(text continues on page 168)

Figure 10-2 Examples of standards of performance.

Position: Production Foreman	
Significant Job Segments	*Standards of Performance*
1. Safety	1. Monthly safety meetings are conducted in accordance with company schedules. 2. Safe operating procedures are followed by all employees. 3. Regular monthly inspections are held in the department in accordance with the approved checklist. 4. Action is taken within five days to correct any unsafe condition. 5. Monthly safety reports are submitted by the fifth of the following month.
2. Controlling costs	1. Waste and scrap are kept below 2% of total production. 2. One cost-saving improvement per month is initiated and put into operation. 3. Overtime costs are held to a maximum of 3% of direct labor costs. 4. All purchases are made in the most economical manner according to a buying plan. 5. Overhead costs are kept within budget limitations. 6. Salary controls are exercised in accordance with the salary administration plan. 7. The ratio of productivity to costs is improved by 1% every six months.
3. Developing subordinates	1. New subordinates are inducted and trained in accordance with a definite plan. 2. Performance reviews are held with all subordinates on an annual basis. 3. The appraisal and performance improvement plan aspects of the performance review program are reviewed with superior. 4. Discussions are held with subordinates at least quarterly to see that performance improvement takes place according to plan. 5. Responsibilities and authority are delegated to subordinates on a planned basis.

Position: Office Supervisor

Significant Job Segments	*Standards of Performance*
1. Written communication	1. All correspondence is answered, and a copy filed, within one week of receiving it. 2. All written communication is handled so that there is minimal misunderstanding. 3. All interdepartmental and intradepartmental memorandums are answered within two working days of receipt. 4. All official memorandums are posted and/or circulated, initialed, dated, and returned to department head within one week of receiving them. 5. Minutes of officially called meetings are distributed to participants within five days after the meeting.

Position: Regional Sales Manager

Significant Job Segments	*Standards of Performance*
1. Developing subordinates	
A. Conducts performance reviews	1. Performance reviews are conducted with all subordinates according to the procedure approved by the sales manager. 2. For new employees, job duties and standards are clarified within the first three months of employment. 3. A complete performance review is conducted within nine months of hiring of each new employee.
B. Coaches	1. Subordinates are coached and worked with on a day-to-day basis to help them perform better on their current jobs. 2. Follow-up is conducted to ensure implementation of performance improvement plan. 3. Selected assignments are delegated to subordinates to help develop them for greater responsibilities.

(continues)

Figure 10-2. (*continued*)

Significant Job Segments	Standards of Performance
C. Trains in products	1. Subordinates understand the products, procedures, programs, and policies that are pertinent to their work. 2. District sales managers know how to use these items. 3. District sales managers put pertinent items into operation.
D. Counsels	1. Subordinates feel that regional sales managers are readily available and glad to discuss problems with them. 2. All personal conversations are kept confidential.
E. General	1. Subordinates clearly understand their jobs. 2. Subordinates are qualified and skilled to perform their jobs. 3. Subordinates know how well they are doing and what improvement needs to be made.

Appraising Performance

If an effective job is done in clarifying what is expected in terms of significant job segments and standards of performance, the appraisal by the boss becomes quite easy and objective. It is a matter of comparing actual performance with definite standards, and the more specific and measurable the standards are, the most objective the appraisal is.

In the book *MBO II*, George Odiorne warns that two kinds of flaws may exist in appraising performances if the standards are vague: the "halo effect" and the "horns effect."[1]

The "halo effect" is the tendency of the boss to overrate a favored employee. This can happen for a variety of reasons:

> ▸ *Effect of past record.* Because the person has done good work in the distant past, performance is assumed to be adequate in the recent past too. Good work tends to carry over into the current rating period.

1. George Odiorne, *MBO II* (Belmont, Calif.: Fearon Pitman Publishing Corp., 1979).

- *Compatibility.* There is a tendency to rate highly people whom we find pleasing of manner and personality—perhaps more than they deserve. Those who agree with us, who nod their heads when we talk, or who—even better—make notes of our words: these people may get better ratings than their performance justifies.
- *Effect of recency.* The person who did an outstanding job last week or yesterday can offset a mediocre performance over the rest of the year by this single act.
- *The one-asset person.* The glib talker, the person with an impressive appearance or an advanced degree, or the graduate of the boss's own alma mater may get a more favorable rating than the person lacking these often irrelevant attributes.
- *The blind-spot effect.* The boss doesn't see certain types of defects because they are just like her own. For example, the boss who loves accounting may overrate another detail person.
- *The high-potential effect.* We sometimes judge the person's paper record rather than the accomplishment for the organization.
- *The no-complaints bias.* Here the appraiser treats no news as good news. The subordinate who has no complaints and says that everything is terrific is likely to go over well.

The *"horns effect"* is the reverse of the halo effect—the tendency to rate a person lower than the circumstances justify. Some specific causes of this are:

- *A perfectionist boss.* Because the boss's expectations are so high, he is more often disappointed and rates a subordinate lower than deserved.
- *A contrary subordinate.* Here the boss vents private irritation with the subordinate's tendency to disagree too often on too many issues.
- *The oddball effect.* Despite all the lip-service to nonconformity, it seldom finds its way into practice when appraisal time comes around. The oddball, the maverick, and the nonconformist get low ratings because they are different.
- *Membership on a weak team.* A good player on a weak team ends up with lower ratings than he would have gotten if playing on a winning one.
- *The guilt-by-association effect.* The person who isn't known well by the boss is often judged by the company she keeps.
- *The dramatic-incident effect.* A recent goof can wipe out the effect of months of good work and give a person a lower rating than deserved.

▸ *The personality-trait effect.* The subordinate who is too cocky, too brash, too meek, too passive, or otherwise lacks some trait the boss associates with a good employee suffers in the appraisal.

▸ *The self-comparison effect.* The person who does the job differently from the way the boss did it when he was back on that job suffers more than a person whose job the boss has never done.

If standards of performance have been effectively established, the halo and horns effects can be eliminated or at least drastically reduced.

From one appraisal time to the next, a manager should be gathering information that will make the appraisal fair and accurate. Otherwise, the appraisal may be based on hazy memory or on only the most recent behavior and accomplishments of the subordinate.

J. C. Flanagan and R. K. Burns developed an objective approach for gathering data for the appraisal; they call it the *critical incident method.*[2] This technique relies on the collection of specific observable job incidents that are judged to be critical because they are related directly to either good or poor job performance. After the incidents are collected and tabulated, components are grouped under one of the headings in a specially designed performance record.

The performance record is accompanied by a manual that describes and illustrates each of the sixteen critical requirements. The supervisor records each incident on the effective (blue) or the ineffective (red) half of the page for the employee involved. The manual states that to be critical, an incident must be directly observed by the supervisor and must clearly show either outstanding or less than satisfactory performance.

In his experience with Delco-Remy Division of General Motors, Flanagan found that most of the recorded incidents were positive. There was speculation that the manager would be much more likely to record negative incidents, but this was not true.

The critical incident method has three basic steps: (1) completing the performance record as critical incidents occur, (2) summarizing them for the rating period, and (3) conducting a performance review interview with the employee. Flanagan and Burns recommend that this three-phase program be carried out at six-month intervals, and they suggest further that the performance review interview should take the average supervisor from half an hour to an hour. Summarizing the method, they say:

A performance record is not a yardstick. It is not a rating method. It is a procedure for collecting significant facts about

2. J. C. Flanagan and R. K. Burns, "The Employee Performance Record: A New Approach and Development Tool," *Harvard Business Review* (September-October 1955).

employee performance. These facts are gathered in such a way that they will be of maximum use to supervisors and management, both in improving the employee's understanding of the requirements of his present job and in developing his potential for more responsible positions. It is not simply a new form but a new approach.[3]

If the critical incident method is used, managers should be sure to look for both positive and negative incidents. Otherwise, the appraisal will become biased, and the subordinate will be unfairly appraised.

In gathering information, the manager should have one objective: to make an accurate appraisal of performance. This information comes from two major sources:

1. Performance records such as quantity of production, quality of work, meeting deadlines and schedules, safety, actual costs versus budget costs, absenteeism, and the number of complaints from customers or co-workers.

2. Other people who have had dealings with the subordinate. This could include the boss, staff personnel, people served by the subordinate, and even people in other departments with whom the subordinate works. If the organization uses project teams on which the subordinate has served, the project leader should be contacted. This should be as objective as possible. Instead of asking, "How do you feel about Harry?" it's better to ask, "What kind of service has Harry given you?" or, "How would you evaluate Harry's performance in regard to this issue?"

In other words, the more sources that are used, the better. But each source should be carefully selected to provide objective data. All these data should then be analyzed and compared with the standards of performance to arrive at an accurate appraisal.

Preparing the Appraisal Form

There are almost as many types of appraisal forms as there are people designing the forms. One approach is shown in Figure 10-3, which uses the following key:

DNMS = Did not meet standard
MS = Met standard

3. Reprinted by permission of the *Harvard Business Review*. An excerpt from "The Employee Performance Record: A New Approach and Development Tool." September–October 1955. Copyright © 1955 by the President and Fellows of Harvard College. All rights reserved.

Figure 10-3. Performance appraisal form.

Job title ——————————————————————— Date ——————————

Name of superior ————————————————————————————

Names of subordinate ————————————————————————————

Significant Job Segments	Standards of Performance*	Appraisal**				Comments on Performance
		DNMS	MS	ES	O	
	1.					
	2.					
	3.					
	1.					
	2.					
	1.					

*What conditions will exist when the job is performed in an *acceptable* manner?
**DNMS = Did not meet standard   MS = Met standard   ES = Exceeded standard
   O   = Outstanding

Performance Strengths   Performance to Be Improved

1.   1.

2.   2.

3.   3.

Performance Improvement Plan

Performance to Be Improved: ————————————————————————

Action to Be Taken	By Whom	When
1.		
2.		
3.		
4.		
5.		

ES = Exceeded standard
O = Was outstanding

This form is based on the use of significant job segments and standards of performance, described earlier in the chapter.

Harnischfeger Corporation (a manufacturer of overhead cranes and hoists, mining shovels, draglines, hydraulic mining excavators, and related replacement parts) has modified this form to use a different key:

DNMR = Did not meet requirements
MR = Met requirements
ER = Exceeded requirements
O = Was outstanding

The reason for the change was that the concept of standard of performance was too complicated to explain and implement. By using *requirements* instead of *standards,* the boss would have to explain the requirements in order to be sure that the subordinate understood what was expected.

Companies vary in their terminology. Some organizations use *unsatisfactory, satisfactory, outstanding,* and *superior.* Others prefer such terms as *unacceptable, acceptable, good, very good,* and *excellent.* Some military units use such words as *good, excellent, outstanding,* and *superior.* Here there are two words that mean something better than excellent. Some organizations prefer a five- or ten-point scale with 1 at the low end of the scale, meaning "poor" or "unsatisfactory," and 5 or 10 at the top level of the scale to mean "outstanding" or "superior." Still other organizations try to describe the gradations—for example:

Poor	Consistently unsatisfactory; doesn't come close to meeting standard
Fair	Occasionally meets standard; usually is slightly below standard
Good	Consistently meets standard; occasionally doesn't meet standard and occasionally is far above standard
Excellent	Consistently far above standard

Other categories and scales are used in the examples in Part II of this book.

If the purpose of performance appraisal is to improve performance, the word *average* should not be used because it invites comparison with other people rather than with the standard. In order to improve performance, it is important to identify, for each person, the level of performance for each standard. This will reveal strengths as well as areas that need improvement. If the purpose of the appraisal is to determine salary increases instead of improve performance, then the word *average* may be used. In this context, individuals' performances are compared with each other.

Using Self-Appraisal

The concept of self-appraisal is required in some organizations, left optional in some, and discouraged or prohibited in others. In a situation where the subordinate does not complete a self-appraisal, the boss makes out the appraisal form, calls in the subordinate for the appraisal interview, and tries to get from the subordinate both understanding and acceptance of the appraisal. The subordinate usually comes to the interview without any specific preparation (although he may have made an informal self-appraisal but has not put it in writing) and may be fearful that it will be an unpleasant experience. She is likely to be on the defensive because the boss will read off the appraisal and ask her to agree or to substantiate any disagreement. Many subordinates will not speak freely; they lack information to substantiate their self-judgments or are afraid to disagree with the boss. Therefore, they might very well express agreement—or rather, refrain from expressing disagreement—even if they don't really agree—and the boss will naively conclude that both understanding and agreement have been reached.

If the subordinate completes a self-appraisal, preferably on the same form the boss uses, the two of them can sit side by side and compare their appraisals. This can create a relaxed climate in which the objective is to arrive at an accurate appraisal. If both have honestly tried to be as objective as possible and if the significant job segments and standards of performance have been clearly stated, the appraisals shouldn't be far apart.

The concept of self-appraisal says to the subordinate: "Your input is important. Maybe you know some things about your performance I don't know. I want to be sure that you have a chance to communicate them to me. And I'll listen to you and consider your input before arriving at a final appraisal."

Several factors should be kept in mind if self-appraisals are going to be used:

1. Subordinates should be given enough advance notice—a minimum of three weeks—so that a fair self-appraisal can be made.
2. Subordinates should be told the reasons for the self-appraisal and how it will be used in the interview.
3. Specific instructions should be given to the subordinates on the form to use and what to do.
4. Subordinates should be urged to make an objective appraisal—not to be overly aggressive (rating themselves higher than justified) or shy (rating themselves lower than justified).
5. Managers should assure subordinates that the self-appraisal will be used to help arrive at a fair appraisal.

The appraisal process must be done in a systematic and objective manner, first gathering data from various sources and then comparing performance with previously set standards. It is important for the subordinate to accept the appraisal as fair. The best way to accomplish this is to have the subordinate prepare a self-appraisal for comparison with the boss's appraisal. Free and open discussion will also help to arrive at a fair appraisal agreed on and accepted by both parties. In case of disagreement, the boss must make the final appraisal, but in most cases agreement can be reached without the boss's exercising this authority.

Conducting the Appraisal Interview

The manner in which this interview is conducted is critical to the success of the performance appraisal program. Following are suggestions of how to prepare as well as how to conduct an interview.

Preparing for the Interview

Both the boss and the subordinate should prepare for the interview. The boss has seven tasks:

1. *To decide on the best time.* The best time is when both parties are able to spend time together without interruption, so it is a good idea for the boss to suggest a time and get approval from the subordinate.

2. *To decide on the best place.* A private office is the best place—either the boss's office or a neutral place. It should be a private place where the door can be closed and people can't look in and see what's going on. Finally, it should be a comfortable place where both parties can relax.

3. *To prepare the facilities.* Arrange the furniture so that the subordinate will feel at ease, perhaps with the chairs side by side instead of across the desk from each other. If possible, have coffee or water available.

4. *To gather information and materials.* Make a complete and objective appraisal. Have the forms and information on hand for the interview.

5. *To plan the opening.* Decide whether to talk about a current event— sports, politics, weather—or to begin by stating the purpose of the interview. Use whatever approach is most natural and will create the best climate for the interview.

6. *To plan the approach.* Here are some alternatives to consider:
   ‣ Begin with strengths and then discuss job segments needing improvement.
   ‣ Go straight through the form, give your appraisal, and discuss one item at a time to get agreement before going ahead to the next item.
   ‣ Ask the subordinate for her appraisal before giving your own. You could do this for the entire form or for each item.
   ‣ Alternate between yourself and the subordinate as to who gives the appraisal first.

There is no right or wrong approach. Your approach might depend on whether the subordinate has made a self-appraisal. Remember that the objective is to get agreement, so use whatever approach is best for you.

7. *To give the subordinate appropriate advance notice.* The subordinate should have enough time to prepare for the interview and should clearly understand the time, place, objectives, and probable length of the interview.

The subordinate should begin to prepare as soon as the date is set. She should:

1. Gather information related to past performance. This includes specific data on activities and accomplishments, as well as reasons why certain things weren't done or were done incorrectly.

2. Complete a self-appraisal if requested by the boss.
3. Arrange for work coverage during the interview. This is important so that the subordinate can concentrate on the interview and not worry about whether the job is being done properly.

Conducting the Interview

The following general principles apply to all performance interviews regardless of the form that is used or whether a self-appraisal has been completed.

1. *Establish and maintain rapport.* Rapport can be defined as the climate in which the interview takes place. The location of the interview is important. It should be conducted in a place where both people can feel relaxed, with comfortable chairs, a minimum of noise, and privacy. If it will help to put the subordinate at ease, the boss and the subordinate should sit alongside each other rather than across the desk. The boss's verbal and nonverbal communications should make it clear that two-way communication will take place and that the subordinate should speak freely and frankly. A cup of coffee might help to create this comfortable climate.

It is debatable whether to begin the interview by talking about hobbies or some current event or whether to begin by saying, "As you know the purpose of this interview is to . . . " If the two people have a common hobby, that may be a good place to start, or if an unusual historical or sporting event just happened, that may be a good opener.

Socializing for a few minutes is well worth the time if it creates rapport. The following list contrasts an interview climate of rapport to an interview climate without it.

Rapport	*Lack of Rapport*
At ease, relaxed	Nervous, fearful, anxious
Comfortable	Uncomfortable
Friendly, warm	Formal, cold
Not afraid to speak freely and frankly	Afraid to speak openly
Believing, trusting	Challenging, proving
Listening	Interrupting
Understanding	Misunderstanding
Open-minded	Close-minded
Accepting criticism without resentment	Resenting criticism
Disagreeing without offending	Arguing, downgrading

2. *Clearly explain the purpose of the interview, and state it in positive terms*, such as: "The purpose of the interview today is for us to discuss your performance and agree on your strengths and areas that can be improved. Then we are going to talk about your future and how we can work together."

3. *Encourage the subordinate to talk.* The interview must include two-way communication. Some subordinates are ready to talk; others are reluctant because of shyness or fear. Establishing rapport will help to overcome this reluctance. In some situations, the boss must ask specific questions to get the subordinate to talk. In others, the subordinate will talk freely with little encouragement.

4. *Listen and don't interrupt.* By *listen*, I mean *really* listen. This means more than merely keeping quiet or not talking; it is an active process of finding out the thoughts and the feelings of the other person. If both parties start to talk at the same time, the boss should quit talking and encourage the subordinate to go ahead. Backing down is quite difficult for some bosses, but it pays off in maintaining two-way communication throughout the interview. It tells the subordinate, "What you have to say is more important to me than what I have to say to you!"

5. *Avoid confrontation and argument.* Even when differences of opinions are expressed, the boss should avoid confrontation and argument. Both parties know that the boss has more authority and power than the subordinate, so there is a chance of ending up in a win-lose situation (the boss wins and the subordinate loses). Winning by the boss might be very costly; it might destroy rapport and result in the subordinate's deciding not to communicate freely and frankly. If this happens, the interview will not achieve its objectives and might even do more harm than good. By keeping the discussion free and open, a win-win situation can be created so that the needs of both people are met.

6. *Focus on performance, not personality.* This is a performance appraisal interview, and emphasis should be on performance, not personality. This does not mean that such items as attitude, integrity, dependability, appearance, or initiative are not mentioned. It does mean that these characteristics are mentioned only as they relate to performance.

7. *Focus on the future, not the past.* This does not mean that past performance will not be discussed, but the emphasis is on what can be learned from the past that will help in the future.

8. *Emphasize strengths as well as areas to improve.* Every employee has strengths as well as areas of performance that can be improved. Recognize and build on these strengths, and also discuss job segments that must be corrected if performance is to improve.

9. *Terminate the interview when advisable.* Don't hesitate to terminate an interview at any point if you think it's a good idea. Any number of reasons could justify the termination: loss of rapport, the boss or subordinate is anxious to go somewhere, quitting time, lack of progress being made, fatigue, or an important interruption. If you end the interview before accomplishing all the objectives you set, agree on when the interview will continue.

10. *Conclude on a positive note.* Be sure that the subordinate leaves the interview in a positive frame of mind instead of resentful toward the negative aspects of the discussion. After the interview is over, the subordinate should say (or at least feel), "Thanks. I'm glad we had a chance to get together and discuss my performance. Now I know where I stand and what I should do in the future. And I know that you are going to work with me."

A warm handshake at the conclusion of the interview is one way to end on a positive tone. Another is for the boss to say, "Thanks for coming in. I feel that this has been a very profitable discussion, and I know I can count on you in the future. I'll be glad to help you in any way I can."

Techniques for Successful Interviews

There really shouldn't be any great surprises in the interview if the significant job segments and standards of performance have been clarified and agreed on as the basis for the appraisal. The subordinate's appraisal, whether mental or written, should be very close to the written appraisal by the manager. The problem the manager faces is to be sure she gets honest agreement or disagreement from the subordinate on the appraisal. Obviously, the establishment of rapport is essential for this. Specific interviewing techniques are also important. Here are some specific suggestions:

1. *Be open.* Show the form to the subordinate. Don't hide it.
2. *Explain your appraisal.* Describe how you arrived at it. If you checked records or talked to other people, say so. If you did it by yourself, say so. Also, be sure to emphasize that you want frank comments from the subordinate because your appraisal may not be accurate. Admit, for example, that the subordinate may have done some things you've forgotten or don't even know about.
3. *Be sure your appraisal is tentative.* Be willing to change your appraisal if the subordinate's input convinces you that you were wrong. Don't be afraid to admit a mistake.
4. *Summarize.* When the entire appraisal has been discussed, go over

it with the subordinate. Have a copy made for the subordinate so that she has the same information you have.

All four of these techniques demonstrate to the subordinate that there is nothing secret about the process. A manager simply wants to come up with a fair and accurate appraisal that will make it possible to work with the subordinate and help improve performance. The manager may want to start with strengths or with the first item on the appraisal form and go straight down the form. Whatever way is most natural and comfortable is the best way. After completing the discussion, the entire appraisal should be summarized.

Developing the Performance Improvement Plan

In the first part of the interview, the boss and subordinate should accomplish the following:

1. Agree on a fair appraisal. If the subordinate feels that the appraisal is not fair, the process will fail.
2. Agree on the strengths that have been demonstrated by the performance. (Three is suggested.)
3. Agree on the weaknesses (areas to improve) that have been demonstrated by performance. (Three is suggested.)
4. Jointly select the one area that should be worked on first. The performance improvement plan will be based on this selection.

Most performance appraisal programs end without any plan of action. They sometimes offer suggestions to the subordinate on what and how to improve, but they don't develop a plan. If improvement is going to take place, a plan is necessary, and it should include what the manager will do, as well as what the subordinate should do. Often the lack of satisfactory performance by subordinates is caused by factors over which they have no control—and many of these factors are controlled by the manager. It is essential for the improvement of subordinates to be a joint venture between managers and subordinates.

An action plan should ask three questions:

1. What action will be taken?
2. By whom?
3. When?

In order to develop this plan, manager and subordinate should independently prepare a list of possible actions to be taken by each of them. In a meeting, the two of them will consider possible actions and integrate them into a plan.

Figure 10-4 shows a performance improvement plan that was jointly developed by Tom Severson, the manager, and John Green, his subordinate supervisor. It was based on the top-priority need of John, "Building an Effective Team."

Figure 10-4. Performance improvement plan.

Employee:	John Green, Supervisor
Boss:	Tom Severson, Department Head
Date:	October 1
Performance to be improved:	Building an effective team

Action to Be Taken	*By Whom*	*When*
1. Evaluate each subordinate as a team player (5 = high to 1 = low).	John Green	October 20
2. If 3 or lower, determine why.	John Green	October 30
3. Read the following: Donald L. Kirkpatrick, *How to Improve Performance Through Appraisal and Coaching,* Chapter 5, "On-the-Job Coaching," (New York: AMACOM, 1982).	John Green	November 15
4. Attend a workshop on "Team Building."	John Green	The next time offered by the Training Department
5. Talk with Supervisor Phil Taylor on his approach to building an effective team.	John Green	October 15
6. Talk with each subordinate rated 3 or below about ways to improve teamwork.	John Green	December 1
7. Set an example by being a good team player with peers in other departments.	Tom Severson	Starting NOW!

Summary

There are several objectives of performance appraisal programs. Most of them become the basis for salary administration. Nearly all of them provide information for personnel decisions on promotion, transfer, and termination, but few of them result in improved performance. Training professionals must realize that the typical performance appraisal program that concentrates on salary administration will not result in improved performance. The chart in Figure 10-5 compares programs aimed at salary administration and those with improved performance as the objective.

Training professionals should take an active part in the development of a program that will result in improved performance. This usually means that there are two different forms and procedures—one for salary administration and one for improved performance. The program described in this chapter is directly aimed at improved performance. The ingredients of such a program require that manager and subordinate agree on what's expected of the subordinate. This can best be accomplished by determining six to eight significant job segments and the standards of performance for each. An appraisal against these standards should be made independently by manager and subordinate. In the ap-

Figure 10-5. A comparison of performance reviews.

	Performance Reviews for Salary Administration	Performance Reviews for Improved Performance
Looking	Backward	Forward
Considering	Overall performance	Detailed performance
Comparing with	Other people	Job standards and objectives
Determined by	Boss, higher management, personnel department	Boss and subordinate together
Interview climate	Subjective, emotional	Objective, unemotional
Factors to consider	Salary range, total money available, inflation, seniority, performance, education	Performance

praisal interview, these appraisals are compared and discussed, and a final appraisal is agreed on. (If the subordinate feels that the appraisal is not "fair," the entire process fails.) The strengths as well as the weaknesses of the subordinate are agreed on, and priorities are established on performance to be improved. The top-priority need is analyzed, and a performance improvement plan is jointly developed that includes action to be taken by both manager and subordinate. No improvement has taken place yet, but a sound basis for coaching has been established.

If the program is going to be successful, the following steps must be followed:

1. Develop a program that is right for the organization.
2. Communicate it so that supervisors understand it.
3. Sell it so supervisors are motivated to do it.
4. Train the supervisors so they know what to do and how to do it.
5. Establish controls to be sure it is done.

One way (and probably the best way) to communicate and sell the program is to involve line managers in the development of the program. A good approach is to establish a performance appraisal task force consisting of line and staff personnel, with the training professional as the chairperson. If the training and personnel professionals don't involve line supervisors in the development of the program, line managers typically look at it as a "personnel program" that they must implement. When line managers are involved, they will see that it is a tool to help them do their job of working with subordinates to get maximum performance.

REFERENCES

Kirkpatrick, Donald L. *How to Improve Performance Through Appraisal and Coaching*. New York: AMACOM, 1982.

Kirkpatrick, Donald L. *Management Inventory on Performance Appraisal and Coaching*. Elm Grove, Wis.: Donald L. Kirkpatrick, 1987. This inventory was developed as a tool to use in a training program. A complementary review set (test, answer booklet, and instructor manual) will be sent on request of:

Dr. Donald Kirkpatrick
1920 Hawthorne Drive
Elm Grove, Wisconsin 53122

11

Coaching for Improved Performance

Chapter 10 described the principles and techniques for planning and implementing an effective performance appraisal program designed to result in improved performance. The program ended with the development of a performance improvement plan. Nothing has really happened except communicating past performance and deciding what should be done in the future. The manager must now become a coach to be sure that improvement takes place. Part of the coaching effort must be aimed at implementing the performance improvement plan. The rest of it will be done on a daily basis.

Coaching on the Performance Improvement Plan

Figure 11-1 contains the coaching schedule for the performance improvement plan worked out between John Green, a supervisor, and Tom Severson, his boss. Tom does not wait to see whether John does what he agreed to do. Rather, Tom contacts him before the agreed-on date to remind him. The figure shows the contacts that Tom will make with John. Also, Tom does not expect John to buy the book he agreed to read. Rather, he gets the book for John. In other words, he encourages, helps, and follows up to see that the action plan is carried out. It is essential that Tom, the boss, does what he personally agreed to do.

Day-to-Day Coaching

In day-to-day coaching, the boss has to set the right example. In one of his essays, Ralph Waldo Emerson wrote, "What you are thunders so that I cannot hear what you say to the contrary!" This statement illustrates

(text continues on page 188)

Figure 11-1. Coaching schedule for a performance improvement plan.

Name: John Green, Supervisor   Boss: Tom Severson, Department Head

Date: October 1

Performance to be improved: Building an effective team

The Performance Improvement Plan   Coaching Contact by Tom Severson

Action to Be Taken	By Whom	When	When	Results
1. Evaluate each subordinate as a team player (5-high to 1-low).	John Green	October 20	October 18	Reminded John to do the evaluations.
			October 21	Went over the evaluations with John.
2. If 3 or lower, determine why.	John Green	October 30	October 25	Asked John for an update on the evaluations.
			October 31	Went over the evaluations with John.
3. Read the following: Donald L. Kirkpatrick, *How to Improve Performance Through Appraisal and Coaching,* Chapter 5, "On-the-Job Coaching," (New York: AMACOM, 1982).	John Green	November 15	October 5	Got a copy of the book and gave it to John.
			November 1	Asked John if he had read it yet. Reminded him of the November 15 date.
			November 12	Set a time on November 16 to discuss the book.
			November 16	Discussed the book with John and highlighted some specific things he should do.

(continues)

Figure 11-1. (*continued*)

Action to Be Taken	By Whom	When	When	Results
4. Attend a workshop on "Team Building."	John Green	The next time offered by the Training Department	October 10	Found out from Phil Jackson, the Training Manager, that the next workshop will be held November 6. Discussed it with John and enrolled him.
			November 3	Reminded John about the course and told him I would discuss the program with him on November 8.
			November 8	Asked John what he had learned and discussed ways to implement the ideas with his subordinates.
5. Talk with Supervisor Phil Taylor on his approach to building an effective team.	John Green	October 15	October 16	Asked John what he had learned from Phil Taylor. Discovered that he had not talked to him. Set the date of October 20 to discuss his talk with Phil.
			October 20	Discussed with John what he had learned from Phil.

Action to Be Taken	By Whom	When	When	Results
6. Talk with each subordinate rated 3 or below about ways to improve teamwork.	John Green	December 1	November 24	Asked John what approach he was going to use in talking with those subordinates rated 3 or lower. He had not planned his approach yet. Set the date of November 28 to discuss the approach
			November 28	Discussed John's approaches and offered suggestions.
			December 3	Asked John for a report on his discussions. Offered comments and suggestions.
7. Set an example by being a good team player with peers in other departments.	Tom Severson	Starting NOW!	October 3	Developed a plan to get together with other managers at my level to discuss cooperation and teamwork. Established a schedule of monthly meetings to discuss problems and suggestions on how we can better work together.

the importance of the example set by the boss. Supervisors are constantly looking at the attitude and behavior of their boss and wondering:

1. What does the boss do about self-development? Does he constantly try to keep up-to-date on technical and management subjects? Does he attend seminars and programs for personal growth?
2. To what extent does the boss support management development activities? For example, does he encourage and stimulate in-company programs that are designed to help the supervisor improve knowledge and skills? Does he encourage subordinates to attend outside management development programs?

Daily coaching is based on observing the performance of the subordinates. If the subordinate performs well, the manager provides positive reinforcement. If the subordinate fails to do something that should be done, the manager calls it to the attention of the subordinate to find out why it wasn't done and to see that it is done. And if the subordinate does something that should not be done, the manager must find out the reason for the mistake and take whatever action is appropriate.

The key to effective coaching is to handle problem situations without causing resentment on the part of the subordinate. Resentment can easily be created by an eager coach who is overly anxious to correct an error. For example, a direct approach to pointing out the mistake and ordering the subordinate to do it right could well end up in resentment. To avoid resentment, a tactful approach is usually required.

If the manager sees an employee make a mistake, there are four possible courses of action to take:

1. Ignore the situation and hope that the subordinate will see the mistake and correct it.

2. Call immediate attention to the mistake and ask the subordinate to do the right thing.

3. Use an indirect approach such as, "How are things going?" If the subordinate knows about the mistake, he may frankly admit the mistake and tell the manager, "Don't worry. I'll take care of it." If the subordinate doesn't realize that a mistake has been made, the answer might be, "Fine. No problems!" In this case the manager will have to call attention to the mistake and ask, "What can we do to correct it?"

4. Use the sandwich approach: praise the subordinate for good work, call attention to the mistake, and end with a positive statement, such as, "I'm sure that this won't happen again." Some people ridicule

this approach; they say that the subordinate will recognize the technique and after the first words of praise will immediately react, "O.K., what have I done wrong?" Obviously the success or failure of the sandwich technique depends on the frequency of its use. If the only time a manager praises a subordinate is to provide the first part of the sandwich, the approach will backfire. But if praise is regularly used by the manager to recognize good work, the technique can be successful. In any case, it must be remembered that praise is recognizing good work that has actually been done, not just using complimentary words when they aren't true.

Among these four choices for correcting poor work, there is no guarantee that any will be successful or unsuccessful. For example, if the manager uses the first approach (doesn't say anything), the worker may or may not recognize the mistake and correct it. Similarly, the sandwich method may be successful with one employee but not with another. The important points are that the coaching must be done to correct the situation—now and in the future—and not cause resentment. Here are some specific suggestions that will help you achieve this.

If the employee has done a good job, the manager has a very pleasant situation. Positive reinforcement should be done immediately. If there are other people within hearing distance, so much the better. They realize that the employee has done something well, and they are pleased to see a boss recognize it. Obviously, they hope to be treated in the same way when they do something worthy of praise. Even if the performance wasn't perfect, a compliment can be sincerely given, and complimenting improvement generally leads to continued effort by the employee and better results in the future.

Some managers compliment warmly when a job is well done. Others ignore it and act as if they thought, "That's what we are paying you for. Why should I have to tell you besides?"

In sporting events, some coaches do not give praise when a player does an exceptionally good job. Other coaches openly show signs of enthusiasm and laud good work. Ara Parseghian is an example of the latter type of coach. When he was head football coach at Notre Dame, and a player made an exceptionally good play, Ara would jump up and down, give his player a hug or pat on the back, and pay him a nice compliment like: "Good play!" That spirit and outward expression brought out the best in his players.

If the employee has done a poor job, the boss should usually correct a situation as soon as it occurs. Sometimes, however, this isn't a good idea; it might not be the right time and place—there may be other people around—and the boss may be emotionally upset. In these situations, it is important to correct the employee as soon as practical but in private. One good approach might be to say, "Can I see you in my office in five minutes?" This gives the manager time to cool down and to do a little preparation for the coaching interview: thinking of some good work the worker has recently done that can be mentioned, trying to determine the reason why the employee made the mistake, and thinking how the interview should conclude. The employee should say or think, "Thanks for calling this to my attention," rather than, "I'll get even with you."

"Coaching is not an option for managers," says Dennis Kinlaw. "It is a large part of their basic managerial functions. It is clear that superior managers and superior leaders engage in coaching and they do it well. The good news is that managers can learn the set of management practices that we call coaching."[1]

Learning to Be an Effective Coach

Coaching is a word commonly used in industry to signify what a manager should do to help subordinates achieve maximum performance. The term, of course, is borrowed from athletics. In order to identify principles and practices as athletic coaches see them, I wrote to a number of them and asked, "What are the characteristics of an effective coach?" Following are some of their direct statements:

J. Frank Broyles, director of athletics, University of Arkansas

In my opinion, an effective coach should be a living example of the virtues he teaches.

Paul F. Dietzel, director of athletics, Louisiana State University

The single most important ingredient is the loyalty the coach displays to his fellow coaches, to his team, and to the organization that he represents. In other words, does the coach have a genuine "like" for the people he or she coaches and an abiding interest in them after they are no longer able to participate for that coach? Maybe that could be spelled out in another way to be called, "Do you really want to be of service to young people?" Whatever it is, that ingredient . . . a genuine concern for the athlete . . . has to be of number 1 importance.

1. Dennis C. Kinlaw, *Coaching for Commitment* (San Diego: University Associates, 1989).

*John Erickson, past president, Fellowship of Christian Athletes
(former basketball coach, University of Wisconsin,
and general manager, Milwaukee Bucks)*

I have always felt that to be effective, a coach must be an excellent teacher and a person of leadership qualities.

*Elroy Hirsch, former director of athletics,
University of Wisconsin*

He must not be afraid of having very sound, good people around him. He must not be afraid that someone underneath him is trying to take over his job. He must surround himself with strength, and, of course, this requires him to be an effective manager of personnel.

Tom Landry, former football coach, Dallas Cowboys

An effective athletic coach must be a teacher, a psychologist, and a motivator. He must possess leadership qualities and, at the same time, he needs the confidence and concentration to operate at maximum efficiency under great stress.

Ray Meyer, former basketball coach, DePaul University

A coach must have patience. He can't expect too much too soon. He is a teacher. Probably the greatest quality a coach can have is understanding. He must understand that each player is an individual and must be treated as such. All players cannot be treated alike. Some you can improve by loud criticism, and others need encouragement. No coach can treat all players alike, for each one is an individual.

Tom Meyer, former baseball coach, University of Wisconsin

A coach must create a climate where criticism can be expressed and viewed as healthy.

Tom Osborne, football coach, University of Nebraska

I believe that the qualities of an effective coach are: good organizational skills, a capacity to work long hours, an ability to communicate effectively with his athletes, an ability to maintain composure and to think clearly in pressure situations, and an ability to communicate a genuine sense of concern for the general well-being of his players.

Joe Paterno, football coach and athletic director, Pennsylvania State University

An effective athletic coach must possess sound moral values and the ability to relate to all types of people. He must be dedicated, loyal, and sincere about his beliefs and philosophies and must be willing to accept success and failure as part of the game. Above and beyond all things he must have a true love for the sport and at all times realize the responsibility he has to his players.

Bart Starr, former football head coach, Green Bay Packers

To begin, I believe he is goal oriented, has a plan by which to accomplish those goals, and a method by which to measure progress along the way. Additionally, he is extremely self-confident, very poised, has the ability to accept criticism and receive coaching himself, has a strong faith in God, and a good sense of humor.

John Wooden, former basketball coach, UCLA

A coach must: communicate with those under his supervision; listen and not be disagreeable when there is disagreement; keep in mind that criticism is to improve, prevent, correct, or help and not to punish; make those under his supervision feel that they are working with him rather than for him; be more interested in finding the best way rather than having his own way; be well organized and not waste time; and be genuinely concerned about his players.[2]

When these statements are analyzed, the word *manager* can be substituted for *coach,* and the word *employee* substituted for *player* in nearly every case.

Lynne Tyson describes the following qualities of an effective coach:

- Has faith in people and a belief that most can improve and grow in a suitable climate.
- Has a true interest in employees.
- Serves as a good role model for subordinates.

2. Donald L. Kirkpatrick, *How to Improve Performance Through Appraisal and Coaching* (New York: AMACOM, 1982).

▸ Has a good understanding of leadership techniques.
▸ Uses these techniques.
▸ Has the ability to empathize with employees—caring enough to help another person grow.
▸ Has knowledge of an effective use of rewards, including money, a pat on the back, a more challenging job, and a letter from the boss.

She then describes seven criteria for becoming a good coach:

1. Have a sincere unselfish interest in helping an employee grow on the job.
2. Develop a "game plan."
3. Earn and maintain team respect.
4. Remember that people learn best by doing.
5. Ask questions so that the worker can arrive at his or her own solution.
6. Establish sub-goals so that both supervisor and subordinate can see gradual progress.
7. Expect mistakes and use them as learning experiences and growth opportunities.[3]

Mike Phipps, a former quarterback, and T. W. Harvey provide the following suggestions for building good relationships with players:

▸ Treat all players fairly.
▸ After chewing a player out, be sure to stop by sometime that day and make him feel like coming back tomorrow.
▸ Support your players.
▸ Try to make every athlete feel important.
▸ If you criticize, do it to the player's face—not downtown. Always end your criticism with something positive about the individual.
▸ Stimulate a desire in the player to be the best.
▸ Always keep control of yourself and make sure your players keep control of themselves.
▸ Don't ever let an athlete loaf, no matter who he is.
▸ Coach before you criticize.
▸ What you teach is the most important, not what you know.
▸ Your practice plans are very important. Know what you are going to do in practice.
▸ Enthusiasm is contagious.

3. Lynne R. Tyson, "Coaching," in William R. Tracey, ed., *Human Resources Management and Development Handbook,* (New York: AMACOM, 1985).

- Fundamentals are the most important factor for an athlete.
- Coaches will never argue in front of players. Any disagreement should be dealt with after practice in the office. Never criticize another coach in front of an athlete, and never let an athlete be disloyal to a coach or teammate.
- Be concerned about injuries of any player.
- Don't ever threaten a player unless you plan to back it up.
- Work with every athlete in our program regardless of what problems may arise.[4]

Again, in nearly all these statements, the word *manager* can be substituted for *coach,* and the word *employee* substituted for *player.*

The Manager as Coach

The manager operates under a number of conditions that are related to coaching:

- The manager must get the best effort and performance from each subordinate.
- In many situations, the manager is concerned with a team of workers as well as with the performance of each individual worker (as in basketball, football, and hockey). In some situations, the manager is primarily concerned with individual workers because each person usually works alone (as in swimming, track, tennis, and golf).
- If individuals performing under a manager do not like the situation, they have options: letting up on performance, complaining, causing dissension among the other workers, and/or quitting.
- Managers have some employees who are better than others and therefore receive higher rewards. Sometimes the subordinates make more money than the manager.
- Managers are under constant pressure to produce with the people and resources that are available. Sometimes accidents, sickness, and other problems reduce the available human resources.
- Managers are concerned about competition. To stay in business, they must meet or beat the competition.
- Managers are constantly trying to help subordinates improve for the benefit of the organization and also for the individual.

4. Mike Phipps and T. W. Harvey, "A Coach's Guide to Good Player Relationships," *The Christian Athlete,* November-December 1987. Reprinted by permission from *The Christian Athlete,* official publication of the Fellowship of Christian Athletes.

▸ Managers have the same opportunities and limitations for rewards that coaches have. Most of them are limited in how much money they can give, but they have ample opportunities to give nonfinancial rewards such as praise, more responsibility, or more freedom or to ask for ideas and give special job assignments.

Because the jobs of manager and coach are similar, the characteristics of an effective athletic coach apply to a manager. Just as athletic coaches have different types of players to work with, managers have employees with differences in attitudes, knowledge, and skills. In both situations, the challenge is to mold them into an effective team in order to accomplish the goals of the organization and to help them accomplish their own goals at the same time.

The coaching relationship between managers and supervisors is continuous. It begins with the setting of goals and follows through to see that the goals are achieved. An athletic coach has a broader objective than to win a game: It is to a team of consistently good players. The manager's role is similar.

Managers need to evaluate their own performance as coaches. The coaches' evaluation form in Figure 11-2 was prepared for this task.

No matter what is done to encourage, stimulate, and assist supervisors in their development, on-the-job coaching becomes a key factor. By example, the boss is constantly coaching subordinates and offering suggestions as to proper behavior. By words and attitudes, the boss is providing leadership, guidance, and direction for subordinates. For the most effective development of supervisors, it becomes essential that the manager:

▸ Set an example by attitudes and personal behavior on the job.
▸ Set an example by self-development through professional organizations, reading, attending seminars and workshops, and other activities.
▸ Support management development activities inside and outside the company.
▸ Take a personal interest in the growth and development of subordinates by encouraging and recognizing any self-development efforts they make and by systematic coaching on the job.
▸ Provide a climate in which subordinates are able to use the new ideas and techniques they have learned. This climate features not only permission to change but also encouragement and positive reinforcement.

(text continues on page 199)

Figure 11-2. Coach's self-evaluation form.

	Weak									Strong
	1	2	3	4	5	6	7	8	9	10
1. I praise my players whenever natural and possible.										
2. I maintain a good balance between being a friend and being the boss.										
3. I work at listening carefully to my players and not doing all the talking.										
4. I'm careful not to criticize in a manner that will alienate or demoralize.										
5. I find something positive to say after each practice and game.										
6. I discipline my players with their best interests at heart—not mine.										
7. I'm open to new ideas and techniques that will make the sport more fun.										

	Weak 1	2	3	4	5	6	7	8	9	Strong 10
8. My players feel comfortable in sharing nonathletic concerns with me.										
9. The growth of my players as total persons is my highest priority.										
10. I let my injured players know I care about them, that they're still important to our program.										
11. I set a good example for my players by the life I lead off the field.										
12. I'm involved in outside activities which allow my players to get to know me and see my humanness.										
13. I act quickly to restore the relationship if I hurt a player through anger or pride.										

(continues)

Figure 11-2. (*continued*)

	Weak									Strong
	1	2	3	4	5	6	7	8	9	10
14. I make it a point to meet with each player at least once before and during the season.										
15. My former players keep in touch and encourage their children to compete.										
16. I don't push my faith on my players, but neither do I hide it.										
17. I'm willing to suspend or remove a star player who's disruptive to the team.										
18. Honesty is at the center of my player relationships.										
19. I encourage my players to think for themselves and not be afraid to fail.										
20. My relationship with God and my family comes before my players.										

Source: Reprinted by permission from The Christian Athlete, *official publication of the Fellowship of Christian Athletes.*

Summary

Coaching subordinates to help them improve their performances is one of the most important skills of a successful supervisor. This chapter has listed many of the qualities that characterize an effective coach. And it was made clear that the qualities of a successful supervisor are similar to those of an effective athletic coach.

The supervisor must coach on a regular basis. The purpose is to improve performance, not only as an individual, but as a member of a team of workers. In addition, supervisors must coach as a follow-up to the performance appraisal process described in Chapter 10. In that chapter, a performance improvement plan (PIP) was developed as the last step in the performance appraisal program. Coaching must be done by the supervisor to be sure the plan is carried out.

12

Selecting and Training
New Supervisors

Supervisors are the key to the productivity and future success of the organization. Selecting new supervisors to replace those lost through retirement, death, transfer, promotion, expansion, and other factors is a major challenge.

In selecting supervisors, special attention should be paid to the "Peter Principle": "In a hierarchy, every employee tends to rise to his level of incompetence."[1] According to Dr. Peter, when an opening for supervisor occurs, the organization usually looks at the employees in that department to determine the most competent person on the job, and that person is usually picked as the supervisor. An analysis of hundreds of cases of occupational incompetence shows that competence in one position "qualifies" them for promotion. And given enough time and assuming enough ranks, each employee rises to and remains at a level of incompetence. A corollary is that people who are incompetent on a job are ineligible for promotion.

This condition of picking the best "doer" to be the supervisor is not as common as it used to be. More and more organizations realize that outstanding performance on a job should not be rewarded by a promotion. It should be a consideration but not the prime requirement. Too many examples of the Peter Principle have occurred to believe that the best "doer" will make the best "manager."

A company can select a first-level supervisor in two ways. The first, and more common, way is to wait until the opening occurs and then select the best available person for the job. This person may be picked from inside, or the company may go outside to hire a qualified person from another organization.

Several problems usually exist with last-minute selection and placement. First, there is seldom enough time to use good selection techniques to pick the best person. There are pressures to find the person

1. Laurence Peter and Raymond Hull, *The Peter Principle* (New York: Morrow, 1969).

immediately and put him or her on the job. Also, emotions are usually high at the time an opening occurs. Many people are wondering, "Will Jane be promoted to the job?" And Jane has freqently been selected because she is the logical person with the most seniority and best knowledge of the people and the jobs to be supervised. Many organizations believe that it is important to promote someone from within the department in order to maintain high morale.

There will be no time to give Jane any prejob training. On Friday she is a worker and on Monday she becomes a supervisor. Beginning Monday, her boss will try to provide extra help, coaching, and other on-the-job training to help her learn the job. However, the pressures to get work done are still there, and Jane is under a terrific handicap because of her lack of management training.

Often with last-minute selection and placement, the person selected is not eager to take the job. However, the manager talks her into it and promises her all the help and encouragement she needs. And she ends up a living example of the Peter Principle.

Many problems of last-minute selection can be solved by the second selection method: identifying and pretraining a group of potential supervisors, so that when an opening occurs, one of these people can be picked to fill the job. This method has three advantages: There is time to consider all candidates carefully; less emotion is involved, so the selection can be more objective; and some management training can be provided before the person takes over as a supervisor.

Selection Principles

The principles and approaches for effective selection are just as important in picking candidates for a supervisor's job as they are for picking engineers or any other key persons. Seven items must be determined and implemented if a good job is to be done in selecting first-level supervisors.

1. *Determine the number of openings.* The first step in planning for this program is to estimate the number and type of openings that will occur in the near future (six months? one year?). This figure should be based on the expected turnover among the current supervisors, as well as on any growth—or contraction—that is expected. The best decision can probably be made by having several persons in key jobs, including the person in charge of a department, discuss the future. The human resources manager and others may also have helpful information concerning retirements, possible transfers, a supervisor's death, or job leaving.

2. *Prepare the job description.* When future openings have been determined, knowledgeable persons should spell out the duties and responsibilities related to those jobs—for instance: planning, communicating, quantity of production, quality of production, maintaining lowest possible cost, maintaining a good safety record, inducting and training new employees, coordinating work with other departments, handling complaints and grievances, assigning work properly, managing change, and the broad area of decision making. If up-to-date job descriptions are available in the company, these can be used with little modification. The importance of looking at the jobs is twofold: it serves as a basis for deciding what kinds of employees are needed and provides a basis for the training program that will be given.

3. *Ascertain the qualifications of candidates.* The candidates' qualifications should be determined from the job descriptions. For example, if one duty is to plan and schedule the work, one qualification must be an ability to plan. If a job responsibility is to train new employees, a qualification must be the ability to teach and train employees. If a job responsibility is to communicate both orally and in writing, the person selected should have the ability to express himself or herself clearly. Other job responsibilities may mean a need for a certain level of intelligence, a certain emotional stability, health requirements, and an ability to get along with people. Other qualifications in line with company policy and future requirements may be related to experience and technical knowledge, a strong desire to be a supervisor, a positive attitude toward the company, and personal integrity.

4. *Specify how many candidates should be selected.* We have now determined the number and type of openings, job descriptions for these openings, and the desirable qualifications of candidates. How many candidates should be selected and trained?

There are two different approaches. One is to train as many people as possible, even if most of them will never be promoted to a management job. This approach has the advantage of giving many people a management orientation and possibly developing better attitudes toward company management. It has the probable disadvantage of creating frustrations and negative attitudes by training many people who will not be promoted.

The other approach is to screen and train a limited number of candidates so that most of them will be promoted to supervision in a relatively short time. For example, if ten openings are likely to be available in the next year, the company may decide to train twenty people for the job. This offers an opportunity to select from a fairly large group of candidates and to promote enough of them to maintain proper attitudes and morale among the rest of the trained candidates. This screening of candidates has the disadvantage of denying the training opportunities to those who are determined by management to be unqualified. Workers who are not selected for the training program may become dissatisfied.

The number of candidates to select is an important decision that must be made by any organization that implements a program for selecting and training potential foremen and supervisors. Generally, it is better to select a limited number of candidates (such as twice as many as will be needed during the next year) than to accept all who are interested and train them.

5. *Decide how to determine qualifications.* Certain selection criteria such as education and previous work experience are easy to determine from available data. In other areas, such as intelligence, mechanical aptitude, knowledge of supervisory principles and practices, and personality, there may be little factual information, so other measures must be used. Qualified persons can give tests to measure some of these criteria effectively. Intelligence can be measured by a paper-and-pencil test, as can mechanical aptitude and knowledge of principles and facts. Whether psychological tests are effective in determining personality is controversial. The personality of an individual can be determined by analyzing previous performance on jobs and behavior under various circumstances. Health can be measured by a medical examination. Leadership abilities and skills can be evaluated by analyzing leadership roles played by the individual, both inside and outside the company. Attitudes toward management, people, and various aspects of the company can be measured by interviewing that person.

In short, a number of different techniques should be used in determining the qualifications that have been established. Factual information should be supplemented with interviews, tests, medical examinations, performance appraisals, and other measures that will help predict future performance as supervisor. If the organization does not have persons who can assess the qualifications of candidates, outside help should be acquired. Reputable psychological consultants can be called on to provide this service.

Some companies use assessment centers to determine an individual's potential for promotion. An assessment center is "a process in which potential supervisors participate in a series of situations similar to a job to which they might be promoted."[2] Their behavior is evaluated by several trained assessors, usually line managers, in a process that usually lasts two to four days. The simulation exercises used are related to the job of supervisor. They include individual problem analysis, including

2. Cabot Jaffee, Fredrick D. Frank, and James R. Preston, "Assessment Centers," in *Human Resources Management and Development Handbook* (New York: AMACOM, 1985).

written reports to explain their actions; one-on-one discussion between the assessor and the potential supervisor; an "in-basket" exercise followed by an interview conducted by an assessor; a leadership activity with two or more subordinates; preparation of a work schedule; and leaderless group discussion. Participants are judged on such skills as planning and organizing, decision making, leadership, perception, adaptability, decisiveness, and interpersonal and written communication. Typically each assessor evaluates each of the participants, and the assessors pool their evaluation to arrive at a final assessment.

AT&T, a pioneer in developing the assessment center, identified 460 supervisors considered to be superior supervisors by their managers. From these supervisors they identified the following areas as the most important:

- Planning the work
- Controlling the work
- Problem solving
- Providing performance feedback
- Creating and maintaining a motivational atmosphere
- Time management
- Informal oral communication
- Self-development
- Written communication
- Knowledge of the Bell System
- Career counseling
- Meeting communication

Care should be taken that the selection criteria and techniques adhere to equal opportunity and affirmative action government regulations.[3]

6. *Establish a procedure for the final selection of candidates.* If many qualifications are established and measures set up to determine them, it is important to decide how the final selection will be made. If these criteria are objective, the selection becomes relatively automatic. If, however, subjective judgment will be important, then the authority and responsibility for selecting the qualified candidates should be clearly defined. Line management has the final responsibility and authority for selection, usually with the advice of human resources professionals.

7. *Draw up procedures for communicating acceptance or nonacceptance of candidates.* If candidates are asked to volunteer or apply for supervisory

3. U.S. Department of Labor, Equal Employment Opportunity, 200 Constitution Ave., Room C-3325, Washington, D.C. 20210.

jobs, it is important to decide how they will be notified concerning their acceptance for the program. If many people have applied, this is very important, especially for those who are not accepted. It is not sufficient, for example, to write a letter and say, "I'm sorry, but you have not been accepted." The letter should tell candidates why they were not accepted and what they might do to become qualified. The offer to discuss the reasons in a personal interview is always appreciated. Those who are not accepted may become discontented, so effective communication with them is important.

BENDIX PRODUCTS, AEROSPACE DIVISION, SOUTH BEND, INDIANA

I was instrumental in developing and implementing an effective approach for selecting first-level supervisors at the Bendix Products Aerospace Division. Although this approach was used in selecting foremen in a manufacturing organization, the principles and techniques can be easily adapted for selecting supervisors in a service or government organization. The only requirement is that the organization be large enough to select a pool of candidates for possible promotion to supervisor.

In cooperation with the general manager and manager of manufacturing, I initiated, planned, and implemented a program for the selection and training of new first-level supervisors (I was the personnel manager). The program contained five steps.

1. *Determination of need.* The following overall plan was developed to select and train new supervisors:
   a. Estimate the number of supervisory openings that would probably exist during the next year.
   b. Determine the number of candidates that should be selected and trained to provide a pool from which new supervisors would be selected.
   c. Determine the qualifications that new supervisors should have.
   d. Agree on the criteria for selecting the candidates for the pool.
   e. Develop a training program to be given to those selected.
   f. Announce the program to all concerned.
   g. Pick new supervisors from the pool of selected and trained candidates.

Based on the analysis of future growth and turnover among supervisors, it was decided that approximately twelve openings would occur within the next year, all of them at the foreman level, the first level of manufacturing management. There was general agreement among the general manager, the manufacturing manager, and me that approximately twice as many candidates should be selected for presupervisory training as would be placed within a year. Therefore, we decided to select between twenty and twenty-five candidates to be trained to become the pool from which new supervisors would be picked.

2. *Selection of candidates.* The job description of foremen at Bendix was used to determine the duties and responsibilities that a new foreman would have. The duties and responsibilities included planning and communicating; quantity of production; quality of production; maintaining lowest possible cost; maintaining a good safety record; inducting and training new employees; coordinating work with other departments such as production control, industrial engineering, personnel, and accounting; handling grievances and assigning work properly.

After discussion among the general manager, personnel manager, and manufacturing manager, it was decided that the following qualifications would be required:

- ▶ No person would be considered unless he completed an application blank showing a strong desire to be considered.
- ▶ Preference would be given to persons age 45 or younger. This was an arbitrary number that was selected because the present age of foremen was very high. The fact that some of these people would move into higher management was also considered. This figure was subject to change if there weren't enough candidates who met it.
- ▶ No candidate would be selected unless he was a high school graduate. (This was a well-established practice at Bendix.)
- ▶ No candidate would be selected unless he had above-average intelligence as measured by the Wonderlic Personnel Test.[4] (This, too, was a well-established practice at Bendix.)

In addition, candidates were required to meet the following standards:

- ▶ Be in good health.
- ▶ Have good performance on past jobs.
- ▶ Have a good attitude toward management and toward the company.

3. *Criteria for selection.* The desire to be a foreman would be measured by the fact that a person has completed an application blank. As part of this process, the applicant agreed to take a battery of tests and to attend training meetings on his own time. The age and education were determined from factual records in the personnel file.

Individual intelligence was measured by the Wonderlic Personnel Test, with a minimum score of 24 established as a cutoff point.[5] This was the same score that was used in selecting foremen prior to the preforeman selection and training program.

In addition, the Minnesota Paper Form Board Test was administered to the applicants to measure mechanical aptitude.[6] The scores were not used as criteria to select or reject a candidate. Rather, the test was given for possible use in future validation of the test.

4. E. F. Wonderlic, *Wonderlic Personnel Test* (New York: The Psychological Corporation, 1983).
5. Ibid.
6. *Minnesota Paper Form Board Test* (New York: The Psychological Corporation, 1970).

The Supervisory Inventory on Human Relations was administered to the candidates to provide information concerning the candidates' knowledge and understanding of human relations facts, principles, and approaches.[7] Responses to each of the eighty items were tabulated to determine which facts and principles should be emphasized in the training program. The test was administered again at the completion of the program to evaluate the effectiveness of the training.

Appraisal forms completed by supervision provided criteria concerning past performance, ability to communicate, attitude toward the company, ability to get along with other people, and other pertinent factors. The health of the individual was measured by the medical records filed in the Industrial Relations Department.

Three criteria (age, education, and score on the Personnel Test) were used as the first screening device, with preference given to those meeting these three criteria. Those who did meet the major criteria were further evaluated by appraisals obtained from immediate supervisors, present and past (Figure 12-1), and by medical records. These additional data were discussed among the general manager, manufacturing manager, and me. Twenty-three candidates met all of the criteria and were selected for the presupervisory training program. The following chart shows the selection statistics:

Number of potential candidates for foremen (hourly employees)	2,000
Number of employees who completed application blank	130
Number of employees who completed the test	93
Number of employees who met the criteria of age, education, and intelligence	29
Number of employees selected for the training program	23

After the final selection of twenty-three candidates, the general manager sent a letter to each person who had applied for the program. Those who were accepted were told that they had been accepted and were given the schedule for the training program.

For those who were not accepted, a letter from the general manager told them that they had not been accepted for this first program. It also told them that if they had any questions and wanted to know why they had not been accepted, they should contact the training supervisor, who would discuss it with them. One-third of those who were rejected did contact the training supervisor to discuss the reason for not being selected.

Figure 12-2 is a copy of the letter that was sent to all 2,000 hourly employees. Figure 12-3 is a copy of the application form.

4. *Preplacement training.* After supervisory candidates are selected, a training program should be planned to prepare them to take the big step from doer to manager; they must be able to see that work is done through others. There are two approaches. One is to provide on-the-job training by a current supervisor. This can be successful if the teacher is an effective supervisor and coach, but it is not practical

(text continues on page 210)

7. Donald L. Kirkpatrick, *Supervisory Inventory on Human Relations* (Elm Grove, Wis.: Donald L. Kirkpatrick, 1990).

Figure 12-1. Performance appraisal form, Bendix Products, Aerospace Division.

Name of candidate _____

Length of time under my supervision   Years _____   Months _____

1. Job performance?
    ☐ Very good   ☐ Satisfactory   ☐ Unsatisfactory

2. Supervision required?
    ☐ A great deal   ☐ Average   ☐ Very little

3. Attitude toward management?
    ☐ Very good   ☐ Average   ☐ Negative

4. How well get along with others?
    ☐ Very well   ☐ Average   ☐ Poorly

5. Does he/she create problems for supervision?   ☐ Yes   ☐ No

    If yes, explain _____

    _____

    _____

6. Absence   ☐ Never   ☐ Occasional   ☐ Frequent
    Tardiness   ☐ Never   ☐ Occasional   ☐ Frequent
    Health   ☐ Excellent ☐ Good   ☐ Poor   ☐ Don't Know

    Comments: _____

    _____

    _____

7. Do you have any evidence that this person has leadership ability? (on the job or outside evidence)   ☐ Yes   ☐ No

    If yes, give details _____

    _____

    _____

    _____

8. How would he/she be in regard to the following items:

Yes	No		Yes	No	
___	___	Would be a good communicator.	___	___	Would accept responsibility.
___	___	Would be too bossy.	___	___	Would be a good organizer.
___	___	Would be easily influenced by employees.	___	___	Would stand up for subordinates.
___	___	Would be a "Yes" person.	___	___	Would give credit.
___	___	Would be overly concerned with details.	___	___	Would be loyal to company.
___	___	Would be a good trainer.	___	___	Would be helpful to employee having a problem.
___	___	Would give instructions clearly.	___	___	Would be capable in handling grievances.
___	___	Would be a "buck passer."	___	___	Would let employees know where they stand.
___	___	Would be cost conscious.	___	___	Would be likely to show favoritism.
___	___	Would be able to influence his/her boss.	___	___	Would have respect of subordinates.
___	___	Would be well liked by subordinates.			

9. To what extent would you recommend this person as a foreman?

☐ Strongly recommend   ☐ Mildly recommend   ☐ Do not recommend   ☐ Uncertain

Additional factors (favorable or not) that should be considered: _____

_____

_____

_____   _____
            Date   Signature of Foreman

_____   _____
            Date   Signature of General Foreman

(continues)

Figure 12-1. (*continued*)

NOTE: The signature of the General Foreman doesn't necessarily mean agree-
       ment with the appraisal by the foreman. It simply means that he has
       seen it.

---

in most organizations. The other method is to provide classroom training, either
internally or at outside supervisory development programs. This was the approach
we took at Bendix. The factors we considered in developing the 18-hour preplacement training program are common to all such programs.

What are the objectives? The objective of the training program is to prepare the
candidates for management jobs. The participants have to learn about management
attitudes, as well as approaches and techniques that supervisors use. At Bendix, we
identified three objectives: (1) to orient participants toward the management job of a
foreman, (2) to improve their understanding of the duties, responsibilities, and desired qualifications of a foreman, and (3) to develop some skills foremen need.

What subjects will be taught? The goal of the subjects taught is to aid in reaching
training objectives. The general subject content for Bendix was determined jointly
by the general manager, the training supervisor, and me, with suggestions from current foremen, general foremen, and superintendents. The specific topics were selected by the training supervisor and me, with pretest responses to the Supervisory
Inventory on Human Relations analyzed to determine specific items to discuss.[8]
Suggestions for other topics came from various other people who were interested in
the training program.

What schedule will be followed? The program was scheduled from 4:00 to 5:30
P.M. on twelve consecutive Tuesdays. The first shift ended at 3:30, and employees
attended on their own time and were not paid. Special arrangements were made for
the few people who worked the second and third shifts.

A number of considerations went into this decision. First were state and federal
laws regarding the training of hourly people for management jobs. In most states,
hourly people can be trained without pay if meetings are held outside working hours,
attendance by employees is voluntary, the course is not directly related to the employees' current jobs, and the employees do not perform any production work during
the meetings. The schedule also had to be convenient for all the candidates.

The length of each meeting, the length of the program, and frequency of meetings were arrived at by considering the objectives of the program and the conve-
nience of candidates.

Where will the meetings be held? The meetings were held in the plant conference room, which was convenient for all participants and was comfortable.

Who will conduct the meetings? Leaders should be selected for their subject
knowledge plus, most important, their ability to communicate effectively. They can
come from both management and the personnel and training department and/or
from outside. In this program, all of the leaders were Bendix employees. The following training program schedule gives details on leaders as well as subjects:

8. Ibid.

Figure 12-2. Letter informing employees of preforeman training program, Bendix Products, Aerospace Division.

TO: Aerospace hourly employees

SUBJECT: Preforeman Training Program

As mentioned in my recent letter we are now ready to offer preforeman training to our employees. This is a program whereby we want to select and train employees who have the potential to become foremen. Then, when new jobs open up, we will fill them from this group. We believe in promotion from within, and are going to try this program as a way of putting into practice what we believe. Here is our program:

1. All candidates will be carefully screened to determine those we feel have the best potential for the job.
   a. The candidate will be given three paper and pencil tests to give us an indication of mental ability, mechanical aptitude, and knowledge of supervisory principles.
   b. We will get a performance appraisal from foremen who have supervised the candidate.
   c. The candidate may be given a medical exam.
2. Candidates will be selected by the general manager, manufacturing manager, and the personnel manager.
3. A training program will be given on the candidate's own time. It will include such subjects as:
   a. The Foreman's Job
   b. Planning and Organizing Work
   c. Understanding and Motivating People
   d. Training Subordinates
   e. Labor Relations
   f. Communications
   g. Aerospace Division Policies and Procedures
4. Graduates of the program will be considered for such positions as openings occur.

Please understand that candidates for this program will be selected on the basis of their potential to become foremen. If you are selected for the training program, we cannot guarantee you a foreman's job after successful completion of the course; however, your chances of being chosen for the position will be greatly enhanced.

We feel that there are many people interested in improving themselves. They will want to complete the enclosed application and return it to Don Kirkpatrick, our Personnel Manager. Your application will be kept in strict confidence. Your applications must be received by December 3 to be considered.

(continues)

Figure 12-2. (*continued*)

If you have further questions, please contact Don directly.

Sincerely,

R. E. Whiffen
General Manager

P.S. Even though the program is designed to select and train future foremen, some of the candidates may be offered other salary jobs in manufacturing, quality control, and production control.

Subject	*Leaders*
The Foreman's Job	Don Kirkpatrick, personnel manager
Management Philosophy and Organization	Richard Whiffen, general manager, plus major department heads in engineering, manufacturing, marketing, and finance
Effective Communication, I	Don Kirkpatrick
Effective Communication, II	Irv Margol, training manager
Planning and Organizing Work	Irv Margol
Understanding People	Don Kirkpatrick
Motivating People	Don Kirkpatrick
Assigning Work	Irv Margol
Delegation	Irv Margol
Training Employees	Irv Margol
Labor Relations	Lou Tiege, director of industrial relations
Discipline and Control	Don Kirkpatrick
Awarding Certificates and Comments	Richard Whiffen

What techniques will be used? This training program used a variety of methods. Presentations by the leaders were accompanied by aids and techniques, including the following:

▸ *Blackboard and flipchart,* to emphasize the important points made by the group, as well as by the leader.
▸ *Films.* During the program, three movies were shown.
▸ *Group discussion and involvement.* The trainees participated extensively in buzz groups with six persons in each group, contributed freely in asking ques-

Figure 12-3. Application form for preforeman training program, Bendix Products, Aerospace Division.

1. Name _____ Department _____

2. Street address _____ City _____ Phone _____

3. Date of birth _____ Date employed by Bendix _____

4. Jobs held at Bendix: _____

   _____

   _____

   _____

5. Jobs held at other companies: _____

   _____

   _____

6. Education
   a. Please circle last grade completed:
         1 2 3 4 5 6 7 8 9 10 11 12   1 2 3 4
                  Grade and high school   College
   b. List any special courses you have taken (night school, correspondence, vocational school, etc.)

      Name of course _____ School _____ Year _____

      Name of course _____ School _____ Year _____

      Name of course _____ School _____ Year _____
   c. Other comments on education: _____

      _____

      _____

7. Leadership activities (list any offices held and other leadership activities):

   _____

   _____

   _____

   _____

   _____

8. Other information that might be important when considering you for a foreman's job:

(continues)

Figure 12-3. (*continued*)

_____

_____

_____

I understand that this application will be held in strict confidence. I also understand that there is no guarantee that I will become a foreman even if I complete the training.

Date	Signature

tions and giving opinions, participated in projects to get them to "learn by doing," and discussed various items of my Supervisory Inventory on Human Relations and Supervisory Inventory on Communication.[9]
- *Case studies.* Several case studies were given to the group in order to get them to think in terms of practical application of the principles discussed.

How will the program be evaluated? Participants completed a reaction sheet at the conclusion of the training program. Figure 12-4 shows their positive reaction.

There are other ways to evaluate, too. If the Supervisory Inventory on Communication is given at the start of the program, it can also be administered at the end of the program, and a comparison made of pretest and posttest responses. Another worthwhile but more difficult way is to compare the performance of supervisors selected from this program with that of supervisors picked in other ways.

5. *Placement in supervision.* The selection process was developed and implemented by the manufacturing manager, general manager, and me. We agreed that future foremen would be taken from the pool of candidates with any exceptions approved by the general manager.

The selection of a specific person to fill a specific opening became the decision of the manufacturing manager. He would consult with his superintendents and general foremen. In order to help him in the decision, a looseleaf notebook was prepared that contained the following information on each candidate in the pool:

- Original application blank showing education, experience, and other information prior to Bendix employment.
- Work history at Bendix showing all departments in which the person worked and jobs performed.
- Application blank completed to apply for the preforeman program.
- Appraisal forms completed by the current and past immediate supervisors.

9. Ibid.

Figure 12-4. Reactions to the preforeman training program, Bendix Products, Aerospace Division.

1. How did the course match your expectations?
   - __0__ Just what I expected.
   - __22__ Generally what I expected.
   - __1__ Not at all what I expected.

   Comments: _____

   _____

2. Was the course held at the proper time? __20__ Yes __3__ No

   If not, when should it have been held: _____

   _____

3. How was the approach?
   - __1__ Too much theory
   - __20__ Right combination of theory and practical application
   - __2__ Not enough theory

4. Were subjects properly covered?

	Should have spent more time	Should have spent less time	OK
1. The supervisor's job	1	0	22
2. Aerospace Organization	8	0	15
3. Communications (two parts)	0	0	23
4. Planning and organization work	3	0	20
5. Understanding employees	1	1	21
6. Motivation	0	0	23
7. Assigning work-delegation	4	1	18
8. Training	8	0	15
9. Discipline and control	5	1	17
10. Labor relations	3	0	20
11. Meeting the department heads	11	0	12

5. What have been the results of the program as far as you are concerned? (Check as many as apply to you.)
   - __23__ Better understanding of Aerospace management, problems, etc.
   - __20__ Better understanding of the foreman's job
   - __13__ More desire to be a foreman
   - __0__ Less desire to be a foreman
   - __15__ Better attitude towards my job as an hourly employee
   - _____ Other (please describe): _____

(continues)

Figure 12-4. *(continued)*

6. Would you be interested in a follow-up program?
   <u>19</u> Yes   <u>0</u> No   <u>4</u> Uncertain

7. Other comments and suggestions:

   _____

   _____

   _____

                              _____
                                      Signature

This information could be studied and the candidate interviewed by the manufacturing manager and anyone else he chose. Usually the interviewing was jointly done by the manufacturing manager and the general foreman, to whom the new foreman would report.

When the person had been picked, the manufacturing manager and I agreed on the offered salary, with the figure depending on the salary range for the job, the current salary of the candidate, and the salaries of other foremen doing comparable jobs. I then contacted the candidate and explained salary, benefits, and opportunities.

During the first year of the program, twelve of the twenty-three candidates were promoted, ten as foremen and two as salaried personnel in production control. All except one accepted the position and salary that was offered. This person had been working in an experimental production department, where the wages of workers and the salary of the foremen were higher than in the production department. He was offered a job as a regular production foreman when he would have preferred the job of foreman in an experimental department. He was assured that if he turned down this job, he would still remain in the pool of candidates. He did turn down the offer. As it happened, an opening occurred as foreman in the experimental department about two months later. He was offered the job and accepted it.

During the first year, only one exception was made to the policy of selecting all new foremen from the pool. In one department, extensive metallurgical knowledge was required on the part of the foreman, and none of the twenty-three candidates had this knowledge. Also, the position was only temporary; the foreman would be returned to the labor force after about six months. Because of these circumstances, the general manager approved the recommendation of the manufacturing manager that a person from that specific department be promoted but only on a temporary basis.

   5. *Evaluation of the program.* The program at Bendix was one of the most effective and satisfying programs that I have been involved in. No one seemed to be

unhappy with it. The union had no objections or negative comments about the program. We kept them informed but did not ask for their input or reactions.

We were very careful to involve current foremen, the general foreman, and superintendents in the program. We explained our approach and asked for their suggestions. We asked them to encourage their good workers to apply for the program. We kept them informed of all aspects of the program and welcomed their comments.

Although the manufacturing manager was reluctant at first to have me, as personnel manager, interfere in his right to select his own foremen, he accepted the program well and became enthusiastic, particularly when he realized that he still had the authority to make the final selection.

Although I do not have tangible data on the success of the program, the overall impression was that the newly selected foremen were well qualified and performed well. During the two years I was at Bendix, none of them left his or her new job.

The Bendix program was intended as a pilot. If the general manager and I had remained at Bendix longer, we would undoubtedly have repeated the program, with a few changes perhaps. We would have opened it up to salaried as well as hourly employees and probably would have changed the criteria for selecting the pool. But we would have continued the three essential elements of the program:

1. Look first for those who have a desire to be a foreman.
2. Develop a pool of selected people.
3. Provide management training before they are placed on a management job.

Two more case studies give examples of similar approaches to training future supervisors. The selection of candidates for the pool was basically the same as the Bendix approach. Following are brief descriptions of the training.

INLAND STEEL PRODUCTS COMPANY, MILWAUKEE, WISCONSIN
R. O. TJENSVOLD, PERSONNAL MANAGER

The preplacement training program consisted of twelve sessions of one and a half hours each. All the meetings were scheduled after working hours on the applicant's own time and without pay for that time. The subject matter had been selected by the plant manager and personnel director in consultation with other interested managers.

During the program, emphasis was placed on informality rather than a schoolroom atmosphere and on group participation instead of lecture. All meetings were conducted by management personnel from the plant with the exception of the session on "Understanding People," which was led by an outside psychologist. Details are described in Figure 12-5.

Class attendance, like all other aspects of this program, was entirely voluntary; however, every participant had to attend sessions 1 and 12 plus at least eight others or else he could be jeopardizing chances for further consideration. Class participation was encouraged, and lack of interest and involvement became a negative factor when considering the person for promotion. A certificate was given to the fourteen who completed the course.

There were a number of indicators of the success of the selection and training program at Inland Steel Products:

▸ The record of attendance at the twelve training sessions exceeded 95 percent, a clear indication of the continued interest among the participants.

▸ After the twelfth session, the participants were asked to comment on the effectiveness of the program as they saw it. Their comments were highly favorable, with some practical recommendations for improvement among the instructors.

▸ The objective of the program was to provide a cadre of potentially promotable candidates for supervision. With the exception of the two who left the company before they might have been promoted, all the graduates of the program moved up within eighteen months from the end of the preplacement training program. Nine went to tasks as production foremen, one moved to an office supervisory job, and the remaining four were upgraded to salaried jobs outside the manufacturing department.

▸ Top management agreed that the program would be repeated whenever future supervisory needs developed.

▸ Other supervisory training was developed at the request of older supervisors who felt that if the program was good enough for trainees, it was good enough for them.

When the results of the evaluations were analyzed, changes in future programs were planned. The most significant changes were in the content of the sessions in order to make them more directly applicable to the specific job of the first-line supervisor. Also, teaching techniques were improved to use more group participation and more audiovisual aids and to do less lecturing. But the approach to the selection process, by self-nomination and screening, remained unchanged because management and candidates felt it was effective.

KEARNEY AND TRECKER CORPORATION, MILWAUKEE, WISCONSIN
DAVE COVERDALE, VICE-PRESIDENT

The training of presupervisory candidates at Kearney and Trecker involved three major thrusts: internal understudy training, external management training, and internal and/or external technical training.

Figure 12-5. Preplacement training program schedule, Inland Steel Products Company.

Inland Steel Products Company

Session and Date	*Subject to Be Covered*	*Leader*
One Nov. 8	**Why we are here . . . and what's ahead** There are many aspects to the job of the Foreman. Most people have to learn this job by trial and error. Here is an opportunity to learn through the accumulated experiences of others.	R. C. McLean
Two Nov. 15	**Survey of Company Organization** The organization charts show the Company structure in its ideal form; the actual relationships are more complex. Job descriptions, especially those of the Supervisor, will be reviewed.	R. O. Tjensvold
Three Nov. 22	**Internal Relationships and Interdependence** The Manufacturing Department does not operate by itself. It is part of that larger organization—the Company. The various departments are considerably dependent on each other to get the total job done.	J. W. Hendricks
Four Nov. 29	**Understanding People** Everything we do is done through people and by people. Therefore, basic to doing every job is our need to understand people.	Dr. E. Russell
Five Dec. 6	**Principles of Communications** People are motivated to act mainly by what they hear or read. How can we improve our skills in communicating in order to get things done?	R. O. Tjensvold

(continues)

Figure 12-5. (*continued*)

Session and Date	Subject to Be Covered	Leader
Six Dec. 13	**Employee Attitudes and Discipline** Some situations call for disciplinary action; many do not. How do we identify what our problems are and how best to deal with them?	L. J. Dunlap
Seven Dec. 20	**Paperwork of the Supervisor** Among the necessary though time-consuming tasks of the supervisor are those of handling mounds of paperwork. Insight is given on why paperwork is necessary and what is involved.	J. W. Hendricks
Eight Jan. 3	**Planning and Organizing Work** Without an organized approach, important tasks may be left unfinished because of time devoted to nonessentials. Let's consider how to identify the important and get it done first.	R. O. Tjensvold
Nine Jan. 10	**Job Instruction** One of the most important duties of a supervisor is training his people. Job instruction training presents a helpful guide to supervisors for this task.	R. O. Tjensvold
Ten Jan. 17	**Analyzing Problems** Before a problem can be solved, it must be identified. Then it can be analyzed for possible solutions.	R. O. Tjensvold
Eleven Jan. 24	**Basic Economics** Part of our understanding of how our Company may be a profitable concern depends on our knowledge of basic economics applied to the organization.	D. R. Axtell

Session and Date	Subject to Be Covered	Leader
Twelve Jan. 31	**Final Review and Questions** A summary session, briefly reviewing the many subjects already touched on, relating them to each other and to the job of the supervisor. Questions from the participants will be answered.	Entire Leader Group led by R. G. McLean

Employees were scheduled into various functions of the organization on a rotational basis for assigned time periods. These schedules were tailored to the background and experience of each trainee so that no one was assigned to a session in an area in which he or she already possessed expertise or experience. The purpose of this internal understudy-type training was twofold:

1. To teach trainees the inner workings of the department, its functions, and its major procedures.
2. To help trainees identify the people in the organization who make things happen and get to know them as human beings they can communicate with in person, rather than as voices at the end of the telephone.

Following an orientation program of a series of half-days rotating through the major manufacturing functions, the employees were assigned to areas such as payroll, industrial engineering, employee relations, and labor relations. These jobs were interspersed with assignments to provide temporary relief help to supervisors in various departments to gain first-hand supervisory experience. This periodic return to the manufacturing environment kept the trainees aware of what was happening in the manufacaturing areas and gave them the opportunity to practice the skills and experiences they had picked up during the training program. Moreover, it served to strengthen their identity as future supervisors.

From time to time, requests were made by various operating departments to have a trainee assigned for a special project. The criteria for such an assignment were the project's length and that it was a learning experience. In other words, the purpose was to provide training, not just to get the job done. This evaluation was made jointly by the training manager and the manager of manufacturing. Such assignments included a special plant layout project, the revamping of a payroll reporting system, and preparation for an arbitration.

The first twenty weeks were spent in areas relating directly to manufacturing supervision. The following eighteen weeks were spent primarily in areas giving a broader viewpoint of the company's overall operations such as marketing and engineering.

The second part of the program was outside management training. Kearney and Trecker is close to the facilities of the Management Institute, University of Wisconsin, as well as Marquette University's adult education program and other fine academic educational institutions. Two courses offered by the Management Institute were required: "Supervisory Skills" and "Leadership Methods." These three-day seminars proved to be invaluable in the development of new supervisors. Also, depending on the need, time, and availability, supervisors were scheduled to attend sessions at the University of Wisconsin and Marquette University on such subjects as problem solving and decision making, management of time, training of new employees, interviewing skills, grievance handling, and discipline.

Candidates were encouraged to continue their education through utilization of the corporation's tuition reimbursement program. Several candidates worked on a degree or two-year certificate program from various institutions.

The third part of the program was to develop technical skills in areas where it appeared that the employee might be eventually assigned. To this end, Kearney and Trecker's Technical Training Department provided training in various machining functions or other areas of shop expertise, such as the customer training school programs on numerical/control programming, maintenance, and the like. Various outside technical institutes provided training that was not available at Kearney and Trecker.

Summary

Many supervisors are ineffective because they do not have the necessary qualities. In most organizations in past years, the primary qualities for being promoted to supervisor were performance on present job, seniority, and cooperation with bosses. Promotion to supervisor was considered a reward for outstanding performance. And typically, the search for a supervisor was restricted to workers in the department that the supervisor would manage.

More and more organizations are realizing that outstanding performance as a "doer" is not a good predictor of performance as a "supervisor." This chapter has suggested concepts, principles, and techniques for selecting first-level supervisors. It has encouraged organizations to avoid "last minute" selection and to develop a plan for selecting. It has also suggested that new supervisors receive some management training *before* they assume the role of supervisor. Emphasis has been placed on the desire to be a supervisor as well as other qualifications.

Case studies from Bendix, Inland Steel, and Kearney and Trecker have illustrated a successful way to select and train supervisors, especially in large organizations.

PART II

Case Studies of Specific Programs

13

A Comprehensive In-House Program at Deere & Company

Many companies do supervisory training on a hit-or-miss basis, conducting programs when they feel the need. These are usually crisis programs, developed to meet an immediate need or solve a critical problem.

Other organizations have well-planned programs. One of the best-planned and implemented programs is at Deere & Company, maker of agricultural and lawn tractors. The following case study sets out the company's statement of mission, philosophy, programs, and the action steps to stimulate changes in job behavior.

DEERE & COMPANY, MOLINE, ILLINOIS
HARRY E. LITCHFIELD, MANAGER, EMPLOYEE TRAINING AND DEVELOPMENT

Statement of Mission and Basic Philosophy

The Employee Training and Development Department has the overall responsibility of improving the effectiveness of present and potential managers through their continued development and training.

In fulfilling this, we systematically determine, create, provide, and evaluate the development and training Company and dealer people need to meet their personal and organizational goals more effectively. We provide opportunities, both internal and external, for these individuals to:

- Increase skills and knowledge needed in present jobs.
- Develop skills and knowledge needed for growth and career advancement.
- Explore innovative management concepts, skills, and technologies.
- Increase personal motivation and confidence.

To this end, we believe that:

▸ Development and training needs are best determined by individuals themselves and their managers.
▸ A systematic approach is used to determine individual and group needs before considering resources, materials, and methods.
▸ The use of internal versus external resources is determined by program objectives, urgency of needs, in-house capabilities, and cost-effectiveness.
▸ Training is "student oriented," focusing on what students should be able to know or do after training.
▸ The development and training evaluation involves measuring the learning, behavior change on the job, and financial return to the organization.
▸ We will have little success unless the students' immediate managers prepare them before the training and later actively support their efforts to apply what has been learned.

We can only offer a system of development and training. Individuals must select what best fits their needs—with the overall goal being more effective job performance.

External Education and Training

All training needs cannot be fulfilled through internal programming and services. Therefore, we provide assistance in determining appropriate external resources, enrollment, and seminar evaluation.

We subscribe to the Seminar Clearinghouse International (SCI). This is a national service and centralized file of seminar feedback evaluations and training resources. We use this service and *Brieker's International Directory,* as well as our own files, to search education and training resources at your request.

Available Programs

Many programs are offered for *all* employees. With the assistance of their bosses, they select the ones that best meet their needs. However, the following three programs are specifically for supervisors.

Staff Supervisory Skills Seminar

Scope

A maximum amount of skill development, participation, and interaction characterizes this five-day, "live-in" seminar. The week includes a general orientation to the Company through exposure to Company officers and the Deere & Company Administrative Center.

Content

- ▸ Challenges of the Supervisor
- ▸ Planning and Organizing
- ▸ Time Management
- ▸ Teamwork
- ▸ Conducting Meetings
- ▸ Communications/Giving Directions
- ▸ Communications/Questioning, Gathering Information, and Listening
- ▸ Managing Change
- ▸ Orientation to Deere & Company
- ▸ Understanding Employee Behavior
- ▸ Increasing Interdepartmental Cooperation
- ▸ Delegation
- ▸ Analyzing and Improving Employee Performance
- ▸ Improving Personal Effectiveness

Participants

It has been designed and developed for first-level staff supervisors who have a minimum of three months' experience on the job. This includes bona-fide supervisors or "permanent lenders of work direction" from technical areas.

Line Supervisory Skills Seminar

Scope

This concentrated, five-day, "live-in" experience provides a maximum amount of skill development, participation, and interaction. A general orientation to the Company is provided through exposure to Company officers and the Deere & Company Administrative Center.

Content

- ▸ Challenges of the Supervisor
- ▸ Planning and Organizing
- ▸ Managing One's Time
- ▸ Teamwork
- ▸ Communications/Giving Directions
- ▸ Listening
- ▸ Communications/Questioning and Gathering Information
- ▸ Increasing Interdepartmental Cooperation
- ▸ Orientation to Deere & Company
- ▸ Current Supervisory Issues
- ▸ Understanding Employee Behavior
- ▸ Analyzing and Improving Employee Performance
- ▸ Improving Personal Effectiveness

Participants

It has been designed and developed for first-level line supervisors who have a minimum of three months' experience on the job.

Supervisory Skills Seminar II: Managing for Performance

Scope

This intensive, "live-in" learning experience is a five-day program for first-level supervisors. Its purpose is to develop managerial skills that will complement those already acquired in either the Line or Staff Supervisory Skills Seminar.

Content

- ▸ Managing Self
  - —Concepts of Peak Performance
  - —Diagnosing Managerial Styles
- ▸ Managing Tasks
  - —Long-Term Planning
  - —Creative Problem Solving and Decision Making
- ▸ Managing Relationships
  - —Developing Employees
  - —Employee Participation at John Deere

Participants

This seminar has been designed for line, staff, and technical supervisory personnel who have already attended a Supervisory Skills Seminar. We offer approximately forty other programs to all employees to meet specific needs. Of these, the following are of special interest to supervisors.

Decision Focus

Scope

Decision Focus is a series of systematic tools used to solve problems and make decisions. It is taught by an outside resource in a two-day workshop where teams use the tools to attack real on-the-job concerns. Complements group problem solving, facilitator skills, and employee participation efforts.

Content

- ▸ Improving ability to describe and analyze problems
- ▸ Increasing skill in identifying criteria and assesssing risks of decisions
- ▸ Building skills to ensure the success of plans by using a method of forecasting obstacles and designing preventive and contingent actions

▸ Improving skill in managing meetings by applying well-chosen systematic tools and strategies

Participants

Managers, supervisors, professional support staff, and technical staff. Although not required, units are encouraged to send teams of three to five people to work on common concerns.

Participative Management and Employee Involvement

Scope

This half-day session is designed to give participants an understanding of their role in participative management and employee involvement and improve their ability to carry out that role in various situations. Through group discussion, video, individual exercises, and role play, participants develop a strategy for participative management and employee involvement in their unique work setting.

Content

▸ The Changing Workplace
▸ Benefits of Involving Others
▸ Overcoming Obstacles
▸ Systematic Approach
▸ Leadership Style Awareness
▸ Action Planning

Participants

This program is designed for those who manage, supervise, or direct others.

Training and Development: The Role of the Manager

Scope

This three- to four-hour program is designed to complement other similar offerings, such as appraisal skills, coaching and counseling, and career development–related programs. It provides an opportunity for managers to explore their employee training and development responsibilities.

Content

▸ Training versus Nontraining Needs
▸ Training Resources
▸ Improving Training Effectiveness

- Development Activities
- Training and Development Strategies

Participants

It has been designed and developed for all managers and supervisors.

Appraisal Skills

Scope

This one and one-half day program increases the participants' skills in giving feedback to employees regarding their performance. It focuses on the overall appraisal cycle, emphasizing skill development in coaching and counseling, as well as the formal feedback session.

Content

- Systematic Approach
- Communication Skills
- Analyzing Performance
- Monitoring and Gathering Information
- Giving Feedback and Constructive Criticism
- Employee Preparation
- Sharing Perceptions of Performance
- Determining Areas of Improvement
- Developing Action Plans

Participants

This program is designed for those supervisors and managers who give appraisals.

Career Development and the Manager

Scope

This six-hour program has been designed to give managers and supervisors an opportunity to improve their ability to assist employees with career development. It clarifies the responsibilities of both the manager and the employee, focuses on a step-by-step approach to the career development discussion, and provides an opportunity for skill building through role play.

Content

- The Manager's Responsibilities
- The Employee's Responsibilities

- A Systematic Approach to Career Development Discussion
- A Career Development Discussion Model
- Roles Required of the Manager
- Practice Session and Action Plan

Participants

This program has been designed for all supervisors and managers whose units have asked Employee Training and Development to help design and implement a career development system.

Exec-U-Speak

Scope

This program has been designed to assist managers in preparing and presenting more effective verbal communications. An intensive two-day program, it focuses largely on development of individual skills and confidence through practice and evaluation sessions.

Content

- Self-Appraisal of Strengths and Weaknesses in Speech-Making
- Basic Concepts and Procedures
- Dealing with Nervousness and Apprehension
- Analyzing Your Audience
- Planning and Organizing the Presentation
- Effective Delivery—Overcoming the Barriers
- The Importance of Visual Aids
- Do's and Don'ts

Participants

Exec-U-Speak is offered to employees who have a desire to become more professional in making verbal presentations of all types.

Effective Writing Skills

Scope

Participants in this one and one-half day program have many opportunities for skill development, participation, and interaction. Improvement of business writing is the central focus, with emphasis on planning and organizing the message in a less formal style.

Content

- ▸ The Fog Index
- ▸ Sentences
- ▸ Words
- ▸ Grammar
- ▸ The Personal Touch
- ▸ Planning and Organizing
- ▸ Writing Workshop

Participants

It has been designed to assist all employees in developing and refining their writing skills.

Effective Writing Skills II

Scope

Effective Writing Skills II is a two-day workshop designed to help participants write more fluently and effectively. It includes practical techniques based on individual functions and needs. In this sense, the course is highly customized for each group of participants.

Content

- ▸ Effective Planning
- ▸ Producing Better Copy With the First Attempt
- ▸ Organizing Materials
- ▸ Shortening Overall Writing Time
- ▸ Avoiding Jargon, Clichés, Wordiness
- ▸ Subject Verb Agreement
- ▸ Detecting Surface Errors
- ▸ Formatting the Page
- ▸ Designing Reports and Proposals

Participants

For all exempt and nonexempt employees, it is recommended that enrollees be graduates of Effective Writing Skills.

Training and Development Philosophy

Instructional Methods

Lectures, question-and-answer discussions, case studies, small-team activities, role play, and other structured participative activities are used in all programs to ensure participant interaction and involvement. Programmed instruction techniques are also used. Many learning aids and handout materials are made available.

Most programs are conducted by Employee Training and Development instructors or by unit trainers who have been certified by our department.

The "Certified Trainer Process" is the hallmark of our department. Its purpose is to provide timely access for an increased number of employees to obtain quality delivery and content of selected programs. In addition to completing an extensive "training-the-trainer" curriculum, candidates for certified trainer status enroll in certified trainer workshops. In these workshops, they are assisted in achieving student-oriented learning results through colleague observation, co-train experiences, classroom feedback, and information sharing.

Application on the Job

The transfer of learning back on the job is of great importance to us as training people. And too often we blame circumstances within the work environment for the participants' inability to use their new knowledge or skills "back at the ranch."

In order to do this, the instructors are told to build into a training program at least two methods that will help initiate or reinforce in-class learning back on the job. Here are suggested approaches:

Before the Program

- Have participants evaluate program goals and objectives.
- Have participants clarify seminar expectations with their supervisor.
- Tie program objectives to on-the-job management objectives.
- Focus on back-home problems and individual motivation.
- Have participants spend some time doing necessary background reading and other prework.
- Have top management kick off the program or attend key sessions.
- Have a preseminar meeting of participants' bosses to help explain program content and their role in the training process.
- Make programs consistent for vertical cross-sections of management.

During the Program

- Have participants frequently answer the questions, "What have I learned?" and "How will I use it?"
- Have participants identify and deal with problems or obstacles to on-the-job application.
- Design modules such that instructors must move consistently and hold participants accountable for their activities.
- Get participants to grade their involvement and contribution each day.
- Provide retention aids as back-home reminders.

After the Program

- Have each participant make an individual contract or action plan, and send each a copy of it later.

- Ask participants' supervisors to review their subordinates' action plans.
- Have participants send the seminar evaluations through their supervisor.
- Conduct follow-up interviews for review and evaluation, and include each participant's supervisor.
- Send out "reminder" mailings of reinforcing information on various program skills at short intervals after the program.
- Conduct a postseminar meeting of participants to discuss or test program skills application.

14

A Comprehensive In-House Program at St. Joseph's Hospital

St. Joseph's Hospital in Milwaukee has implemented a well-planned and comprehensive training and development program for supervisors and those recommended for supervision. It begins with Prevision, a program that provides an introduction to management for nonsupervisory employees who have been approved for the course by their boss. For those who are already supervisors, a Management Institute of numerous courses has been developed. Finally, as a refresher, one-hour classes are offered on various hospital and supervisory subjects.

ST. JOSEPH'S HOSPITAL, MILWAUKEE, WISCONSIN
GEORGE J. KOLEAS, MANAGER, HUMAN RESOURCES DEVELOPMENT

A coordinated training and development program has been implemented at St. Joseph's Hospital, Milwaukee, to fill the needs of staff at all levels of the organization. The following beliefs and practices are in keeping with our organization philosophy of Human Community Development:

Human: Respecting the sacredness of life and the dignity and worth of every person.
Community: Creating caring communities in which the needs are being met of those serving and those being served.
Development: Providing opportunities for personal and professional growth.

Mission Statement for the Department of Human Resources Development

To assure that there are educational opportunities internally and externally for the personal and professional growth and development of staff to assist them in the continuous improvement in the quality of patient care.

This mission is supported through a variety of training initiatives including the following:

- ▸ Prevision. This is an introduction to management. It contains basic concepts of management for nonsupervisory personnel who aspire to become supervisors.
- ▸ Management Institute. Provides ongoing educational opportunities for supervisors, managers, and other individuals with high potential. The objective of these programs is to provide insights into the science and art of management.
- ▸ The Continuing Education Program. Contains a wide variety of courses available to all employees to upgrade skills and advance their knowledge.
- ▸ Ad Hoc Training. This is designed and provided to meet specific needs identified by supervisors and managers in collaboration with the human resources development staff.

Prevision: Introduction to Management

Following are details on course titles and teaching staff:

- ▸ All classes are held on Mondays for five consecutive weeks.
- ▸ All classes will be held from 12:00–1:00 P.M. in Room M105.
- ▸ Class limit is 25.
- ▸ Must have manager/supervisory approval to be registered for the program.
- ▸ Must attend all five classes and pass a computer simulation which is due within three (3) weeks of completion of session.
- ▸ Functions as a prerequisite to the Management Institute.

Class Title	Instructor
Management Overview	Mary Poehls, human resources generalist/ training specialist
Planning, Organizing, and Staffing	Nancy Christensen, human resources generalist
Leadership and Motivation	Jeff Mehring, supervisor, safety/security
Communication	Katie Graceffa, human resources generalist

Class Title	Instructor
Controlling and Decision Making	Mary Poehls, human resources generalist/ training specialist

The Management Institute

  I. Orientation
    A. Mission
    B. Upgrade current management skills
    C. Mentor employees to fill management/supervisory roles
    D. Facilitate communication and understanding of roles between management and staff levels
  II. Requirements to Enter Program
    A. Completion of Prevision or waiver
    B. Permission and signature of current manager or supervisor
    C. Hired as a manager/supervisor with previous related education and/or experience
    D. Must attend mandatory orientation offered in June/January and Module 1, the Principles of Management, before being allowed to enroll in future modules
  III. The Management Institute Program
    A. Scheduled by fiscal year—July/June
    B. Twenty-two classes offered
    C. Approximately one and a half years to complete
    D. Eight National Continuing Education Credits
    E. Certificate in Management
    F. Must complete fifteen classes
      1. Thirteen required—noted by number only
      2. Five electives—noted by number and letters
    G. All classes held in Room M105
  IV. Module Design
    A. Typically three to four hours classroom training and one-hour presentation worth .4 or .5 continuing education units (CEU)
    B. Integrate theory to application on the job
    C. Class size twelve to fifteen participants; limit twenty-five
    D. Contents of courses
      1. Lecture
      2. Learning activities/discussions
      3. Action plans/assignments/tests
    E. Requirements to pass a module
      1. Attend all classes
        a. Automatically dropped if you miss first class
        b. If unable to attend a class, contact instructor either prior to start of class or within two days after the class
      2. Complete required assignments

Following are the course offerings in the Management Institute.

Course	CEUs Accredited	Instructor
Mandatory Orientation		Mary Poehls, training specialist
Introduction to the Principles of Management	.4	George Koleas, manager of training and human resources development
Organizing and Delegating	.4	George Koleas, manager of human resources development
Time Management	.4	Mary Moat, director of nursing/ medicine
Managing Employees With Special Problems	.5	Tom Vanden Heuvel, manager of employee assistance programs
Management Planning, Monitoring, and Evaluation	.5	Marjorie Wilbur, director of planning, WFSI-Milwaukee, and Kathleen Murray, business development manager
Selecting New Employees	.4	Sherri DuCharme, human resources generalist
Improving Your Listening Skills	.4	Marge Roth, supervisor of infection control
Managerial Communication Presentation Skills	.4	Mary Poehls, training specialist
Managing Financial Services	.5	Susan Pitta, controller
Decision Making: Problem Solving and Problem-Solving Tools	.5	George Koleas, manager of human resources development
The Future of Management: Participation and Team Building	.4	Mary Poehls, training specialist
The Human Resources Legal Environment in Health Care	.4	Bob Weiss, vice-president of human resources
Statistics	.5	Brian Kay, budget manager
Managing Conflict	.4	George Koleas, manager of human resources development
Establishing a Climate for Motivation	.4	Bob Weiss, vice-president of human resources
Managing Stress	.4	Mary Poehls, training specialist
Coaching, Counseling, and Appraising Employee Performance	.5	George Koleas, manager of human resources development

Course	CEUs Accredited	Instructor
Managing Change	.4	George Koleas, manager of human resources development
Managerial Communication: Writing Skills	.4	Rick Romano, director of public affairs
Discipline and Appeal Handling	.5	George Koleas, manager of human resources development
Using St. Joseph's Data for Decision Making	.4	Gene Markiewicz, director systems and data processing
Managing in a Multicultural Environment	.4	George Koleas, manager of human resources development

The Continuing Education Program

▸ All Continuing Education course offerings are one hour and are held on Thursdays, with the exception of Self-Paced Skill Development sessions, which are scheduled on Mondays, Tuesdays, and Thursdays from 1:30–2:30 P.M. or 3:30–4:30 P.M.
▸ Must have manager/supervisory approval for each class registered.
▸ Class limit is twenty-five.

Course	Instructor(s)
Self-Paced Skill Development: Practical Reading and Writing	Community and hospital employee volunteers
Change	George Koleas, manager of human resources development
Icebreakers: Gaining Your Audience's Attention	Mary Poehls, training specialist
Stress Management	Mary Poehls, training specialist
Personal and Career Development	George Koleas, manager, human resources development
Marketing Yourself: In Writing and in Person	Mary Poehls, training specialist
Franklin Time Management[a]	George Koleas, manager, human resources development
Coaching and Counseling	George Koleas, manager, human resources development
Guest Relations: Dealing With Difficult People	Don Green, director of safety and security
Franklin Time Management User Group[b]	George Koleas, manager, human resources development

Course	Instructor(s)
Franklin Time Management User Group[b]	George Koleas, manager, human resources development
Guest Relations: Telephone Courtesy and First Impressions Coordinator	Cathie Callen, media/guest relations
Developing Positive Assertiveness	Mary Poehls, training specialist
Developing Self-Esteem	Mary Poehls, training specialist
Deming's 14 Points	George Koleas, manager, human resources development
Team Development	George Koleas, manager, human resources development
Team Development Workshop[c]	George Koleas, manager, human resources development
Business Writing	Public affairs staff
Special Event Planning	Public affairs staff
Two-Way Communications	Mary Poehls, training specialist
Active Listening	George Koleas, manager, human resources development
PC Hardware and Disk Operating System	Joe Orlando, DP Electronics Tech, and Pam Bruening, decision support specialist
Microcomputer Applications	Pam Bruening, decision support specialist
St. Joseph's Computer Systems	Larry Noldan, software systems supervisor, and Joan Kurszewski, supervisor systems development
Constructive Criticism	George Koleas, manager, human resources development
Balancing Work and Family	Jeanne Faupl, sick bay coordinator
Constructive Feedback	George Koleas, manager, human resources development
Holding Effective Meetings	Mary Poehls, training specialist
Time Management	Mary Poehls, training specialist

[a]Requires five or more students enrolled—$90.00 materials cost. You must register six weeks prior to course in order to receive Franklin Planner. Alternative dates may be scheduled.
[b]Must have completed Franklin Time Management Group.
[c]Must have completed Team Development course.

To ensure that needs are being met, we conduct an annual Employee Climate Survey and periodic needs assessments. The purpose of these surveys is to ensure that programs are being provided that fulfill the organizational philosophy as well as the mission of the human resources department.

15

A Twelve-Day Certificate Program for Supervisors

Few organizations use a well-thought-out approach to supervisory training and development. Typically training professionals decide to put on a program because of a specific need or pressure from a chief executive who has heard about a program that another organization has offered—"Management by Objectives" or "Leadership" or "Diversity in the Work Force" or "Empowerment" or "Total Quality Improvement" or something else.

The Management Institute (MI) of the University of Wisconsin uses a different approach. In 1944, MI offered a program called "Human Relations for Foremen and Supervisors." Because of requests and research of the needs of supervisors, MI continually revised and added programs to cover all of the topics that supervisors need to be effective. This resulted in a twelve-day program of benefit to supervisors in all types and sizes of organizations. It is beneficial to new supervisors, as well as those who have been in supervision for many years but have never been taught how to be "managers" instead of "doers." Here is a description of this program.

MANAGEMENT INSTITUTE, UNIVERSITY OF WISCONSIN, MILWAUKEE
RONALD J. BULA, DIRECTOR, CENTER FOR HUMAN RESOURCES PROGRAMS, SANDRA L. WELLER, PROGRAM MANAGER, CENTER FOR HUMAN RESOURCES PROGRAMS, AND JOHN W. HANIN, PROGRAM ASSISTANT, CENTER FOR HUMAN RESOURCES PROGRAMS

Organizations have discovered that first-line supervisors are the key people in accomplishing maximum results. They influence not only how the job gets done but also the morale and culture of the organization. In addition to having a management perspective and the "right" attitude, they need up-to-date knowledge and skills in performing their jobs. They need to know how to work with people to get the job done. In most cases, they have been promoted from "doers" (and probably excellent ones!) to supervisors with little or no training on how the new job differs from the previous job. Because of the lack of understanding about their new roles and responsibilities, they frequently become frustrated and do not perform well. Organizations that invest in their supervisors have a real payoff. Not only will these supervisors learn the knowledge and skills needed to do their jobs, but they will also have a feeling of confidence, importance, and loyalty to upper-level management who have demonstrated their concern to help them be successful.

The supervisors are told that "management" is "a science and an art." The "science" of management is concepts, theory, principles, and techniques. This they will learn in the programs. The "art" of management is application back on the job. This they must keep constantly in mind so that the organization's investment pays off in improved performance.

Program Content

Twelve days of training are required to complete the certificate. The required aspects of the program can be met in two ways. Supervisors can attend two three-day programs or a one-week workshop. The remaining six days can be selected from a list of elective courses. This allows supervisors to focus on programs which meet their particular needs. Here are the details.

Required Courses

There are six days of required courses in units 1 (three days) and unit 2 (three days). Or units 1 and 2 can be combined in a week-long seminar, "The Total Supervisor."

Unit 1, Leading and Working With People
   The following subjects are covered in this three-day program.
   a. Making It in Management
       Supervisors look at the whole picture of what it means to be a successful supervisor and how it's different from being a worker. Learning what is required and why it's important gives the participants a wide-angle view of their expectations and performance.
          ‣ Dealing with responsibilities, roles, and pressures of managing
          ‣ Developing the management perspective
          ‣ Understanding, developing, and adopting your leadership style
   b. Growing Personally As an Ongoing Process
       It's not enough to attend a management seminar if development stops there. There has to be a challenge to keep growing. This session provides an incentive for supervisors to see how and where to keep improving. Each person completes a plan for personal development, including a step-by-step guide for future improvement in their performance.

- Introducing the elements of life/work planning
- Identifying personal and professional goals
- Developing a strategy for greater life and work satisfaction

c. Understanding and Getting Along With People on the Job
Employees are people with feelings, hopes, and fears. Supervisors who understand this are powerful assets to their organization. They manage employees as individuals, helping them overcome their weaknesses and develop their strengths.
- Identifying what supervisors should know about their people
- Getting to know them
- Learning the essentials of human relations
- Assessing yourself and your interpersonal style

d. Creating the Climate for High Motivation and Achievement
This session shows supervisors practical ways to provide leadership that creates a climate for high performance.
- Understanding the elements of effective job performance, rewards, and job satisfaction for employees
- Identifying what the supervisor can do to create a climate of high motivation
- Handling today's motivational problems and opportunities

e. Improving Your Communication Effectiveness
Knowing to whom to communicate, why, when, and how are as important as what's being communicated. In this session, supervisors have an opportunity to learn and practice effective communication—written, oral, and nonverbal.
- Clarifying the meaning of communication
- Identifying communication barriers
- Learning the requirements for effective communication
- Planning for effective communication
- Learning methods and techniques
- Getting feedback to verify understanding

f. Managing Change Without Anxiety
Change is an everyday fact of life, and so is the anxiety that goes with it. Planning and preparing to manage change is a critical management function. This session teaches managers how to obtain their employees' acceptance and support of change and contribute to its successful implementation.
- Understanding the supervisor's role in managing change
- Understanding why employees resist/resent change
- Understanding why employees accept/welcome change
- Understanding the three keys for managing change

Unit 2, Mastering Supervisory Skills
The following subjects are covered in this three-day program.

a. Solving Problems and Making Decisions
This key part of the supervisor's job is covered in depth with case histories,

group assignments, and practice sessions to build understanding and confidence. Supervisors learn specific techniques that improve their abilities as problem solvers and decision makers.

- ‣ Understanding systematic approaches to problem solving
- ‣ Defining problems and analyzing causes
- ‣ Generating, selecting, and weighing alternatives
- ‣ Implementing decisions
- ‣ Deciding when to use participative problem solving

b. Preventing and Handling Complaints and Grievances

Every organization, whether union or nonunion, faces problems that lead to complaints by employees and can turn into serious problems or grievances. Supervisors learn the important differences between complaints and grievances and how to recognize common sources and causes. They acquire practical concepts and skills for handling complaints so these situations don't get out of control.

- ‣ Defining gripes, complaints, and grievances
- ‣ Determining relationships and causes
- ‣ Understanding prevention versus cure
- ‣ Investigating complaints and grievances to arrive at an acceptable resolution

c. Maintaining Order and Discipline

Discipline is not a reaction to something bad that's already happened. It's a continuing process of recognizing, preparing for, and dealing with small situations that can develop into major problems. Once supervisors start thinking of discipline as problem prevention rather than punishment, they're more comfortable and adept at handling it in a consistent and fair manner.

- ‣ Developing an enlightened approach to discipline
- ‣ Establishing order through modeling: clarifying expectations and building rapport
- ‣ Communicating corrective actions and praise to produce the right results
- ‣ Handling major disciplinary problems

d. Orienting and Training Employees

The first few weeks on a new job can make or break an employee. Through good orientation (introducing employees to policies, procedures, and the organization) and effective training based on objectives, follow-through, and evaluation, supervisors hold the key to the new employee's success. Learning the systematic approaches that are presented in this session enables supervisors to perform their role effectively.

- ‣ Understanding why it is necessary to orient and train employees properly
- ‣ Understanding how employees learn
- ‣ Learning the principles of instruction
- ‣ Learning the four-step method for training
- ‣ Practicing the four-step method

Elective Courses

The second half of the certificate program, also lasting six days, is designed so that participants can structure their own learning experiences around the topics that most closely meet their needs. They can select programs that enhance or expand their supervisory skills.

Most of the supervisors who complete the twelve-day requirements attend units 3 and 4, each lasting three days, or "The Effective Manager," a week-long course that combines units 3 and 4.

Unit 3, Developing Administrative Skills
The following subjects are covered:

- ▸ Planning and Organizing
- ▸ Time Management
- ▸ Direction and Delegation
- ▸ Improving Performance through Appraisal and Coaching

Unit 4, Improving Communication Skills
The following subjects are covered:

- ▸ Interviewing Skills that Produce Results
- ▸ Managing Conflict
- ▸ Organizing Productive Teams
- ▸ Communication Barriers, Principles, and Approaches
- ▸ How to Conduct Productive Meetings
- ▸ How to Write Effectively

The following additional elective programs allow the participants to select topics that more closely meet their personal needs:

The Supervisor and the Union (two days)
Assertiveness Training (one day)
Negotiation Skills (one day)
Dealing With Difficult People (two days)

Instructors

The full-time faculty and ad hoc instructional staff not only have the educational background and teaching experiences needed to make programs top quality, but they also have a broad range of ongoing "real world" business experiences. They are or have been practitioners in their areas of expertise. It is a combination of theory, practical experience, and teaching skills that make the courses effective.

Methods and Techniques

The latest concepts, theories, principles, and techniques are presented and discussed in the programs. The instructors make the meetings interesting, enjoyable, and practical by using much group involvement. The most frequently used aids and techniques are videotapes, case studies, supervisory inventories, exercises, and buzz group assignments. The participants learn from each other, as well as from the instructors. Practice is included in many of the sessions.

Certificate

A paper certificate is awarded for each three-day program. A supervisor who completes the twelve-day requirement receives a wooden plaque for the office wall. A photograph is taken and sent to participants and their managers.

Evaluations

In every program the participants complete reaction sheets that ask for their evaluation, as well as comments and suggestions. The ratings are consistently in the "very good" to "excellent" range. These reaction sheets are carefully analyzed by the instructors to be sure they are meeting the needs of the participants. Probably the best measure of the effectiveness of the programs is that most participants return to complete the twelve-day certificate. In addition, their recommendations back at the office or plant result in additional people attending. Many organizations have sent all of their supervisors (and even their bosses) to the programs.

Summary

The Management Institute has gained a reputation for presenting high-quality programs that meet the needs of the supervisors who attend. During 1991, for example, 299 supervisors attended. Twenty-five percent of them came from states other than Wisconsin.

For detailed information on these programs, contact:

Management Institute, University of Wisconsin—Milwaukee
929 North 6th Street
Milwaukee, Wisconsin 53203
414/227-3220

16

Evaluation of a Training Program for Supervisors and Foremen at the Management Institute, University of Wisconsin

Chapter 8 described four stages for evaluating the effectiveness of training programs:

> ▸ *Reaction*. How well did the participants like the program (a measure of customer satisfaction)?
> ▸ *Learning*. What attitudes were changed, and what knowledge and skills were learned?
> ▸ *Behavior*. What changes in behavior took place as a result of attending the program?
> ▸ *Results*. What final results (increased production, reduced costs, improved quality, reduced turnover, increased return on investment, increased sales, reduced accidents) occurred because of attending the program?

Following is a case study of an evaluation of a program that was conducted numerous times by the Management Institute, University of Wisconsin. The purpose of the evaluation was to determine the amount of behavior change that took place when the participants returned to their jobs. In addition, an attempt was made to measure results.

In reading the case, note especially the research design, which can be adapted to any evaluation of this type.

MANAGEMENT INSTITUTE, UNIVERSITY OF WISCONSIN, MILWAUKEE
DONALD L. KIRKPATRICK, PROFESSOR EMERITUS

Since 1944, the Management Institute of the University of Wisconsin has presented three- to five-day institutes for foremen and supervisors. These programs have been attended by representatives of companies throughout the midwestern United States. Each program has been evaluated from the standpoint of the reaction of the participants. Consistently, the participants have been enthusiastic about the subjects, the leaders, and the benefits.

Evaluations have also been made of the learning of the participants. Pretests and posttests have been given to measure the amount of learning of the principles, facts, and approaches that have been taught. These evaluations revealed significant changes in knowledge and attitudes.

Following is a description of an evaluation project designed to measure changes in behavior that took place on the job as a result of participating in a supervisory training program.

The Program

The institute "Developing Supervisory Skills" was presented in Milwaukee, Wisconsin, on three consecutive Tuesdays and repeated for a different group on three consecutive Wednesdays. In attendance were fifty-seven lower-level management people from various management people from various organizations in southeastern Wisconsin.

The program featured six three-hour sessions covering the following topics:

1. Order Giving
2. Training Employees
3. Appraising Employee Performance
4. Preventing and Handling Grievances
5. Decision Making
6. Initiating Change

The leaders were staff members of the Management Institute, the University of Wisconsin.

Teaching methods included lecture, guided discussion, buzz groups, role playing, films, case studies, and other visual aids.

Research Design

A questionnaire was completed by each participant to obtain information on the participant, his company, and his relationship with his immediate supervisor. Specific information was obtained on:

1. *The participant.* His job, experience, education, age, why he is attending the program, what he hopes to learn.
2. *The company.* Size, type, climate for change.
3. *The participant's boss.* Years spent as boss, the climate he sets for change, his involvement in sending the man to the institute.

Interviews were conducted with each participant within two to three months following the institute. The interviews were conducted in the participant's company to obtain information regarding changes in behavior that had taken place on the job. In addition, interviews were conducted with the participant's immediate supervisor as another measure of changes in the participant's behavior.

The Group Being Evaluated

Complete information was obtained from forty-three of the fifty-seven participants in the institute. Only these forty-three are included in the research results. The following data describe the forty-three participants and their organizations. The information was obtained from the questionnaire they completed at the start of the institute.

Organizations of Participants

1. Size
   - **4**   0–100 employees
   - **3**   500–1,000 employees
   - **10**   100–500 employees
   - **26**   More than 1,000 employees
2. Products
   - **15**   Consumer use
   - **11**   Industrial use
   - **12**   Both
   - **5**   Other
3. How would you classify top management?
   - **31**   Liberal (encourages change; invites and responds to suggestions)
   - **3**   Conservative (discourages change)
   - **9**   Middle-of-the-road
4. How would you classify your boss?
   - **35**   Liberal
   - **0**   Conservative
   - **8**   Middle-of-the-road
5. How often does your boss ask you for ideas to solve departmental problems?
   - **19**   Frequently
   - **19**   Sometimes
   - **5**   Hardly ever

6. To what extent will your boss encourage you to apply the ideas and techniques you learn in this program?
- **14** To a large extent
- **14** To some extent
- **1** Very little
- **14** Not sure

Participants

1. Title
- **33** Foreman or supervisor
- **8** General foreman or superintendent
- **2** Other

2. Education
- **12** Less than high school
- **21** High school
- **10** More than high school

3. Previous attendance at University of Wisconsin institutes
- **38** None
- **2** One
- **1** Two
- **1** Three
- **0** Four
- **1** Five

4. Before attending this institute, how much were you told about it?
- **3** Complete information
- **8** Quite a lot
- **20** A little
- **12** None

5. Attendance at in-plant training programs?
- **28** Yes
- **15** No

6. How many people supervise?
- **1** 0–5
- **9** 6–10
- **6** 11–15
- **8** 16–20
- **19** More than 20

7. Whom do you supervise?
- **26** All men
- **11** Mostly men
- **6** Mostly women
- **0** All women

8. What kind of workers do you supervise?
   14   Production (nonskilled)
   13   Production (semiskilled)
   11   Production (skilled)
   2   Maintenance
   9   Office
   4   Other

9. To what extent do you feel that you will be able to improve your supervisory performance by attending this program?
   21   To a large extent
   22   To some extent
   0   Very little

Research Results

The purpose of the research was to evaluate changes in on-the-job behavior that resulted from attendance at the institute. It was felt that information from both the participant and his immediate supervisor would contribute to the research. A comparison of responses from participants with those of their supervisors was also considered part of the research—in other words, how much agreement on changes in behavior was observed by the immediate supervisor in comparison with the changes in behavior expressed by the participant himself.

The results were described below in two categories: "A"—those relating to overall behavior—and "B"—those relating to each of the six subjects covered in the institute.

The following figures given are percentages. Wherever two figures are given, the first figure is the percent of the response from participants, and the second figure is the percent of response from the participants' immediate supervisors.

Overall Changes in Behavior and Results

1. To what extent has the program improved the participant's working relationship with his boss?
To a large extent 23 – 12
To some extent 51 – 32
No change 26 – 56
Made it worse 0 – 0

2. Since the program, how much two-way communication has taken place between the participant and his subordinates?
Much more 12 – 5
Somewhat more 63 – 46
No change 25 – 44
Somewhat less 0 – 0
Much less 0 – 0
Don't know 0 – 5

3. Since the program, is the participant taking a more active interest in employees?

Much more 26 — 5
Somewhat more 67 — 49
No change 7 — 44
Somewhat less 0 — 0
Much less 0 — 0
Don't know 0 — 2

4. On an overall basis, to what extent has the participant's job behavior changed *since* the program (Figure 16-1)?

5. In regard to the following results, what changes have been noticed *since* the participant's attendance in the program (Figure 16-2)?

The responses to these five questions indicate that the program improved relationships between the participant and his boss, as well as those between participants and subordinates. In nearly all instances, the participant indicated more of a positive change than his supervisor did. In questions 1 and 2, for example, approximately 75 percent of the participants indicated a positive change, while 51 percent of their supervisors indicated a positive change.

In question 3, there is a large difference of opinion (93 percent of the participants expressed a positive change while 54 percent of their supervisors noticed such a change).

In question 4, all nine of the items revealed a positive change on the part of more than 50 percent of the participants as expressed by participants as well as their supervisors. The most significant changes were expressed in "order giving," "decision making," and the attitude of the participant toward his job.

Question 5 shows less positive change than was revealed in questions 1–4.

Figure 16-1. Changes in participants' job behavior.

Supervisory Areas	Much Better	Somewhat Better	No Change	Somewhat Worse	Much Worse	Don't Know
a. Order giving	25–12	70–65	5–14	0–0	0–0	0– 9
b. Training	22–17	56–39	22–39	0–0	0–0	0– 5
c. Decision making	35–14	58–58	7–23	0–0	0–0	0– 5
d. Initiating change	21– 9	53–53	26–30	0–0	0–0	0– 7
e. Appraising employee performance	21– 7	50–42	28–36	0–0	0–0	0–12
f. Preventing and handling grievances	12– 7	42–40	46–46	0–0	0–0	0– 7
g. Attitude toward job	37–23	37–53	26–23	0–0	0–0	0– 0
h. Attitude toward subordinates	40– 7	42–60	19–30	0–0	0–0	0– 2
i. Attitude toward management	42–26	26–35	32–37	0–0	0–0	0– 2

Figure 16-2. Other changes noted in participants' behavior.

Performance Benchmarks	Much Better	Somewhat Better	No Change	Somewhat Worse	Much Worse	Don't Know
a. Quantity of production	5– 5	43–38	50–50	0–2	0–0	0–5
b. Quality of production	10– 7	60–38	28–52	0–0	0–0	0–2
c. Safety	21– 7	28–37	49–56	0–0	0–0	0–0
d. Housekeeping	23–14	32–35	42–46	0–5	0–0	0–0
e. Employee attitudes and morale	12– 7	56–53	28–32	2–5	0–0	0–2
f. Employee attendance	7– 2	23–19	67–77	0–0	0–0	0–0
g. Employee promptness	7– 2	32–16	58–81	0–0	0–0	0–0
h. Employee turnover	5– 0	14–16	79–79	0–5	0–0	0–0

Employee attitudes and morale showed the highest positive change, while employee attendance, promptness, and turnover showed the least positive changes.

Changes in Behavior Relating to Each Subject

The responses to the questions on "order giving" (Figure 16-3) reveal a high degree of positive change, particularly as expressed by participants. These changes cover all aspects of the order-giving process.

As many as 28 percent of the participants' supervisors answered "don't know" to items dealing with the participant and his dealings with subordinates.

It is interesting to note that approximately 90 percent of the supervisors are personally involved in training their new and transferred employees (questions b and c in Figure 16-4). Sixty percent train the workers "usually" or "always." The situation did not change as a result of the program.

Questions d through i indicate that the participant is putting more effort and time to see that the training is done more effectively. Question a shows that these efforts are paying off in terms of better-trained employees.

According to question a in Figure 16-5, approximately two-thirds of the participants conduct formal appraisals with subordinates. As a result of the institute, the greatest positive change occurred in the participants' efforts to determine employees' goals and objectives. Also, the participants are praising employees more, as well as placing more emphasis on future performance.

Sixty-nine percent of the participants supervise unionized employees. Questions b and c in Figure 16-6 show very little change in terms of the participants' role in settling grievances. Question e shows considerable change in favor of management's viewpoint regarding grievances and complaints.

The responses to f show very little change in the number of complaints, but g shows some tendency for the grievances to be less serious.

Probably the most significant behavior change appears to have occurred in the participants' success in satisfying complaints before they became formal grievances (question h). This was one of the major objectives of the session on "preventing and handling grievances."

Figure 16-3. Changes in participants' order giving.

Order Giving	Much More	Somewhat More	No Change	Somewhat Less	Much Less	Don't Know
a. *Since* the program, is the participant taking more time to plan his orders?	17—23	58—60	16—12	7—0	0—0	X— 5
b. *Since* the program, is the participant taking more time to prepare the order receiver?	24—17	71—57	5—19	0—0	0—0	X— 7
c. *Since* the program, is the participant getting more *voluntary cooperation* from his employees?	26— 0	37—56	37—23	0—0	0—0	X—21
d. *Since* the program, is the participant doing more in the way of making sure the order receiver understands the order?	51—21	44—44	5— 7	0—0	0—0	X—28
e. *Since* the program, is the participant taking more time to make sure the order receiver is following instructions?	21—16	60—58	19—12	0—0	0—0	X—14
f. *Since* the program, is the participant making more of an effort to praise his employees for a job well done?	24— X	50— X	26— X	0—X	0—X	X— X
g. *Since* the program, is the participant doing more follow-up to see that his orders were properly carried out?	37—21	39—42	23—26	0—0	0—0	X—12

Note: An *X* means the question was not asked.

Questions a and b in Figure 16-7 reveal that 88 percent of the participants are making better decisions as the participants see it and 80 percent as the participants' supervisors see it. According to the responses to question e, 40 percent of the participants are more involved in departmental decisions than they were prior to the institute. Question f indicates that most of the participants are getting their subordinates more involved in the decision-making process, also.

(text continues on page 259)

Figure 16-4. Changes in participants' involvement in training new employees.

Training Employees	Yes	No	Not Sure
a. *Since* the participant attended the program, are his new or transferred employees better trained?	63—46	9—0	23—43
	No new or transferred employees: 6—11		

Training Method	Participant Always	Participant Usually	Participant Sometimes	Participant Never
b. *Before* the program, who trained the workers?	16—13	42—45	34—31	8—11
c. *Since* the program, who trained the workers?	15—18	45—42	32—29	8—11

Progress in Training Effectiveness	Does Not Apply	Much More	Somewhat More	No Change	Somewhat Less	Much Less	Don't Know
d. *Since* the program, if someone else trains the employees, has the participant become more observant and taken a more active interest in the training process?	14—11	22—16	40—27	24—30	0—0	0—0	X—16
e. *Since* the program, if the participant trains the employees, is he making more of an effort in seeing that the employees are well trained?	8—5	42—24	42—42	8—18	0—0	0—0	X—11
f. *Since* the program, is the participant more inclined to be patient while training?	8—11	24—5	47—50	21—20	0—3	0—0	X—11
g. *Since* the program, while teaching an operation, is the participant asking for more questions to ensure understanding?	8—21	27—14	46—46	19—8	0—0	0—0	X—11
h. *Since* the program, is the participant better prepared to teach?	8—11	29—18	47—52	16—8	0—0	0—0	X—11
i. *Since* the program, is the participant doing more follow-up to check the trainees' progress?	0—0	41—21	38—49	21—14	0—0	0—0	X—16

Note: An X means the question was not asked.

Figure 16-5. Changes in participants' appraisal of employee performance.

Appraising Employee Performance					
a. Is the participant required to complete appraisal forms on his subordinates? Yes: 62—69 No.: 38—31					

	Does Not Apply	Large Extent	Some Extent	Little	Don't Know
b. *Before* the program, if the participant conducted appraisal interviews, to what extent did he emphasize past performance?	48—40	10— 5	40—12	2—14	X—29
c. *Before* the program, to what extent did the participant try to determine the goals and objectives of his employees?	0— 0	5—15	65—52	30—30	X— 3
d. *Before* the program, to what extent did the participant praise the work of his employees?	0— 0	8—12	77—52	15—18	X—18

	Does Not Apply	Much More	Somewhat More	No Change	Somewhat Less	Much Less	Don't Know
e. *Since* the program, is the participant doing more follow-up to see that the objectives of the appraisal interview are being carried out?	48—40	10— 5	24—21	14—19	2—0	0—0	X—14
f. *Since* the program, during an appraisal interview, is the participant placing more emphasis on future performance?	48—40	24— 7	17—10	10—14	0—2	0—0	X—26
g. *Since* the program, is the participant making more of an effort to determine the goals and objectives of his employees?	0— 0	22—15	60—50	18—18	0—0	0—0	X—18
h. *Since* the program, how much does the participant praise his employees?	0— 0	22—10	40—38	38—38	0—2	0—0	X—12

Note: An X means the question was not asked.

Figure 16-6. Changes in participants' handling of grievances.

Preventing and Handling Grievances				
a. Do participant's employees belong to a union?	Yes: 69—69		No: 31—31	
	Participant Always	*Participant Usually*	*Participant Sometimes*	*Participant Never*
b. *Before* the program, if an employee had a grievance, who usually settled it?	10—12	64—38	24—43	2—5
c. *Since* the program, who usually settles employee grievances?	10—12	69—48	21—38	0—2
d. *Before* the program, to what extent did the participant defend management versus the employees in regard to grievance problems?	Always defended management: 34—17 Usually defended management: 22—39 Acted objectively in view of the facts: 44—20 Usually defended the employees: 0—10 Always defended the employees: 0—0 Don't know: 0—15			

	Much More	*Somewhat More*	*No Change*	*Somewhat Less*	*Much Less*	*No Union*	*Don't Know*
e. *Since* the program is the participant more inclined to the management viewpoint regarding grievances and complaints?	19—14	31—29	48—48	10— 5	0—0		X—9
f. *Since* the program, has there been a change in the number of grievances in the participants' department?	2— 5	7—14	81—71	2— 0	0—0		X—5
g. *Since* the program, has the degree of seriousness of grievances changed?	0— 0	2— 2	74—74	24—12	0—7		X—5
h. *Since* the program, has the participant been better able to satisfy employee complaints before they reach the grievance stage?	17— 7	31—52	26—24	0— 0	0—2	26—14	

Note: An *X* means the question was not asked.

Figure 16-7. Changes in participants' decision making.

Decision Making			
a. *Since* the program, is the participant making better decisions? (Participants only)	Yes: 88	No: 2	Don't Know: 10

b. *Since* the program, is the participant making better decisions? (Supervisors only)	Much better—12 Somewhat better—68 No change—10		Somewhat worse—0 Much worse—0 Don't know—10

	Frequently	Sometimes	Hardly Ever	Don't Know
c. *Before* the program, how often did the participant's boss involve or consult him or her in the decision-making process in the participant's department?	40—65	45—30	15— 5	
d. *Before* the program, to what extent did the participant involve or consult employees in the decision-making process?	24—26	57—38	19—24	X—10

	Much More	Somewhat More	No Change	Somewhat Less	Much Less	Don't Know
e. *Since* the program, how often does the participant's boss involve him or her in the departmental decision-making process?	13—23	25—17	60—55	3— 3	0— 3	X— 0
f. *Since* the program, how often does the participant involve employees in the decision-making process?	26— 0	38—43	33—33	3— 7	0— 3	X—14
g. *Since* the program, does the participant have less tendency to put off making decisions?	0— 0	0— 0	36—33	36—40	28—22	X— 5
h. *Since* the program, is the participant holding more group meetings with employees?	12— 5	26—17	62—55	0— 0	0— 0	X—24
i. *Since* the program, does the participant have more confidence in the decisions he makes?	29—19	60—60	12—21	0— 0	0— 0	X— 0
j. *Since* the program, is the participant using a more planned approach to decision making (more time to define the problem and develop an answer)?	40—14	50—71	10— 7	0— 0	0— 0	X— 7
k. *Since* the program, does the participant take more time to evaluate the results of a decision?	24— 3	60—62	14—12	3— 0	0— 0	X—24

Note: An X means the question was not asked.

Each of the other questions on decision making also indicates that most of the participants are applying the principles and approaches that were recommended in the institute.

Questions a and b in Figure 16-8 reveal the situation prior to the program. There is a general agreement between participants and supervisors that approximately 85 percent of the participants "sometimes" or "frequently" asked subordinates for suggestions and informed them of change and the reasons for it.

Likewise, there is agreement that a large majority of the participants are doing more of the following:

1. Follow-up on change (77%–88%)

Figure 16-8. Changes in participants' initiation of change on the job.

Initiating Change	
a. *Before* the program, when the need for change arose, how often did the participant ask his subordinate for suggestions or ideas regarding the change or need for change?	Frequently: 21–21 Sometimes: 64–52 Hardly ever: 14–21
b. *Before* the program, how often did the participant inform his or her employees of the change and the reason for it?	Frequently: 50–26 Sometimes: 36–55 Hardly ever: 14–14

	Much More	Somewhat More	No Change	Somewhat Less	Much Less	Don't Know
c. *Since* the program, is the participant doing more follow-up to the change process to make sure it is going in the right direction?	38–17	50–60	12–12	0–0	0–0	X–12
d. *Since* the program, how often has the participant involved his or her subordinates by asking them for suggestions or ideas?	17– 2	43–40	40–38	0–7	0–0	X–12
e. *Since* the program, is the participant doing more in the way of informing employees of impending change and the reasons for it?	33–10	38–45	29–26	0–2	0–0	X–17

Note: An X means the question was not asked.

2. Asking for ideas (42%–60%)
3. Informing subordinates of changes and reasons (55%–71%)

All of these behavior changes were in line with the objectives of the institute.

Summary and Conclusions

The reactions to the institute on "Developing Supervisory Skills" were highly favorable. A tabulation of reaction sheets revealed the following (figures are in percentages):

Immediate Reaction to Institute by Participants		*Reaction to Institute as Measured Two Months Later*	
53	Excellent	**29**	Excellent
47	Very good	**71**	Very good
0	Good	**0**	Good
0	Fair	**0**	Fair
0	Poor	**0**	Poor

The purpose of the research project was to measure changes in behavior that took place on the job because of attendance at the institute. Personal interviews were held with participants as well as with their immediate supervisors. Each participant knew that his boss was also going to be interviewed concerning changes in behavior.

Of the original fifty-seven participants in the institutes (two sections with twenty-eight in one section and twenty-nine in the other), forty-three pairs of data (from the participant and boss) were complete and are included in the research report.

The research data indicate that positive changes in behavior had taken place in nearly all phases of the job that were related to the subject content of the institute. These changes were revealed by participants as well as by their supervisors. The participants tended to indicate slightly more positive changes than did their supervisors.

In addition to the positive changes in behavior, the research also indicates significant positive results in terms of quantity and quality of production, safety, housekeeping, and employee attitudes and morale. Some positive results were indicated in the reduction of employee absenteeism, tardiness, and turnover.

The "Developing Supervisory Skills" institute that was researched is presented on a regular basis by the Management Institute. Although modification and updating are made on a continuous basis, the subject content, instructors, teaching approaches, and teaching aids are similar. Also, the profile of each participant is very much the same as those in the group studied in this research.

Although the results of this research cannot be directly applied to future "Developing Supervisory Skills" institutes, one can conclude that this kind of institute is probably resulting in favorable on-the-job behavior of the participants. This research, in fact, bears out the numerous unsolicited comments by participants and higher-level management that positive behavior changes have taken place. The high number of repeat enrollments from participating organizations indicates the same conclusion.

17

General Electric Medical Systems' Front-Line Leadership Development Program

One organization that has consistently been a leader in the training and development field is General Electric. Following is a case study describing how the Medical Systems Division of GE developed a dynamic leadership development program for its supervisors and mid-managers. (This program was recognized by the American Society of Training and Development in 1991 as a National Award Winner for Management Development.)

GE MEDICAL SYSTEMS, MILWAUKEE, WISCONSIN
KEVIN WILDE, HUMAN RESOURCES MANAGER

According to Kevin Wilde, the overall leader of this training effort, the primary objective was to improve the performance of GE's supervisors—their front-line leaders—to meet the increasing demands of the new work environment. These key challenges included:

- ▸ Greater complexity in manufacturing process and standards
- ▸ Higher emphasis on quality, cost, and cycle time
- ▸ Expanding employee involvement and empowerment

To meet these challenges, a comprehensive training and development plan was created (see Figure 17-1). "Our work was guided by a number of key principles," said Wilde. "First, *involvement*: We were constantly looking for ways to involve people in the creation of the program. Through the use of steering committees, task forces, training, and presentation opportunities, we involved supervisors, manufac-

Figure 17-1. General Electric's Front-Line Leadership Program development steps (1989–1990).

Overall Objective: Improve performance of GEMS supervisors by executing a series of programs impacting three key domains:

Supervisors

Objective: To improve business knowledge (how-to's) and interpersonal leadership skills.

⑥ **Leadership Effectiveness Survey (11/90)**
To reassess leadership skills through performance feedback from employees and peers, creating new self-development plans.

⑤ **Business Modality Understanding Course (5/10/90)**
To improve understanding of modality marketplace, customers, business strategy, and manufacturing operation.

④ **Performance Management Course (3/90 – 4/90)**
To improve understanding of disciplinary practices and interpersonal skills in tough one-on-one situations such as substance abuse and sexual harassment.

③ **Finanacial Understanding Course (10/90)**
To improve understanding of business operations/ measurements and grow ownership for business strategy and changes.

② **Coaching Clinic (11/89 – 2/90)**
To assess baseline of leadership skills and areas for personal development.

① **Leadership Skills Model Guide (9/89)**
To commmunicate new performance expectations.

Shop Managers

Objective: To improve coaching skills and role modeling.

⑤ **Leadership Effectiveness Survey (11/90)**
To assess manager leadership skills through performance feedback from supervisors and peers.

④ **Leadership Instructors Certification (2/90)**
To certify a select group of managers in the Zenger-Miller Frontline Leadership Program to instruct and provide positive role models.

③ **Coaching Workshop (2/90)**
To improve coaching skills, including setting performance expectations, encouraging development, and recognizing positive results.

② **Coaching Clinic Assessors (10/89 – 2/90)**
Improve coaching skills of performance assessment and feedback.

① **Leadership Skills Model Development (9/89)**
For coaching baseline.

Performance Environment

Objective: To improve the system and processes that impact supervisory leadership performance.

⑤ **Problem-Solving Task Force (1990)**
To involve supervisors in solving system issues affecting performance, including:
•Communication processes
•Recognition and Career Advancement

④ **In-Plant Learning Library (11/90)**
To establish four in-plant leadership learning libraries, including workbooks and video tapes from the Finance, Performance Management, and Business Modality courses.

③ **New Supervisor Assimilation (7/90)**
To provide a disciplined process for bringing new supervisors up to speed quickly on leadership and performance expectations.

② **Talent Upgrade**
To reassign or outplace poor performing supervisors not able to adjust to the new environment and replace them withpromising talent better equipped for the challenges.

① **Leadership Skills Model Application (Ongoing)**
•For new supervisor selection
•For performance appraisals

turing management, human resources, and support-staff personnel. The training was accomplished *with* the supervisors and not *at* them.

"Second, it was *strategic*: Before we began any training, we had a hard look at what we expected from supervisors and what the workplace of the future would demand. A skills model was created that served as a foundation and guide for all training and development.

"Third, it was *comprehensive*: A series of training programs were directly aimed at the supervisors over a two-year period. In addition, we worked to develop the support system around the supervisor, including a coaching workshop for their managers, a learning resource library in each plant, and a talent upgrade effort.

"Finally, it entailed *self-responsibility*: Once the leadership model was created, we chose to use an assessment center approach to test the current supervisors' skills. Each supervisor experienced a two-day workship where, on the first day, they were challenged by a variety of problems and situations that would show how well they would measure up to the new leadership model. On the second day, they received feedback on their performance and were guided through a process where they established a self-development plan. They were asked to review these plans with their manager and establish one-on-one coaching sessions to support their ongoing development. This assessment process, called the Coaching Clinic, was a great success and provided the needed positive momentum for the training that followed."

Target Audience

The target audience was divided into two groups: primary audience and secondary audience.

Primary audience: GE Medical Systems (GEMS) manufacturing supervisors (sixty), plus service supervisors (twelve) for some portions of the training. Overall, 58 percent hold college degrees, 70 percent have more than five years of company service, and 60 percent have two or more years on the job. This population can be classified as follows:

- ▸ *Eager learners:* Forty percent of the supervisors—generally hold technical degrees, have less than two years on the job, and less than five years with the company.

    These supervisors are eager to learn, will be very supportive of the program. Their skills and aggressiveness will help motivate the other supervisors to improve.
- ▸ *Experienced skeptics:* Sixty percent of the supervisors—generally do not hold four-year college degrees, have more than ten years with the company, and five years as a supervisor.

    These supervisors will be cautious about training and will need motivation to develop. (The assessment center will be aimed primarily for these people.) They must be involved in the development of course work to build ownership and relevance.

Secondary audience: Twenty manufacturing and service shop managers—the managers of the supervisors. Their backgrounds are diverse, but less than half have held the position of shop supervisor. Based on the initial data gathering and analysis of the performance appraisals they give supervisors, they are weak in setting performance expectations and coaching skills.

This group will need to be involved in the design and delivery of training, as well as to receive training relevant to their jobs.

Front-Line Leadership Program

The various steps in the program are listed under two categories: "Developmental Event" and "Rationale and Results." The eleven sections consist of the following:

Developmental Event	*Rationale and Results*
1. Initial data gathering, July 1989	
Interviews with manufacturing managers, shop managers, key employee relations managers, and a cross-section of supervisors	Objective To determine leadership expectations and the current state of leadership training
Collection and analysis of supervisor performance appraisals	Findings Little leadership training for past five years Performance expectations higher than current level of performance Appraisals were too general—did not focus on leadership behaviors
2. Leadership Skills model, September 1989	
Shop managers create a seven-dimension leadership skills model	Objective To create ownership and involvement and begin communicating clear leadership standards for the 1990s
An all-supervisors meeting is held to gather their inputs and communicate the higher performance expectations	
	Results Leadership skills model created, and serves as a basis for all future course work, appraisals, and new supervisor selection

Developmental Event	*Rationale and Results*
3. Finance course, October 1989 A business course is taught, covering: —business economic concepts —GE Company financial measurements —GEMS measurements and concepts —manufacturing measurements and the role of the supervisor	**Objective** To build financial understanding and business ownership in the supervisory ranks (weakness indicated from step 1 assessment interviews) **Results** A five-week, twelve-hour course for all supervisors taught by GEMS financial managers, with follow-up meetings between plant supervisors and financial analysts; many supervisors also presented their learnings to their employees
4. Coaching Clinic, November 1989–February 1990 A skills assessment center is offered, involving: —one-on-one coaching situations —group problem-solving settings —performance feedback from assessors —a personal leadership development plan	**Objectives** To motivate supervisors to increase their leadership skills through intensive feedback and a specific developmental action plan To identify the collective training needs of the supervisors, per the leadership skills model To increase the coaching skills of shop managers **Results** Seventy-one supervisors participated in eight coaching clinics. They received performance feedback from the assessors (shop managers) and created personal development plans. Further, the supervisors shared their plans with their managers and agreed to action items. Prior to the clinics, twenty shop managers received eight hours of training in performance judgment and constructive feedback (the skills of coaching).

Developmental Event   *Rationale and Results*

The overall results of the clinic indicated that supervisors needed the
most help in group leadership situations and presentation skills.

5. Coaching Skills training, February 1990

A coaching skills course is taught, offering:
—recognizing positive results
—giving constructive feedback
—supporting and helping others learn

Objective

To increase the coaching skills of
shop managers and ensure the training of supervisors is supported

Results

Two eight-hour workshops are held
for a total of twenty shop managers.
The managers are enthusiastic about
upcoming training.

6. Leadership Instructor certification, February 1990

A four-day instructor certification program is held for the front-line leadership program.

Objective

To develop the internal capacity to
teach and model superior leadership
skills

Results

A select group of twelve shop managers, supervisors, and human resources managers are certified and
will teach leadership modules
throughout the program. In fact, the
group will also teach leadership
skills to lead technician and hourly
group leaders.

7. Performance Management course, March–April 1990

A leadership skills course is taught,
covering:
—performance expectation setting
—constructive feedback
—recognizing positive results
—GE work rules and practices
—appraisals and coaching

Objective

To increase supervisory skills in handling the most difficult one-on-one
situations and provide resources to
support confrontations with low per-
formers

Developmental Event	*Rationale and Results*
—employee assistance program (EAP) —substance abuse —sexual harassment	Results Seventy-two supervisors participated in the nine-week, thirty-six-hour program. A follow-up survey of supervisors and their managers reported that: —all supervisors cited personal growth in the nine key performance objectives (their managers concurred) —seventy specific situations were cited where course material was immediately applied, including EAP referrals, constructive feedback, and positive recognition.

8. Business/Modality course, May, October 1990

A modality-specific course, teaching: —product and market strategy —GE modality organization and business plan —manufacturing operation today —manufacturing values and vision	Objectives To increase supervisory knowledge and ownership of the business, the realities of competition, and the rationale behind business changes To encourage the continued transition of the supervisory role from foreman to coach by having the participants teach the material to their employees Results Sixty-two supervisors participated in business courses for their modality. The courses ran an average of four sessions and sixteen hours. Strong personal improvement was cited in each of the five key course objectives, with over 70 percent of the supervisors teaching the material to their employees.

9. Leadership talent upgrade, ongoing

An effort to upgrade the supervisory talent pool, staffing the organization	Objective To replace low-performing supervi-

Developmental Event	*Rationale and Results*
with new technical supervisors who have promising leadership skills	sors with talented new supervisors more able to meet the leadership challenges of the 1990s

Results

Higher performance standards were instituted based on the leadership skills model and potential actions tracked through the 1990 manpower review process.

10. New supervisor assimilation, November 1990

A series of leadership tools are established to improve supervisory performance, including: —an assimilation process —performance management training —in-plant learning library	Objectives To bring new supervisors quickly up to speed in critical leadership and performance areas To provide senior supervisors new growth opportunities

Results

A detailed new supervisor training package has been established covering thirty-three learning areas, such as safety procedures, key disciplinary practices, and performance recognition. The program is overseen by the immediate manager, and a senior supervisor provides a mentoring role.

An in-plant learning library has been established for new and current supervisors. Workbooks and videos are stocked for such programs as:
—Performance Management course
—Finance course
—Modality/Business course

11. Leadership Effectiveness Survey, November 1990

A leadership survey is given to employees and peers of GEMS manufacturing supervisors.	Objective To provide a new level of performance feedback to supervisors that will serve as a basis for a new per-

Developmental Event	*Rationale and Results*
	sonal development plan and an indication of collective training needs.
	Results
	The survey results showed significant improvement in a number of areas, including: —Leadership —Communication —Team work

Follow-Up Procedures

Throughout the Front-Line Leadership Program, a variety of feedback tools were used to assess progress and identify needed follow-up actions. Follow-up procedures included:

- ▸ Participant feedback survey at the end of each course. The survey asked supervisors to rate their skill and knowledge against specific course objectives before and after the course.
- ▸ Application situations—participants were asked to cite specific cases where they applied course material on the job. The reports from the Performance Management and the Business/Modality courses report numerous examples of applications.
- ▸ Shop manager feedback surveys six weeks after the Performance Management course was used to verify the gains reported by the supervisors and the situation applications.
- ▸ Leadership Effectiveness Survey in November 1990 indicated that the supervisors received positive reviews from their employees and peers. Specifically, the collective results reported scores of 80 percent or more on the following dimensions:
  - —Organizational relationships
  - —Decision making
  - —Concern for customers
  - —Communication
  - —Personal accountability
  - —Employee empowerment
- ▸ Periodic interviews, phone calls, and opinion surveys were used to judge supervisory reaction to program activities.

Results

"As the program unfolded, we tried to capture supervisory performance data to determine whether we were meeting our objectives and any mid-course corrections necessary," said Wilde. "Assessing bottom-line impact of leadership development and training as an isolated variable is difficult. For example, during the last twelve months, employee unpaid absenteeism has been reduced from 3.2 percent to 2.7 percent—a 15 percent improvement, saving $220,000 in labor costs. One could attribute the improvement to the training supervisors received through the Coaching Clinic and the Performance Management class. However, the decrease can also stem from a drop in product volume and overtime from one major plant. In another example, productivity in one of the plants increased from 60 percent to 82 percent. It is hard to separate the impact of improved leadership skills from productivity gains due to new products, procedures, and volume gains.

"A more useful view of the results from the Front-Line Leadership Program is to look for impact indicators":

Finance course. Over 75 percent of the supervisors cited significant knowledge gains in the following key concepts: ROI/ROS, income statement and balance sheet, GE growth strategy, GE Medical Systems productivity programs, and globalization programs. A sample reaction:

"I have a greater ability to communicate to my direct reports and peers. I am able to relate to the financial measurements and how my unit performance will influence these measurements."

Coaching Clinic. Over 95 percent of the supervisors voluntarily met with their managers after the clinic and created a leadership development plan. Eighty-six percent of the participants reported that the Coaching Clinic exercises enabled them to demonstrate their leadership skills and received useful feedback. Sample reactions:

"The program was a challenge. Overall, it was useful and a good starting place to initiate one's personal development plan."

"It was good. I learned something about myself and how to improve."

"This is one of the best programs I have ever gone to. I learned something about myself that no one has even pointed out to me before."

Performance Management course. Supervisors reported a 39 percent gain in skill and knowledge in the nine key learning objectives. A separate survey of their managers concurs, citing a collective 49 percent skill and knowledge gain. Furthermore, documented application of course material on the job includes: constructive feedback (sixteen cases), setting performance expectations (sixteen, recognizing positive employee results (fifteen), and employee assistance program referrals (twelve). A sample reaction:

"I found every module very interesting and informative. I have referenced my [performance management] book several times when I've had situations arise when I need help."

Business and Product Understanding course. Supervisors reported a 42 percent gain in skill and knowledge in the ten key learning objectives. A sample reaction:

"I was asked questions by hourly employees on the sales and marketing aspects of the business. Through this course, I was able to explain and use segments of the [Business and Product Understanding course] manual to give my people a fair and concise answer to their questions."

Overall program survey. In October 1990, all supervisors were asked to reflect on their growth and learning over the past year. They attributed the largest portion of their skill increase due to the following:

- 40 percent Performance Management course
- Business and Product Understanding course
- 10 percent Coaching Clinic
- 6 percent Manager Coaching

Sample observations:

"The Front-Line Leadership courses and sessions have been very helpful in my development as a new supervisor."

"This training was overdue and well received. It exceeded previous training."

"I have learned to give empowerment to my employees."

"I have used the things from these classes with my employees and at home."

Final Comment

"GE Medical Systems has led an intensive campaign to increase the leadership performance of its front-line supervisors," observes Wilde "While we have been happy with the progress so far, making a significant, sustaining improvement in an organization's leadership capability is not achieved overnight. In the long run, real success will entail multiple efforts over a sustained period of time to upgrade the overall performance of a leadership team. We are pleased with our results so far, but we need to continue and do more."

18

A Management Skills Class at First Union National Bank of North Carolina

A comprehensive management training program was planned and implemented at First Union National Bank in Charlotte, North Carolina. The basic program, Management Directions, is followed by another called Manager as Developer and Executive Leadership.

FIRST UNION NATIONAL BANK OF NORTH CAROLINA, CHARLOTTE, NORTH CAROLINA
KATHRYN HEATH, VICE-PRESIDENT AND MANAGER OF MANAGEMENT AND LEADERSHIP DEVELOPMENT, HUMAN RESOURCES DIVISION

First Union's Management Directions course is the first in a series of three programs to help develop managers. Management Directions is a basic supervisory course providing skill-based training on key behaviors essential to being a successful manager. It is also a building block to our second program, Manager as Developer. The outcome of our second program is to help managers understand themselves as managers, learn how to develop a team, and learn how to coach their people. Our third course is Executive Leadership. The outcome of this course is to help managers increase their self-awareness, realize their impact upon their staff, become more strategic, and drive and lead change in our tumultuous environment.

First Union's Management Directions class is therefore a course to address and practice basic management skills. The course helps the participants learn information that will enable them to be successful managers at First Union. First Union's philosophy is that new managers and supervisors have a transition to make from their old roles as peers. Management Directions is to help people in their transitions into new roles and confront the challenges that are part of those roles.

Course Objectives

The Management Directions training program is designed to help participants develop and enhance the fundamental skills they will need to supervise a staff. During this training program the participant will learn:

1. Management skills essential to being an effective manager.
2. Policies and procedures critical to a manager's success at First Union.
3. Self-awareness through the use of an Image Study (anonymous survey from employees) and a management style survey, which provide important feedback for improving management performance.

Who Attends?

New supervisors and managers are nominated by their manager to be in the class. Anyone who is a new manager is put into the program. All new teller supervisors are also trained in a similar program that is slightly adapted to their specific roles. The class is made up of first-time supervisors, branch managers, and assistant branch managers. The course is voluntary and no one has to attend.

Policies

Policies from the *Supervisors' Handbook* are reviewed in a self-paced unit that participants do outside the class. They are reviewed in class through the use of case studies. It is First Union's belief that it is not helpful to lecture on these policies, but more helpful for people to work through them themselves.

Trainers

First Union's Training and Development Department is divided into three sections. One of the sections is Management and Leadership Development. The trainers in this area conduct the Management Directions training. All trainers have either banking experience or training experience. They have all been managers.

Quality Improvement to the Program

First Union redesigned the program to reflect a work/family dimension. We think it is important for managers to continue to be more sensitive to alternative work schedules and to the demands that a large percentage of our work force have with dual career families. We also include "negotiating" and "career counseling." Both topics have become increasingly important with the introduction of flexible work schedules and the flattening of the organizations' hierarchies.

Management Involvement

Before the program starts, a preworkshop skill assessment form (Figure 18-1) is answered. After the program, a mailing is done to the managers to summarize the course and ask them please to follow up with their employees. First Union's belief is that no real behavioral change will occur unless the participant's manager is involved. We can provide an entertaining, challenging training program, but if it is not followed up and reinforced in the work plan, it is a wasted four days.

Following is an outline of the four-day course called Management Directions.

Day 1

I. Transition to Manager
   A. Video
   B. Exercise—"Ten Phrases"
II. Communication Skills
   A. Exercise: "What Does It Mean?"
   B. Building rapport—exercise: "Nonverbal Rapport"
   C. Active listening—exercise: "Did You Really Hear Me?"
   D. Assertiveness—exercise: "Stereotypes"
   E. Feedback
   F. Personal Profile Inventory
   G. Exercise
   H. Role-play exercise

Day 2

I. Time Management
   A. Delegating
II. Policies and Procedures
   A. First Union guidelines—exercise: "Attitudes"
   B. Employee assistance program
   C. STEP II
   D. Discipline process—exercise: "What's the Next Step?"
   E. Work/family programs
III. Conflict Management
   A. Video
   B. Conflict model
   C. Exercise: "Fishbowl Role Play"
   D. Role-play exercise

Day 3

I. Image Studies
II. Coaching
   A. Video
   B. Exercise: "Management Action Planner Profile"

Figure 18-1. Preworkshop skill assessment form, First Union National Bank of North Carolina.

To workshop participant:

Before attending a Training and Development workshop it is necessary for you and your manager to have a discussion about the goals you each have for the workshop.

After this preworkshop conference, please complete the questions below and have your manager sign this form. Please bring this to class with you.

- Active Listening
- Assertiveness
- Conflict Management
- STEP Planning and Usage
- Delegation
- Giving Feedback
- Performance Problem Solving
- Motivation

Using the above list as a guide, what management skill areas are your strengths and what areas would you like to improve upon as a manager?

Strengths:

Areas to Improve:

_____   _____
Manager's signature   Date

_____   _____
Employee's signature   Date

To manager:

Through experience, the Training and Development Department has learned that preworkshop conferences *greatly* enhance the benefits of any training program. We appreciate your taking the time to have this conference and for your support in reinforcing your employees' efforts to improve their skills.

III. Negotiating
   A. Exercise: "Finding Win/Win"

Day 4

 I. Follow-Up Image Studies
   A. Exercise
 II. Managing Change
   A. Exercise: "Stress Test"
   B. Exercise: "Personal Transitions"
III. Empowerment
   A. Video
   B. Exercise: "Proactive Pushes"
IV. Wrap-Up

19

An Internal Training Program on How to Manage Change at Dana Corporation

One of the most popular courses in the 1990s has been, and will continue to be, Managing Change. Professional trainers in more and more organizations realize that supervisors need training in how to make decisions and get them accepted and implemented by their subordinates. The following case study describes the approach used by Dana Corporation, a manufacturer of various parts for the automobile industry.

DANA CORPORATION, TOLEDO, OHIO
LARRY LOTTIER, DEAN, BUSINESS SCHOOL, DANA UNIVERSITY (A CONTINUING EDUCATION PROGRAM FOR DANA EMPLOYEES)

Following is an abbreviated lesson plan of our approach to training our supervisors on how to manage change.

1. Lecturette: Do people resist change? A poll of the group results in a usual overwhelming yes. Then we develop the concept that people do resist *some* changes, but, more important (especially for supervisors and managers to realize), people resist *being* changed.
2. Explain the "valley of despair" concept.
   a. Begins with the status quo.
   b. Shows a dip of performance into a "valley" when changes are planned such as new people, tools, processes, materials, etc.
   c. Improvement in performance occurs when the new things become more familiar and are accepted.

3. Discuss the five steps to successful behavior change.
   a. Desire
   b. Knowledge
   c. Visualization
   d. Planning
   e. Action
4. Discuss William James's suggestions for getting people to change their habits.
   a. Launch a new behavior as strongly as possible. First you must define exactly what that behavior is to be. Then think of ways to practice the new behavior with gusto. Public announcement is a good technique.
   b. Seize the first opportunity to act on the new behavior. Remember, your new actions will not be comfortable, so you will have to be extremely conscious of what you are doing.
   c. Never let an exception occur until the new behavior is firmly rooted. Once you make an exception, your resolve is broken, and it is more difficult to begin again.
5. Administer Kirkpatrick's Management Inventory on Managing Change.[1] In teams, discuss the items that are most pertinent.
6. Discuss and list on flipcharts the changes each person is going to make back on the job. Focus on changes:
   In you
   In your department to improve the work situation
   Be specific and write changes in the present tense beginning with "I now . . ."
7. Have each team present its flipchart report.
8. Each individual completes the form called "A Contract With Myself," which contains the following sentence fragments to finish:
   a. What I learned in the workshop was . . .
   b. Goals I plan to achieve as a result of what I learned are . . .
   c. The evidence I have accomplished these goals will be . . .
   The name and address are written on the bottom of the form. One copy of the completed form is kept by the supervisor and one copy given to the class instructor.

Several handouts are given to the supervisors for future study. One of them contains the following suggestions from Gordon Lippitt on how to turn resistance into acceptance:[2]

1. *Involve employees in planning the change.* Resistance to change will be less intense when those to be affected, or those who believe they might be affected, know why a change is being made and what the advantages are. This can be done most effectively by letting them participate in the actual planning. Besides helping them

1. Donald L. Kirkpatrick, *Management Inventory on Managing Change* (Elm Grove, Wis., Donald L. Kirkpatrick, 1987).
2. Gordon Lippitt, *The Change Resistors* (Englewood Cliffs, N.J.: Prentice-Hall, 1981).

to understand the when, what, where, and why of a change, participation eases any fears that management is hiding something from them. In addition, participation can stimulate many good ideas from those who probably are best acquainted with the problem that necessitates the change. It also alerts a supervisor to potential problems that might arise when the change is implemented.

2. *Provide accurate and complete information.* When workers are kept in the dark or get incomplete information, alarms and rumors start to circulate. This creates an atmosphere of mistrust. Even when the news is bad, employees would rather get it straight and fast than receive no news at all. Lack of information makes them feel helpless, while the whole story—even if it's unpleasant—lets them know where they stand.

3. *Give employees a chance to air their objections.* Change is more easily assimilated when a supervisor provides an opportunity for employees to blow off steam. A gripe session also gives supervisors useful feedback that may reveal unsuspected reasons for opposition. For example, a man may balk at using another machine only because he will be moved away from a window.

4. *Always take group norms and habits into account.* When change is contemplated, a supervisor should ask himself if it will:

- Break up congenial work groups.
- Disrupt commuting schedules or car pools.
- Split up long-standing luncheon partners.
- Unfavorably affect anticipated vacations, priorities, preferences.
- Require temperamentally incompatible employees to work together.

5. *Make only essential changes.* Most employees can tolerate only so much change. When they are confronted with many trivial or unnecessary changes, their reaction will be irritation and resentment. Even more important, they will be less receptive to major changes.

6. *Learn to use problem-solving techniques.* Research in behavioral science furnishes some useful guidelines in solving problems that arise from implementing change. First, identify the real problem. A supervisor may think, "If I could only get Mary to retire, the morale of the group would improve." But deep-seated problems rarely are caused by a single individual in a group. Second, be aware of timing. It is much easier to influence people favorably toward data processing equipment before it's installed than afterward. Third, help people solve problems to their own satisfaction. They will react negatively to such advice as, "You shouldn't take that attitude," or attempts at persuasion like, "I'm sure when you have all the facts, you'll see it my way."

Adjusting to change is difficult enough under the best of conditions. The supervisor can make it far easier for his subordinates—and for himself—by taking positive steps to forestall potential resistance. Resistance to change will be less intense when those to be affected, or those who believe they might be affected, know why a change is being made and what the advantages are.

The supervisors are encouraged to discuss with their bosses the program and the contract they completed. In addition, the instructor sends a follow-up letter about four weeks after the program. The letter:

1. Reminds them of the program and the form they completed.
2. Asks for feedback on what they have done.
3. Encourages continued application of what they learned.

Additional reading related to the program is enclosed with the letter.

20

A Program on Effective Writing at Warman International

Crucial for the office supervisor and middle-level manager today is the ability to write effective business letters, memos, and informal reports. Crucial, yes, but rarely do management education programs provide writing instructions that get results. Courses typically place too much emphasis on principles of writing rather than on practice. They spend too little time reviewing and criticizing correspondence and discuss broad principles instead of building specific writing skills needed by the organization. One program that has broken this mold was developed for Warman International, a manufacturer of slurry pumps for the mining and utility industries.

WARMAN INTERNATIONAL, INC., MADISON, WISCONSIN
BUCK JOSEPH, ASSOCIATE PROFESSOR OF MANAGEMENT, DIRECTOR OF EXECUTIVE DEVELOPMENT, MANAGEMENT INSTITUTE, SCHOOL OF BUSINESS, UNIVERSITY OF WISCONSIN, MADISON

Warman International, Inc., a small but growing manufacturer, produces slurry pumps for the mining and utility industries, pumps called the "Cadillacs" of the field. Young, growing, and confident of their ability to produce a high-quality product, Warman's managers wanted their business letters and memoranda to reflect their professionalism and get better results. Their technical sales engineers, project engineers, technical sales assistants, and administrative assistants were competent professionals; but the quality of their correspondence was unsatisfactory. They were especially in need of learning how to:

- Plan correspondence with a stronger results orientation.
- Create a more positive tone in their writing.
- Develop a deeper and broader understanding of the needs of their audiences and techniques of addressing those needs.
- Create technical but clear and readable work.
- Write more persuasive sales letters.

To meet these needs, I developed and implemented the following program.

Program Planning

To assess writing needs, several techniques were used:

1. Interviews were conducted with the personnel manager and utility sales supervisor to learn their perceptions of the current writing strengths and weaknesses of the target clientele group.
2. Three unedited samples of correspondence from each program participant were analyzed.
3. Discussion was held with administrative assistants, middle-level managers, and the general manager to determine the desired results from the writing program.

Armed with this information—an inventory of the existing situation and what Warman wanted—I created a course.

Writing Effective Business Letters and Memos

Session 1

1. Orientation
   - Climate setting
   - Program goals, methods, focus
2. Planning for Results
   - Understanding the importance of clarity of purpose in written communication
   - Clarifying the results we wish to accomplish through the communication
   - Understanding audience needs

Session 2

Organizing for Impact
- Keys to structure: purpose statements, lead sentences, headings and subheadings
- Organizing the middle: strategic paragraphing
- Sequencing for readability and emphasis

Session 3

Developing a Positive Tone in the Letter or Memo
▸ The "you" attitude
▸ Building in empathy
▸ Saying "no" tactfully

Session 4

1. Keys to Readability
   ▸ Assessing readability
   ▸ Reducing sentence length
   ▸ Reducing wordiness
2. Summary, evaluation

In planning the specific schedule, I considered the following principles:

1. Timing and duration of a writing program are critical to its success.
2. Intensity of instruction over a short period of time (two to three months) seems to work best.
3. Sessions should be spaced just far enough apart to allow for practice, review, and critiquing by the instructor, but not so far apart as to destroy group climate and program continuity.

Thus, Warman personnel and I scheduled sessions to run for three hours a day every two weeks. We agreed that the group size and program objectives would require four group sessions. Following the second and fourth sessions would be a unique feature: time for one-on-one consultation with the instructor. These thirty-minute sessions were designed to help the trainee receive straightforward, objective feedback from the trainer on writing strengths and areas needing improvement.

Climate Setting

Creating a positive learning climate was critical to the success of the program. To remove anxiety, fear of criticism, and defensiveness, I used the following approach:

▸ Introduced myself and my role in a personal way and asked for their help in understanding the slurry pump industry in exchange for my help in improving their writing abilities.
▸ Created the understanding that the goal of the program was to help them improve their writing by small degrees, not to perfect their abilities.
▸ Indicated that except for grammar, punctuation, and spelling conventions, no clear, concrete rules for effective writing exist. Our objective was to discuss and learn what will work for Warman.
▸ Pointed out that open, honest discussion is essential to program success.

▸ Memorized participants' names during their self-introductions and used first names throughout the program.
▸ Informed participants that my criticism of their writing would be balanced— strengths as well as areas needing improvement would be noted.
▸ Assured them that my comments on their writing should not be interpreted as evaluations of their total beings, but only of their current skill level in writing.

Methods

In order to make the session interesting, as well as effective, we used the following methods:

▸ Analysis of samples of letters and memos by small teams (three to four members) for strengths and weaknesses.
▸ Small group identification of "must-know" factors of our audiences.
▸ Individual and small group work on revising of samples, building in the "you" attitude, and sensitivity to reader needs.
▸ Listening teams, reporting on key information communicated in the film *Writing Letters That Get Results*.
▸ Reviewing examples of positive models (memos and sales letters) through passouts and overhead transparencies.
▸ Sharing and peer critiquing of participants' original drafts and revisions.
▸ Reviewing overhead transparencies made of participants' revised work, followed by group discussion of strengths.
▸ Individual work on revising for conciseness and clarity.
▸ Using hypothetical case studies, such as The Case of the Fledgling District Supervisor (Figure 20-1).

Consultation Sessions

A one-on-one consultation day was interspersed between sessions 2 and 3 and also followed session 4. During these days, I met with each participant to answer any questions and to provide feedback on his writing. Both the participants and I found these opportunities rewarding. Balanced criticism and honest, objective evaluation marked the sessions.

Evaluating the Program

The best measure of the success or failure of a writing program is the degree of change in the participants' writing. For Warman, I conducted three types of postprogram assessments:

▸ I compared participant samples written before the program with those written following the instruction, using a checklist as a basis of evaluation (Figure 20-2).

▸ Participants analyzed their before-and-after samples for improvements and reported their judgments to me.

▸ Participants' superiors did the same.

All assessments indicated that the level of writing skills was improved significantly because of this program.

Figure 20-1. A case study used in the writing program at Warman International.

The Case of the Fledgling District Supervisor

You are the General Accounting Supervisor of Flexnor Corporation, responsible for the work of six district supervisors. Four field accountants report to your newest supervisor, Jack Adams.

Recently, several complaints from the field have landed on your desk. Customers are dissatisfied with the services of the four accountants in the Southeastern District, Jack Adams's territory. Inaccuracies, delays in getting the jobs finished, and, above all, rudeness comprise the complaints.

In addition, each complaint mentioned previous unsuccessful contacts with Jack Adams about these problems. You have heard nothing from Jack about these difficulties. In fact, you have had little face-to-face contact with him during the first six months on the job because of the two thousand miles separating you. You do have a performance appraisal scheduled with him, but you feel this problem cannot wait until that date, three months away. Unfortunately, you cannot meet with him now and have decided that telephoning him would be inappropriate.

During the next forty-five minutes—

1. Write a memo to Jack Adams, seeking to:

_____

_____

2. Prepare a letter directed to the disgruntled customers for the purpose of:

_____

_____

_____

Figure 20-2. Writing assessment checklist, Warman International.

Introduction

1. Does the letter or memo contain a subject line?   _____ Yes   _____ No
2. Does it *clearly* indicate the work's subject matter?   _____ Yes   _____ No
3. Does the introduction convey clearly the work's purpose?   _____ Yes   _____ No
4. Does it clearly forecast the content *and* organization of the body of the letter or memo?   _____ Yes   _____ No
5. Does it convey the "you" attitude?   _____ Yes   _____ No
6. Does it convey enough background information or context?   _____ Yes   _____ No

---

Body

7. Does the overall design move from the general to the particular?   _____ Yes   _____ No
8. Are headings, subheadings, numbers, or bullets used effectively to divide the body?   _____ Yes   _____ No
9. Do the individual sections and paragraphs fit the purpose and organization forecasted by the introduction?   _____ Yes   _____ No
10. Is enough information included in each section, subsection, and paragraph?   _____ Yes   _____ No
11. Do the paragraphs' opening sentences clearly organize and forecast their contents?   _____ Yes   _____ No
12. Are clear transitional markers present between paragraphs?   _____ Yes   _____ No
13. Do the paragraphs contain extraneous information?   _____ Yes   _____ No
14. Are the paragraphs kept short for readability?   _____ Yes   _____ No

---

(continues)

Figure 20-2. (*continued*)

Closing

15. Does the letter or memo contain a
    closing paragraph?   _____ Yes   _____ No
16. Does it indicate clearly what the
    reader should do, say, or think as a
    result of the letter or memo?   _____ Yes   _____ No
17. Does it relate directly to the
    purpose of the work?   _____ Yes   _____ No

Language and Tone

18. Does the work convey a positive,
    courteous, friendly, but
    professional tone?   _____ Yes   _____ No
19. Is the language level appropriate to
    the audience and purpose?   _____ Yes   _____ No
20. Are simple, familiar words used?   _____ Yes   _____ No
21. Do any words require definition?   _____ Yes   _____ No
22. Does the letter or memo convey a
    negative message about the author
    and organization?   _____ Yes   _____ No

Sentences

23. Are the sentences concise?   _____ Yes   _____ No
24. Do they clearly communicate their
    meaning?   _____ Yes   _____ No
25. Are they arranged in a coherent,
    logical order?   _____ Yes   _____ No
26. Do they vary in length?   _____ Yes   _____ No
27. Are their ideas properly
    subordinated?   _____ Yes   _____ No

Mechanics

28. Does the memo or letter contain
    distraction-free mechanics?   _____ Yes   _____ No
    ‣ grammar   _____ Yes   _____ No
    ‣ spelling   _____ Yes   _____ No
    ‣ punctuation   _____ Yes   _____ No

Overall Assessment:

_____

21

Use of Outside Consultants at A. O. Smith Corporation and Johnson Motors

The top management of many organizations decides that the training of first-level management is important to their organizations' future success and growth. If they do not have qualified management development personnel in their organization, they call on outside professionals for assistance in planning and implementing the program. This situation existed at A. O. Smith Corporation, a manufacturer of automobile frames, grain silos, and water heaters, and at Johnson Motors, manufacturer of Johnson outboard boat motors.

A. O. SMITH CORPORATION, MILWAUKEE, WISCONSIN
D. W. HARRIS, FORMER DIRECTOR OF INDUSTRIAL RELATIONS

Recently, we became increasingly concerned with the image of the company being projected by the supervisors at our Milwaukee plant. We had been growing and expanding, and while we were growing and expanding many of our old-time supervisors were fading from the scene.

We realized that our supervisory organization was strong and effective, and some of our supervisors had genuine warmth and feeling for leading people and insight into the way people reacted. However, others were pretty cold fish who couldn't care less how people reacted to them as long as they got the job done. Of course, there was a broad range between these extremes. We discussed and explored several possibilities in our staff meetings. We decided to find an effective way of giving our management employees some comprehensive and practical human relations training that would make them responsive to the needs of people.

We knew that Don Kirkpatrick, professor of management development at the University of Wisconsin—Extension, had had an outstanding record in the industrial human relations field and had professional experience as an industrial relations executive. We knew that he was capable as a management development professional who would give the program more glamour and prestige than if we used someone from our own ranks. We conferred with Don, told him our needs, and he suggested a series of subjects.

This human relations course was reviewed by our group vice-president's staff in a capsule one-day conference at the Milwaukee Athletic Club. It was enthusiastically received, and the staff quickly agreed that it should be given to all 672 members of the management group at our Milwaukee Works. This was done in layer-by-layer order so that no one would attend the series without knowing that his boss had covered the same ground before him.

We scheduled the groups every other week for eight meetings of one and one-half hours each to cover the entire human relations series. Plenty of advance notice was given to participants so that each one could work his calendar and have no conflict in attendance. These meetings covered such subjects as responsibilities of a manager, how employees learn, indoctrination and training of new employees, motivation of employees, discipline, and upward and downward communication.

We were impressed not only with Don's broad, comprehensive knowledge of the subject and his ability to present it well but by the thoroughness with which he saw to it that all the mechanical details were worked out. These included projectors, screen, easel, Hook 'n Loop board, name cards, pencils, crayons, and insisting that a janitor clean the ashtrays and wash the blackboards after each session. When it was time to start, Don saw to it we were ready. Don is a warm person with an active, friendly sense of humor. No one would ever think of calling him Dr. Kirkpatrick. Our supervisors at all levels responded well to his leadership.

The groups were kept small (under twenty) to permit maximum participation in the discussions at each meeting. It took us a full year to cover the entire organization.

The feedback has been favorable, and the association and discussions in the eight sessions have improved communications and relationships between people on the same level and between levels. It has also given our supervisors a better insight into human behavior and freshened their outlook and approach to handling people problems with understanding. This has helped us maintain a good relationship with our work force.

An interesting control that Don established was the use of the Supervisory Inventory on Human Relations as a pretest at the first session and as a posttest in the final session so that the individual could evaluate the progress that he had made in the course of each session and so that management could see what had been gained in total.[1]

This was motivating to the individual and convincing to management that the money was well spent. There was real progress in management effectiveness because of the training program.

---

1. Donald L. Kirkpatrick, *Supervisory Inventory on Human Relations* (Elm Grove, Wis.: Donald L. Kirkpatrick, 1990).

JOHNSON MOTORS, WAUKEGAN, ILLINOIS
ED SCHROEDTER, FORMER VICE-PRESIDENT, INDUSTRIAL RELATIONS

In the last several years, Johnson Motors has expanded rapidly in terms of manpower. This created management problems for which our management, particularly first-line supervision, was not prepared. We felt that improved management techniques for our more than 200 supervisors would have a significant positive effect on the performance of our division.

Our top management group was unanimous in our decision to provide quality training for this group. We realized that we needed outside help to plan and implement an effective program for the first-line supervisors and to make recommendations for the development of the entire management organization. After considering several possibilities, we selected personnel from the Management Institute, University of Wisconsin—Extension because of their vast experience and national reputation in supervisory development and training.

Our top management met with Donald Kirkpatrick to plan the details of the program, including subject content, notebook materials, schedule, teaching approach, and instructional staff. The program was implemented in three phases:

Phase 1. A capsule program was conducted for the top management group by Dr. Kirkpatrick.

Phase 2. The capsule program was conducted for the department heads by Dr. Kirkpatrick.

Phase 3. The entire program of eighteen hours was conducted for all remaining management personnel. The instructors included the following people from the Management Institute staff: Norm Allhiser, Brad Boyd, Don Kirkpatrick, Ed Pickett, and Earl Wyman.

The program consisted of nine sessions of two hours each offered on company time at company facilities in Waukegan. The sessions were held every other week. There were twenty-five to thirty supervisors in each group. The specific subjects were:

Session 1: The Management Job
Session 2: Understanding Employees
Session 3: Motivating Employees (Part I)
Session 4: Motivating Employees (Part II)
Session 5: Inducting New Employees
Session 6: Training Employees (Part I)
Session 7: Training Employees (Part II)
Session 8: Effective Communication
Session 9: Self-Improvement

Dr. Kirkpatrick's Supervisory Inventory on Human Relations (SIHR) was given on a pretest basis to help determine specific training needs to use as a discussion tool.[2] The SIHR was also administered at the end of the program as a posttest for evaluation purposes. The basic approach was informal guided discussion. Other methods and techniques that were used included films, visual aids, role playing, case studies, and presentation by the instructor.

Reaction sheets, as well as the pretest and posttest of the SIHR, were used to determine the effectiveness of the leaders, subject content, and the program in general.

At the suggestion of Dr. Kirkpatrick, an implementation committee was organized at the beginning of the program. It consisted of one representative from each of the nine training groups. The main purpose of the committee was to assist with the on-the-job implementation of practical ideas that were discussed in the classroom situation. Each participant was encouraged to offer his comments and suggestions to his class representative. The committee met regularly with the division manager and the director of industrial relations to discuss their ideas.

Upon completion of the program, the committee prepared a comprehensive report that reflected the sentiments of all the seminar participants. The report did not include as many constructive suggestions as we had hoped. We learned that in many cases, the committee had been used as a grievance committee by the supervisors instead of the purpose for which it had been intended. In our experience, the committee probably did more harm than good, and I would suggest to other organizations that very careful consideration be given to the purpose, organization, and use of such a committee before deciding to use it.

In general, the training program was effective by making our supervisors more aware of their responsibilities, shortcomings, and some principles and approaches for becoming more effective managers. All participants requested additional training so they could respond to the challenges of the job and improve their contribution to the success and progress of Johnson Motors.

REFERENCE

Parry, Scott, and William B. Ouweneel. Chapter 47 in *Consultants: Training and Development Handbook,* 3d ed. New York: McGraw-Hill, 1987.

2. Ibid.

22

A Course on People Management at ServiceMaster

A one-week course for middle and upper-level managers was designed and implemented at ServiceMaster. Why is this case study included in a book on supervisory training and development? Three reasons stand out:

1. Middle and upper-level managers must set an example for their subordinate supervisors. They must be leaders to emulate and to inspire the supervisors to be leaders.

2. When supervisors return to their jobs after attending a training program, their bosses (managers) must provide a positive climate for changes in behavior. In order to do this, their managers should receive the same kind of training that the supervisors do so they are in a good position to be mentors and coaches.

3. By attending a management training program, middle and upper-level managers can participate in developing subject content for courses for the supervisors who report to them.

ServiceMaster is an international company offering various types of services, including office cleaning, insect extermination, lawn sterilization, and food service for hospitals, nursing homes, and universities.

SERVICEMASTER, DOWNERS GROVE, ILLINOIS
WILLIAM NEWELL, TRAINING AND EDUCATION COORDINATOR

Unit V of our nine-unit program for middle and upper-level managers is called People Development. The objective is to provide concepts, theories, principles, and techniques to make our managers more effective in dealing with the people in their departments. In attendance at the February 1992 program were twenty managers from all over the United States.

The subject content of this five-day program was determined jointly by our managers, our training and development professionals, and Dr. Donald L. Kirkpatrick, professor emeritus, University of Wisconsin, our primary conference leader. To supplement his teaching, three executives of ServiceMaster discussed our philosophy, principles, and approaches: W. W. Hargreaves, vice-president for people; C. W. Stair, president, management services; and R. A. Armstrong, senior vice-president.

Dr. Kirkpatrick covered eight subjects in the program:

1. The Job of a Manager—Objectives and Functions
2. Leadership Styles
3. Understanding and Motivating Employees
4. Managing Change
5. Orienting and Training Employees
6. Performance Appraisal
7. Coaching
8. Effective Communication

The group was involved in many discussions during the program, in both small groups and the general session. A number of videotapes were shown and discussed, including those describing principles of leadership, motivation, and communication.

Four of Dr. Kirkpatrick's inventories were administered, scored, and discussed:

1. Management Inventory on Leadership, Motivation, and Decision-Making
2. Management Inventory on Managing Change
3. Management Inventory on Performance Appraisal and Coaching
4. Supervisory Inventory on Communication

After completing an inventory and before scoring it, selected items were assigned to the participants to work in groups and reach consensus on the better answer. The inventories were then self-scored, and the selected items were discussed.

Extensive reading by the participants supplemented the classroom instruction. The readings included the following ServiceMaster materials: *Principles of Leadership, Principles of Learning,* and the *1990 Annual Report.*

The participants also read the following three books by Dr. Kirkpatrick:

How to Manage Change Effectively (San Francisco: Jossey-Bass, 1985).
How to Improve Performance Through Appraisal and Coaching (New York: AMACOM, 1982).
No-Nonsense Communication, 3d ed. (Elm Grove, Wis.: Dr. Donald Kirkpatrick, 1991).

Special assignments from these books were given for outside reading.

The reactions to the program were highly favorable. Following is a tabulation of the responses from the participants:

THE INSTRUCTOR: Dr. Donald Kirkpatrick	Poor	Fair	Good	Excellent
Understood the subject matter.				20
Presented materials in a clear and interesting way.			1	19
Made goals and objectives clear at beginning of classes and followed that plan.			9	11
Stimulated discussion and involvement within the group.		1		19
How would you rate the instructor?			2	18

Some of the comments were:

Outstanding. The best seminar I've been to.

Made everyone feel comfortable about getting involved.

Great balance between video, quiz, lecture, and exercises.

Communicated material very clearly.

Excellent. Makes learning enjoyable.

Excellent. Enjoyed sense of humor.

Very well done. Good handouts.

Excellent style. Saw some very general application to my present responsibilities.

All the presentation material was excellent. Not only was it understandable, but got the entire group involved.

Outstanding. Very practical.

Excellent. Dr. Kirkpatrick's techniques and delivery were excellent. One of the best presenters I've ever had. Thank you!

Dr. Kirkpatrick did an excellent job. Have him back!

A description of the philosophy and policies of ServiceMaster is included in Chapter 3. Because of the positive reaction to the program, we are planning to use Dr. Kirkpatrick in a number of follow-up programs with supervisors and managers.

REFERENCES

Kirkpatrick, Donald L. *Management Inventory on Leadership, Motivation, and Decision Making.* Elm Grove, Wis.: Donald L. Kirkpatrick, 1992.

Kirkpatrick, Donald L. *Management Inventory on Managing Change.* Elm Grove, Wis.: Donald L. Kirkpatrick, 1987.

Kirkpatrick, Donald L. *Management Inventory on Performance Appraisal and Coaching.* Elm Grove, Wis.: Donald L. Kirkpatrick, 1987.

Kirkpatrick, Donald L. *Supervisory Inventory on Communication.* Elm Grove, Wis.: Donald L. Kirkpatrick, 1990.

23

A Safety Training Program at DuPont

Regulatory attention is increasingly focused on workplace safety. Organizations are facing scrutiny at all levels, and future regulations will likely require even more detailed record keeping and auditing of safety efforts. To achieve workplace safety, safe behavior must become part of the organizational culture; it must be considered business as usual and have the unwavering commitment of top management. Following is a description of a comprehensive training program that has been effective in achieving workplace safety.

The DuPont Company is known for its development and production of various chemical products.

DuPont COMPANY, WILMINGTON, DELAWARE
ANTHONY F. CANTARELLA, DEVELOPMENT PROGRAMS MANAGER

DuPont has created a strong safety culture and earned a worldwide reputation for on-the-job safety performance, in part by applying the concepts of a safety training program it developed, the Safety Training Observation Program (STOP).

STOP, a behavior modification program, works in every workplace environment because it's based on fundamental safety principles. The key tenet of STOP is simple: it teaches how to "observe for safety." Its objective is to eliminate workplace injuries by enabling and encouraging all employees, from senior management to hourly employees, to recognize and eliminate unsafe acts and conditions. The program's safety activities establish safety as equal in importance to cost, productivity, and quality.

Two versions of STOP are available; when used together, they can improve the safety awareness and skills of every employee. STOP for Supervision trains managers, line supervisors, and team leaders to systematically and positively observe, correct, and prevent recurrence of unsafe acts wherever they occur in the workplace. STOP for Employees focuses on developing safety awareness and self-auditing skills in all work areas and activities in order to help employees fulfill their personal safety responsibility. To help global organizations communicate their safety philosophy effectively, both STOP programs also are available in French and Spanish. The programs are translated in the international language version for clarity.

Training is conducted over a period of eleven to twenty-two weeks, depending on the size of the organization and its safety needs. Participants are taught how to examine and observe the safety aspect of their job—for example, work posture, tool usage, and established operating procedures. Videotapes, self-study workbooks, group discussions, and on-the-job applications help facilitate learning. While focusing on individual responsibility for safety, STOP promotes a team effort, ultimately encouraging positive interaction among employees and between management and employees. This allows every person in the organization to develop safety management skills and contribute to safety performance.

Based on these principles, DuPont has developed its STOP for Ergonomics. Like the original STOP, this program's goal is the same: to eliminate injuries and occupational illnesses. However, STOP for Ergonomics focuses on injuries that have resulted because of the demands of a work environment. Carpal tunnel syndrome and "trigger finger," as well as many back injuries and disorders, are examples of injuries resulting from ergonomic risk factors. STOP for Ergonomics can improve safety performance, helping everyone in the organization identify and reduce ergonomic risk factors.

Management needs to be highly committed to safety for STOP to be most effective because it should be implemented using the technique of cascade teaching. The STOP for Supervision program is first presented to upper management on the site. Then these managers present the same material to those who report directly to them, and so on, down to the first-line supervisor level. STOP for Employees utilizes the same technique, with previously trained supervisors serving as program leaders. Cascade teaching helps reinforce the idea that safety is a line function. There is an added impact when the program is presented to employees by their manager, knowing she has just gone through the same process with her manager. There is probably no faster way to spread safety commitment throughout an organization.

STOP clearly communicates management's commitment to safety and provides a basis for ongoing safety improvement. Even after the formal training ends, employees continue to develop positive safety attitudes along with improved auditing and self-auditing safety skills. A safe workplace can't be created by a single training program or management decree, but STOP can be effective for any organization that is serious about improving its safety performance, whether it is just beginning a formal safety program or fine-tuning an existing one.

This program is available for purchase from DuPont:

> DuPont Safety Services
> Training Materials
> P.O. Box 80800
> Wilmington, Delaware 19880-0800
> 800/532-SAFE

Bibliography

Many books have been written about training and development. Here is a list of eleven of the most comprehensive ones to provide concepts, theories, principles, and techniques to professionals in the field.

Bard, Ray, Chip R. Bell, Leslie Stephen, and Linda Webster. *The Trainers' Professional Development Handbook.* San Francisco: Jossey-Bass Publishers, 1987. 325 pages. An excellent reference book with a detailed list of resources of books; professional journals and periodicals; professional organizations; conferences, workshops, and academic programs; training exercises and group experiences; audiotapes, films, and videos; on-line databases; and microcomputer courses and training programs.

Buyer's Guide and Consultant Directory. Alexandria, Va.: American Society for Training and Development, 1992. 230 pages. An annual directory of organizations and consultants in human resources development. It provides a list by subject and by the organization/individual providing the service.

Craig, Robert L., ed. *Training and Development Handbook,* 3d ed. New York: McGraw-Hill, 1987. 878 pages. A handbook divided into five sections: (1) The Training and Development Function, (2) Program Design and Development, (3) Media and Methods, (4) Training Applications, and (5) Resources. The forty-nine chapters contain principles, concepts, and techniques for training professionals to consider as they plan and implement programs in supervisory training and development.

Kirkpatrick, Donald L. ed., *More Evaluating Training Programs.* Alexandria, Va.: American Society for Training and Development, 1987. 280 pages. Contains articles by Kirkpatrick as well as all of the articles on evaluation that appeared in *Training and Development Journal* from 1976 to 1986. Covers philosophy and concepts, reaction, learning, behavior, results, and federal government references. The philosophy, principles, and techniques imparted by this book will be helpful in program evaluation.

Mitchell, Garry. *The Trainer's Handbook: The AMA Guide to Effective Train-*

ing, Second Edition. New York: AMACOM, 1993. 432 pages. A problem-solver for all trainers at all levels. A brush-up guide for experienced trainers; a look-up reference for novices.

Nadler, Leonard, and Zeace Nadler, eds. *The Handbook of Human Resource Development,* 2d ed. New York: John Wiley and Sons, 1990. A comprehensive handbook with thirty-one chapters written by many well-known human resources development professionals.

Odiorne, George, and Geary Rummler. *Training and Development: A Guide for Professionals.* Chicago: Commerce Clearing House, 1988. 450 pages. Contains a chapter on the learning theories of such well-known researchers and authors as Pavlov, Skinner, Thorndike, Lewin, and Maslow. Also includes chapters on determining training needs, role playing, case studies, management games, video-based training, and evaluation.

Svenson, Raynold, and Monica Rinderer. *Training and Development Strategic Plan Workbook.* Englewood Cliffs, N.J.: Prentice-Hall, 1992. Twenty-five chapters that discuss the assessment of training needs, delivery strategies, resources, and measurement of training results. Includes over 160 spreadsheets, checklists, forms, and examples.

Tracey, William R., ed. *Human Resources Management and Development Handbook.* New York: AMACOM, 1985. 1,550 pages. Contains 108 chapters that cover all aspects of the human resources function. Many different authors have provided principles, concepts, and techniques. Of particular interest are chapters 62–93, which relate to supervisory training and development.

Tracey, William R. *Designing Training and Development Systems,* 3d ed. New York: AMACOM, 1992. 532 pages. Concrete guidelines for developing training programs that work. Covers twenty-two key topics a human resources manager, trainer, or course developer needs to know to achieve outstanding training.

The Trainers Resource Directory. Hopkins, Minn.: Linton Publishing Co., 1992. 1,100 pages. A comprehensive handbook with detailed information on training organizations and individuals by name, type of service, state in which located, and the person to contact.

Index

records
  advantages and disadvantages of, 75
  past, 168
reports, 75
resentment, 188
Resources for Organization, as source of learning instruments, 116
responsibility
  of boss, 7, 8
  of manager vs. team leader, 18
  of supervisor, 7, 8
  for supervisory training, 7–11
  of top management, 7, 8–9
  of training professionals, 8, 9–11
results
  evaluation of, 144–151
  objectives of, 77–78
review and application law, 34
review courses, 81–82
rewards, 158
Robinson, Dana and James
  on behavior change, 144
  on training program evaluation, 147
role playing, 106, 112–113
Rummler, Geary, on determining training needs, 64–70

safety, supervisory inventory on, 58
Safety Training Observations Program (STOP), 296–297
safety training program, 296–297
St. Joseph's Hospital program, 235–240
sandwich approach, 188–189
selection
  criteria for, 206–207
  principles of, 201–205
self, attitudes toward, 143, 144
self-appraisal, 174–175
self-comparison effect, 170
self-development program, 19
self-directed learning, 36
self-esteem, 36
self-evaluation form, coaching, 196–198

self-responsibility, 263
seminars, 80
separation of variables, 145
ServiceMaster
  people management course of, 292–294
  training program principles of, 24–26
skills
  from classroom training, 93–94
  level of, 31
  objectives for, 77
Starr, Bart, on effective coaching, 192
statistical process control, viii
Stewart, William, job analysis of, 44–45
subordinates
  contrary, 169
  in determining needs, 42, 43
"Supervisor Review: Improving Our Working Relationships," 46–51
supervisors, vii
  attitudes of, 4
  challenges to, vii
  communication of, 50
  competence of, 48
  integrity and fairness of, 50
  in needs determination, 42
  participative leadership by, 50–51
  placement of, 214–216
  principles in development of, 158
  responsibility of, 7, 8, 86
  selection and training of, 200–222
supervisory inventories, 57–58, 115
supervisory needs, determination of, 205
supervisory training programs
  evaluation form for, 154–155
  maximum benefits from, 153–157
Swierczek, Frederic, on behavior evaluation, 141–143
systematic training programs, 15–16

task analysis, 66–69
teacher, law of, 33